To my husband, Jim,
whom I love more with each passing year,
whose never-ending support encourages
and inspires me beyond words.
You are my best friend.
You even rallied behind me when
I dreamed up the topic for this book.
I love you dearly. You're perfect . . .
just the way you are.

Contents

PART ONE

READY

CHAPTER ONE

....

Can We Talk?

If someone were to tell you that you could have better, more meaningful communication with your partner, or that you could hug and touch him without his thinking sex was imminent, or you could get him to realize that, unlike the oven, the house isn't self-cleaning, wouldn't you want to know *how?* Even if you were somewhat skeptical about getting through to your partner because he's so set in his ways, wouldn't you still be curious as to whether you've been missing something? What if you were told that *there really is a way* to inspire your man to be more loving, to become more involved with the kids, or to remember to put _____ (the toothpaste cap, his clothes, his wet towel—fill in the blank) where it belongs. Wouldn't you be first in line to find out exactly what you need to do? Of course you would.

How do I know? You're a woman. I'm a woman. My friends are women. Lots of my clients are women. Many of my relatives are women. Women are familiar territory to me. I understand them really well. I've noticed that breasts aren't the only thing we have in common. Most women want to change their men. We want them to compliment us more, to be more affectionate, to assume more responsibility at home, to lighten up when things get tense, to quit thinking they know the Right Way to Do Things, to talk more, to be the one who arranges for a baby-sitter for a change, to stop snoring. I could go on forever. So many changes, so little time. A woman's work is never done.

But here's the sixty-four-thousand-dollar question. If we're so determined to change our men, why are we so lousy at it? Why

·3·

aren't we more skilled at getting them to be the kind of partners we really want? For starters, when things aren't going well, we spend far too much time analyzing things to death and finding fault instead of finding creative solutions. Because we assume that knowing who or what is to blame for our unhappiness is the first step in improving the quality of our lives, we become hell-bent on discovering the real underlying causes of our relationship problems. Unfortunately, as you're about to see, this is a huge waste of time—for two reasons.

First of all, regardless of how much you know about the causes of your relationship problems, it won't help you figure out what to do to fix things. For example, have you ever rifled through women's magazines, searching for articles about your man's personality and taking every pop psychology quiz imaginable, hoping to shed light on your partner's irritating behavior? "No wonder we have problems," you tell yourself. "He's got a 'Type A' personality" or "He's a workaholic." Well, maybe the pop quizzes demonstrate unequivocally that he does have a Type A personality or that he is a workaholic, but does knowing this help you one iota? Do you now know what to do to get him to be more laid-back or to work less? Does diagnosing him help you get unstuck? I doubt it.

But you don't let that stop you. You continue searching for causes, looking for other things to blame. You tell yourself, "It must have been his upbringing." "His family was dysfunctional." The culprits, you surmise, are your mother and/or father-in-law. "They spoiled him, so obviously he expects to be waited on hand and foot" or "He never stops criticizing me. He's just like his father." In the heat of an argument, you assign blame by calling him by your father (or mother) -in-law's name. I've never met a man who, after being accused of having the same undesirable trait as his parent, reflects upon his behavior and genuinely says, "Thank you for your insightful comments, dear. I'll work on that." Most men (most people, for that matter) become defensive when blamed and counterattack. Hardly the response you want.

Although you undoubtedly notice that blaming your partner, his personality, his parents, or all of the above is a dead-end endeavor, you still don't know what to do next. In frustration, you turn to your friends. You pick up the phone or meet for lunch and you vent. You complain. You commiserate. They understand. They empathize. And, best of all, they agree. They can't believe he's acting like such a jerk. "What in the world is he thinking?" they chime in unison. "Why doesn't he just admit you're right and he's wrong?" they wonder. You thank your friends for their "objectivity" and support and you end the conversation feeling bolstered to do more battle. Stronger? Perhaps, but not necessarily wiser. Here's why.

While you're busy collecting data, formulating your diagnosis, and trying to think of a more palatable way to make your case against him, you fail to notice that another precious day has slipped away. You're no closer to having more joy in your life than when you started. He's no more enlightened, loving, or interactive than he was years ago. In fact, if anything, there's more distance between you. In short, without realizing it, you've now become an expert on *why* your partner *isn't changing* and a novice at knowing what to do about it.

Second, even if you are convinced you're right about why he behaves the way he does, it's absolutely meaningless because he won't agree with you. Think about it. In times past, when you shared your diagnosis with him, did he buy it and embark on a journey of intense self-improvement? Despite the mounting evidence against him, didn't he still think that *you* were the one who was off base? I bet he did!

Nevertheless, you spend the next few months or years trying to convince him of his shortsightedness and the reasons for it. Unfortunately, the harder you work at this, the more he blames you. And, what's worse, in the midst of this blaming and counterblaming, you're waiting for him to change and he's waiting for you to change. You don't have to be a rocket scientist to recognize the fruitlessness of both partners believing that relationship improvement is predicated on the other person changing first! Stalemate.

It's no surprise that our requests for change fall upon deaf ears. Beyond not wanting to be criticized and the certainty that *they* are always right, there are other reasons why men don't respond the way we'd like. The most common is the misguided notion that "talking things out" will be of help. What do the experts tell us to do if we're unhappy with our mates? "Tell him how you feel. Talk things out. Share feelings openly." Well, have you ever mustered up the courage to tell your partner how you *really* feel about something—that it hurts your feelings when he acts a certain way, that you'd appreciate it if he would truly consider how important something is to you? What was his response? In addition to the fact that he seemed put out by what you said, perhaps you also noticed that he remained totally unchanged the next time you encountered that situation. Apparently, he heard nothing. I'm not surprised. You're not alone. But why doesn't this strategy work?

Perhaps you've noticed that the man in your life probably doesn't pick up the phone to have lengthy conversations with his friends. He doesn't "do lunch" to catch up on the latest intimate details of his buddy's life. Long silent periods are just fine with him. Watching a movie together or reading while sitting in the same room is his idea of feeling close. He's convinced that talking is merely a necessity in life.

We're different. Verbal communication is our lifeline. We don't feel close to our partners unless we've had a good talk recently. Intimate conversation allows us to merge together. Although these differences in men and women aren't, in and of themselves, stumbling blocks to good relationships, they can present major problems if they are ignored or overlooked. And all too often, that's precisely what happens.

For example, we too frequently assume that men *are* like us; that they feel relieved after hashing things out in conversation. Actually, men generally do whatever they can to steer clear of lengthy, intimate tête-à-têtes, because they're not as comfortable with talking as we are. It's why men withdraw when women want to talk about relationship issues. It's not because they don't love us or care about our feelings. It's just that it feels unsettling to them. They're out of their domain.

Yet, with all this emphasis on the importance of "talking things out," it's hard for us not to think that our mates are holding back when they resist conversation or ignore what we're saying to them. We can't help but feel offended and hurt. We assume they're not committed to making the relationship work. We assume they're selfish and unloving. Right?

Look, just because your man is sick of talking, or doesn't seem to hear a word you say, you shouldn't take it to mean that he doesn't care about your feelings. It may just mean that he's gotten word-saturated, and it's time for you to switch gears. You need to internalize that verbal means are certainly not the only, or the best, strategy for influencing your man. If you've ever heard yourself say, "I talk until I'm blue in the face" or "I've told you a million times," your partner is tuning you out. He hears only what he wants to hear. You've heard of blind spots? Well, he's got "deaf spots." His deaf spots are your requests for change. It's time for you to stop relying solely on words to be heard. It's time to learn alternative methods for getting through to him.

A final reason that men aren't too receptive (to say the least) to our "suggestions" is that they seem to have radar for anything that smacks of being controlled. The need to be self-determining is an incredibly powerful force in their lives. They want to be in charge of themselves. Men often feel weak if they accept influence or advice from others (does your partner ever ask for directions if he's lost?). That's why they seem to get bent out of shape when we offer our opinions. They don't like being told "what to do." In fact, research suggests that men's number-one complaint about their partners is that women are always trying to change them. Guys don't appreciate this "nurturing" quality in us. They feel nagged, controlled, and henpecked, and stubbornly resist even the most benevolent, well-meaning advice.

So, you may be asking yourself, "Since men don't like being changed, why read a book instructing women to do the very thing men most detest about being in a relationship?" The answer is simple. I'm here to tell you that not all efforts to change men are created equal. Some strategies simply work better than others; they don't leave men feeling nagged or coerced. And, as a result, men are more responsive and accommodating. Women need to learn these "male-friendly" methods of persuasion and stop doing what doesn't work.

I want you to know that once armed with these "male-friendly" methods, no matter what you've been told by the experts, your friends, your mother, or even your partner; regardless of the roadblocks you've encountered on the path to relationship bliss; no matter how frustrated you might have felt in the past, *you really can change your man*, you really can. You can create the kind of relationship you've always wanted. You can rekindle the love you felt when you first met. You can get him to be more communicative and involved. You can influence him to be more sensitive to your feelings. It could happen.

If you're thinking, "Yeah, right, the only way I'll ever get that kind of treatment is if I trade him in for someone new," you're wrong. Trade-ins aren't practical. New men need training, too. That's why I'm going to teach you how to *transform* your man into the "new and improved" version you've been hoping for. So, if remaining stagnant has lost its appeal, you've come to the right place! That's because you're about to learn effective, down-to-earth, easy-to-understand, simple-to-implement strategies for changing your man. Want to know what makes me so certain about all of this?

I'm a marriage and family therapist who has been practicing a radically different approach to problem-solving since the early eighties. Unlike most experts, I believe that finding solutions to life's dilemmas doesn't have to be difficult, painful, or even time-consuming. I practice a method called Solution-Oriented Brief Therapy, which is based on unorthodox but commonsense principles.

Traditional therapists believe that the key to resolving problems in your life lies in understanding the forces in your childhood. In theory, once you recognize how the past has influenced you, you'll know *why* you do what you do and your problems will disappear. Well, I bet you know a lot of people who recognize exactly *why* they're depressed but can't seem to break free of their depression. Or perhaps you have a friend who has great insight into her less-than-perfect childhood and recognizes *why* she overeats, yet continues to raid the refrigerator night after night.

You see, despite what the pros might say, learning how the past shapes who you are as an adult (and it does) may be an interesting or provocative endeavor, but it won't get you solutions. You can analyze things until the cows come home, but it won't make problems go away. What's worse, when you're busy analyzing what's caused your problems, you fool yourself into thinking you're actually doing something about them, when nothing could be farther from the truth.

When I finally realized this, I made a promise to myself to stop dissecting the past (which is unchangeable) and start dissecting the future instead. I began to help people identify how they want their lives to change and the specific steps they need to take to make those changes happen. No introspective journeys into the past or painful probing for lost memories. No parent-bashing or finger-pointing. Just blame-free strategies for changing one's life in the here and now. At last, immediate solutions to long-standing problems. What a relief! You see, without analyzing the past, you can fast-forward into the future. Solutions are right around the corner if you're headed in the right direction.

I became incredibly passionate about this new approach and started teaching others to "think solutions." First, I trained other therapists. Then, wanting to spread my message even farther, I wrote a best-selling book based on solution-oriented principles to help couples divorce-proof their marriages: *Divorce Busting: A Step-by-Step Approach to Making Your Marriage Loving Again.* I wanted *Divorce Busting* to be both an appeal to those contemplating divorce to reconsider, and a handbook for getting shaky relationships back on firmer ground. The response to this book has been overwhelming. I've received thousands of letters and calls thanking me for having revitalized people's love for each other. I can't imagine anything more rewarding than those expressions of gratitude.

One of the reasons for the book's popularity was the fact that it was based on the very pragmatic, yet unorthodox idea that one person can change a relationship single-handedly. As you can imagine, this notion was very appealing to readers whose marriages were teetering on the brink of divorce because, as is often true in those cases, one partner is more interested than the other in putting forth the effort required to resurrect an ailing relationship. I can't tell you how many marriages I've seen rebuilt when the person most interested in making things better stopped pointing fingers and started taking productive actions. Time and time again, I've observed relationships having near-death experiences resurrected by the one determined person who was willing to tip over the first domino.

After seeing extremely conflictual relationships rebound from the brink of disaster, I couldn't help but think of how many more people—people with less serious, garden-variety relationship problems—could benefit from knowing that relationship change is inevitable if they're willing to stop blaming their partners and take the first step. The possibilities were mind-boggling. I couldn't wait to tell people. Thus, the genesis of this book.

Now, despite what I just told you, I can hear you saying, "I thought the only person you can change is yourself. You can't change other people." Well, it simply isn't true. You most certainly *can* change other people, but—and here's the big but—*you must begin by changing your own actions first.* Relationships are such that if one person changes, the other person must change as well. Want to know how I know?

Through all the years that I've been practicing couples' therapy, much of the time I work with only one partner, frequently the woman. Although initially she may be skeptical about the possibilities for change because her partner won't come for therapy, I tell her not to worry—I've got a plan. With a little prompting, she goes home and experiments with new ways of approaching him. Her experiments pay off. Without his ever coming in, without their even talking things over, he begins to change right before her very eyes. She can't believe I hadn't called her partner to coach him. She's certain I must have sent a letter of instruction home to him without her knowing it.

Well, I don't send letters home or tutor guys over the phone. And it isn't magic. It's simple: she changes/he changes. I've seen it work that way time and time again. I've seen it in my practice. I've read about it in letters from readers of *Divorce Busting*. I practice it with my husband. I know that it works. That's why I'm going to teach you exactly what you need to change to get your partner to be more responsive to you. I'll help you determine what to do and what to say so that your partner truly hears you and takes action. I'll guide you in tipping over the first domino so that you'll get more of your needs met. This is a book about change, and you, my friend, are going to start the ball in motion all by yourself!

The fact that one person can spark change in another person is really great news for women. Since most men aren't overly interested in "working on" relationships (having in-depth, emotionally laden discussions, going to therapy, taking relationship-enhancing seminars, or reading self-help books), knowing that you can effect change single-handedly enables you to take the energy you spent trying to convince your mate there's a problem and that he's the cause of it and funnel this energy into a vastly more productive direction. This means you can take charge of your life rather than just wishing and hoping your man will change. You can start planning your next step to having a more fulfilling love life.

So, if you've been waiting for the man in your life to stop being so stubborn and finally admit he's wrong and start doing things your way (the right way, of course), I suggest you quit waiting. You're wasting time. I can think of a hundred things you could be doing that would get him off dead center. Once you figure out how to approach him differently, change will be imminent. You don't need a commitment from him to change or an agreement to work on things together. You don't need to leave heavily highlighted relationship books lying around the house in the hopes he might read them. You can trigger change in him single-handedly! In fact, you can change him without his even knowing it!

But I must warn you. I've said it before and I'll say it again: some man-changing strategies work better than others. What works for you might not work for your best friend or neighbor down the street. What works one day might not work next month. The point is, I'm going to teach you many different techniques to reach your man and help you determine which strategies work, which don't, when to shift gears if what you're doing isn't working, and what you can do instead. I'm going to help you become more systematic about the ways you approach your partner. I'll guide you in doing more of what works and less of what doesn't.

On the surface of things, discarding strategies that don't work seems too obvious to mention. But trust me when I tell you that it simply isn't so. One of the biggest mistakes women make when they're experiencing relationship problems is that they rely too heavily on their emotions to guide them. We do what "feels right," whether it works or not. We're not strategic. Even rats know better.

If you put a rat at the bottom of a maze in front of five tunnels and you put cheese in one of these tunnels, the rat will explore all the tunnels, looking for the cheese. If you put the cheese down tunnel five each time you do the experiment, eventually the rat will remember that the cheese is down tunnel five and go there first each time. In other words, the rat will stop looking for the cheese in the other four tunnels.

If you then decide to put the cheese down the second tunnel, the rat will go up the fifth tunnel, notice there's no cheese and then go back down. The rat may do this two or three more times, but it will soon figure out that the cheese is no longer there and start exploring the other tunnels again until it finds the cheese. The major difference between rats and women is that rats will stop going up tunnels that have no cheese. Women, on the other hand, will go up the fifth tunnel forever. Women will spend months, even years, going down empty tunnels in relationships even if they're in pain, because, unlike the rat who's just focused on the prize, we lose sight of *why* we're doing what we're doing.

Pam was one woman who forgot to keep her eyes on the cheese. After years of feeling criticized and controlled by her husband, she believed she had no alternative other than leaving her marriage. When she informed her husband, Hal, of her decision, he made a desperate plea for her to work on their relationship. She decided to give him another chance. Like most women who feel controlled by their partners, Pam grew determined to become more assertive, forcing Hal to be accountable for his actions.

In the months that followed, Hal truly worked overtime to become the person Pam wanted him to be; he was more loving, attentive, respectful, and involved with their children. Although Pam appreciated his changes, she withheld positive feedback. Instead, each time Hal said or did something that displeased Pam, she called him on it. In fact, the only time she discussed their relationship was when she was unhappy with his actions. It wasn't long before Hal felt discouraged. Since he felt her needs were a moving target, he eventually stopped trying. The loving marriage Pam had always wanted was now slipping through her fingers. I knew Pam needed to be reminded of the cheese.

Once alone with Pam, I applauded her decision to become more forthcoming with Hal and told her that the success of their marriage hinged upon her being more open and honest than she had been in the past. However, I asked whether she thought she was getting anywhere focusing solely on Hal's faults and not his strengths. Although she admitted that things deteriorated between them each time she criticized him, she felt compelled to persist because of her promise to herself to take a stronger stand with Hal. Ironically, the very thing she was doing to improve her relationship with Hal was actually driving him away.

I told Pam that, if she wanted to, she could have Hal eating out of the palm of her hand. Predictably, she liked that idea a lot and was open to hearing my suggestion. I supported her sharing her negative feelings with Hal, but advised her to stop censoring her positive feelings. "Catch him in the act of doing what you want him to do and reward him in some way," I told her. "Let him know you appreciate what he's doing. Compliment him, hug him, write him a note." She agreed to give it a try.

Within a very short time, she saw a remarkable change in him. Once again, he was putting his heart into making their marriage work. Pam even noticed that Hal was more receptive to her comments when her feedback to him was less than complimentary. For the first time, she believed her marriage was on the right track. Pam learned the difference between being right and doing what works.

If your man is the controlling sort, I can see why Pam's story might be somewhat puzzling to you. After all, conventional feminist wisdom and mainstream psychotherapy have impressed upon women the need to voice their negative feelings whenever they're upset. That's why many women who have grown weary of feeling overpowered begin scrutinizing their relationships and call their partners to task every chance they get. Well, I may be the bearer of politically incorrect news, but here goes. In reality, voicing your discontent each and every time you're displeased is a fail-safe prescription for marital-relationship disaster!

But don't panic! I'm not suggesting that if you feel resentful or fed up to simply stuff your feelings inside. As a strong-willed, independent woman who's been in a relationship with a macho-type, strong-willed man (my husband) for twenty-six years, I know the importance of speaking one's mind. I know how vital it is to be self-determining, to have your voice heard. Thanks to my being a native New Yorker, I have little trouble speaking out and taking a stand, but I've come to define real assertiveness in a different way.

To me, real assertiveness means being able to decide if, how, when, or where I make my needs known. Typically, when I express my feelings to my husband, it is not a knee-jerk reaction to having my buttons pushed. Generally, I choose my battles wisely and plan my approach in order to increase the odds that I'll get the kind of response I want. It seems to be working pretty well so far. Consistent with this philosophy, I help women gain control over their lives, not by speaking out reactively, but by learning truly effective ways of reaching the men they love. I show them how to achieve greater happiness by teaching them how to get smart, instead of getting even.

Perhaps the challenges you're facing aren't as extreme as Pam's. Maybe your relationship is basically sound; you just want to smooth out the rough edges. That's exactly what I'm going to help you do. The methods you're about to learn vary. Some are like a stick of dynamite; others, a gentle nudge. Which methods you use will depend on your particular situation and your personal preference. There's something here for everyone. Well, not exactly for everyone. For every woman.

Now, perhaps you're wondering, "Since *either* person can take charge of changing the relationship, why is this book directed specifically at women?" There are several reasons. First of all, think about the people in your life who are important to you—your kids, other family members, or your partner. When these people or relationships require attention, who's most likely to take action? You. Right? That's because women tend to be the primary caretakers in relationships. When it comes to kids, we wipe more noses, change more diapers, give more kisses and hugs, and spend far more sleepless nights nursing sick children back to health or waiting for the sound of adolescents beating the clock and rushing home for curfew. That's because we're the moms.

If you have an aging or ailing parent, research suggests that, whatever the size of the family, it is usually a daughter who assumes responsibility for the parent's care. We may tire of it, but we do it anyway because more than anything, we value caring for others. Or what about your family? Have you ever asked yourself, "Who's at the hub of family get-togethers?" "Who picks up the phone to check in most often?" "Who sends the Hallmark cards?" No doubt a woman. You see, unlike men, who typically define themselves through achievement, women (even high-powered, career-oriented women) value relationships, communication, and nurturance. Our relationships are the yardsticks by which we measure success.

Just think about your interactions with your man. Isn't it true that if things go well in love, we feel centered and satisfied, ready to take on the challenges of the world? But if our relationship is strained or distant, our need for synergy becomes paramount. Nothing feels quite right when love is out of sync. That's why getting along is so important to us. Simply put, for women, "Relationships 'R' Us."

Because of this need for connection and closeness, we take frequent, if not daily, temperature readings of how well we're getting along with our partners. We ask ourselves, "Are we spending enough time together?" "Have we had a good talk recently?" "Is he paying enough attention to me?" When the relationship flounders, we tenaciously try to set things back on course. We don't like to settle for mediocrity and are quite willing to "work on the relationship" until it shines.

It's not that men don't value relationships. They really do. But when it comes to taking the lead in improving things, they think we're so qualified for the job, they don't even bother applying. Plus, when the going gets rough, men are so much better at putting relationship problems out of their minds than we are. They're great at distracting themselves; they go to the gym to work out, they make business calls, play golf, veg out in front of the TV, have a beer, or whatever. They tell themselves, "This too shall pass." And life goes on.

At least for them it does. But I bet you're not as good at putting your relationship on the back burner as he is. When things aren't just right with our significant others, we women don't sweep things under the carpet or work up a sweat in an aerobics class. We lose sleep. We pig out on Häagen-Dazs ice cream. We stop eating altogether. We obsess. We get depressed. We *become* the problem. We immerse ourselves in a tireless search for answers to our relationship dilemmas. We're simply wired that way.

So, I'm no fool. I'm going straight to the top. I'm talking to you—the person who is the real engine of your relationship. If I wanted to write a cookbook, I'd direct it at the true lover of the culinary arts. If I wanted to write the definitive sports book, I'd have the sports fanatic in mind. If I'm going to pour my heart and soul into writing a no-nonsense manual for relationship change, I want to make certain it gets in the hands of the person most likely to put it to good use—and that's you.

There's another reason I've written this book for women. Since the publication of my book *Divorce Busting*, I've had the opportunity to touch people's lives in profound ways. I've helped warring couples love again, enabling them to renew their commitment to one another and keep their families together. However, despite my best efforts, some relationships have fallen through the cracks. Although this, in and of itself, is not particularly remarkable, what is remarkable is the definite pattern I noticed; it is primarily *women* who are walking out of their marriages. In fact, a journalist recently coined the phrase the "Walkaway Wives." Here's a behind-the-scenes look at what the Walkaway Wife syndrome is all about.

After years of trying unsuccessfully to improve an unhappy marriage, a woman eventually surrenders and convinces herself that change isn't possible. She ends up believing there's absolutely nothing she can do to influence her partner to be more responsive, since everything she's tried hasn't worked. That's when she begins to carefully map out the logistics of what she considers to be the inevitable—getting a divorce.

While she's planning her escape, she no longer tries to improve her relationship or modify her partner's behavior in any way. She resigns herself to living in silent desperation until "D day." Unfortunately, her husband views his wife's silence as an indication that "everything is fine." After all, the "nagging" has ceased. That's why, when she finally breaks the news of the impending divorce, her shell-shocked partner replies, "I had no idea you were unhappy." This response serves as further evidence of her husband's unfathomable insensitivity to her feelings, and the decision to dissolve their relationship becomes etched in stone. Even when her husband undergoes real and lasting changes, it's usually too late. The same impenetrable wall that for years shielded her from pain now prevents her from truly recognizing his genuine willingness to change. The relationship is over.

I know countless women who have said *"Au revoir"* to their partners. I've witnessed their struggles up close. They aren't cold, unfeeling people. They didn't take their decisions to leave lightly. They dreaded disbanding their families. They simply saw no other alternative. Unfortunately, many of these women eventually regretted their decisions. But it was too late. I want to change all that. I'm utterly convinced that all this pain can be avoided if women have access to practical, effective information about the mechanics of change earlier in their relationships, so they don't ever get to the point of no return.

Do you know someone who is a Walkaway Wife? A neighbor, a relative, or a friend? Is it you? Have you been secretly fantasizing about sharing an apartment with your cat or a new, flawless man? Have you been wondering what your life would be like without him around? Stop it. The only reason you've been thinking that way is because you've been feeling at a loss as to what to do next. Well, there are no coincidences. You picked up this book for a reason. *Getting Through to the Man You Love* is the ounce of prevention you'll need to ward off stockpiled resentment, toxic apathy, and irreversible hopelessness.

Your relationship challenges might be minor compared with Walkaway Wives'—your man's quirks are annoying but commonplace. And though you might feel frustrated about your partner's apparent allergy to change, perhaps you've never really thought about parting ways. Perhaps you're just someone who has had a gnawing feeling that things between you and your partner could be better. Maybe you've noticed more distance than in times past and you've been stymied because your efforts to get through to him have been unappreciated or misconstrued.

Well, regardless of the nature, depth, or complexity of your partner's foibles, you're about to learn effective methods for modifying him. In fact, once you start implementing these strategies, you'll be surprised at how yielding your partner really can be. You might also be surprised by your new, overriding feeling of empowerment.

Okay, have I piqued your curiosity about man-changing yet? Do you want to know how to lead a horse to water *and* make him drink? Well, that's what the rest of this book is about. Let me outline what you're about to learn.

Since the basic premise of this book is that you can effect relationship change single-handedly, the next chapter, "Changing Your Leopard's Spots," explains more fully how this is possible. Although you may have your doubts now, once you learn the mechanics of relationship change, you'll become a believer. You'll learn how, by making definite shifts in your usual way of approaching your partner, you can get him to respond more lovingly to you. In fact, once you witness how a change in you sparks a change in him, the only remaining question will be "Why did I wait so long to do this?"

The following chapter will make you feel as if I've been hiding out in your living room, eavesdropping on all of your conversations and interactions. That's where I'll describe what irks women most about men—their lack of interest in communicating, their tendency to misprioritize work, family, and outside interests, their insistence on being right, their rigid parenting style, their foolish belief that housework is synonymous with women's work, their inclination to spend too much or too little money. Shall I go on? Suffice it to say, I'll cover a broad range of male idiosyncrasies. But that's not all.

In addition to outlining the problems men pose in our lives, I'll explain, as best I can, why men behave the way they do. If you're going to battle, you've got to know the territory. In order to change your man, you first need to enter his world and learn how he thinks and feels. You need to know what makes him tick, what piques and holds his interest, what drives or motivates him, and what turns him off so that he no longer responds to you. Knowing how men are wired unlocks the mystery of how to influence them.

But before you get carried away with false hope, I want you to know that there are some things about men that *aren't* changeable, and this chapter will address these issues as well. For example, although I probably can help you influence your man to engage in more conversation, it may never be his favorite thing to do. He may become a better listener or a better conversationalist, but he may never get the same charge out of your talks that you do. And instead of your trying to convince him of the value of communication in life, it's *you* I'm going to convince to acknowledge his efforts to talk, however small. That's because I believe that the sooner you figure out what's changeable and what isn't, the more efficient you'll become at channeling your energy productively.

Once you better understand the problems confronting you, why your partner handles things the way he does and which aspects of his behavior are alterable, you'll want to know where to begin the process of change. That's easy. You start by setting concrete goals. Even if you think you know exactly what you would like to change about your mate, I bet you'll be surprised to find that your goals are only half-baked. I will teach you the basics of solution-oriented goals-setting in chapter 4. You'll create a target so clear that missing it will be virtually impossible. And to make certain that you won't get sidetracked, chapter 5 will remind you of paths to avoid as you embark on your journey toward relationship change.

Next, you'll need a step-by-step map to guide you in accomplishing your goals. You'll learn specific techniques you can put into practice immediately. First, you'll read about the basics of behavioral change. In fact, you'll discover that much of what you need to know about changing your man can be learned from a good dog-training manual. Think I'm joking? I'm not. I'm dead serious. The truth is, if you've ever trained a dog, you know more than you think you do about training your man. You can get him to sit, stay, and come, too.

After the primer on behavioral change, you'll learn seven techniques for influencing your partner that are primarily action-oriented. Why action-oriented? Since men are less verbal than women, it makes sense that we stop depending on words, lectures, and verbal appeals to influence them. No matter what we say or how we say it, men think we're nagging. Even when we're incredibly diplomatic, they still think we're bitching and so they tune us out. On the other hand, men are less inclined to ignore messages relayed to them through action. That's why, although there's a short chapter entitled "Smart Talk: How to Talk So Men Will Listen," action-oriented techniques take center stage. You'll learn exactly what you need *to do* to get his attention, and quickly, I might add.

The next item of business is learning how to keep the positive changes going. You can't rest on your laurels when it comes to changing your man. You need to go on a maintenance program. Forever. And although forever sounds like an impossibly long time, it really isn't. Once you've gotten the ball of change rolling, it's quite simple to keep it rolling. I'll teach you everything you need to know about making the positive changes stick.

Finally, since some men are impervious to even the most well-planned, well-executed strategies aimed at changing them, I'll help you assess what to do if nothing seems to work. However, with a bundle of determination and a modicum of luck, you won't ever have to read this chapter.

One more thing you should know. Despite the fact that their identities have been changed to maintain their anonymity, all the women you'll read about in this book are real. The methods they used to change their men are also real, as are the changes they inspired in their partners. Now it's your turn.

After all this, perhaps there's still a teensy part of you that is having a hard time admitting that changing your man is part of your master plan. You feel that if you were to admit a desire to change him, it would be too presumptuous or selfish. Well, girlfriend, cast your inhibitions to the wind. You can finally admit it. It's just between you and me, and I won't tell anyone. Every time I told a woman about my plans to call this book *Getting Through to the Man You Love*, she laughed out loud and said, "When can I get my copy?" So, don't worry. You're not alone in your desires. We all feel that way. Having said that, just because you can better accept your ambitious goal of changing your man, it doesn't mean you have to flaunt your intentions. In fact, this book is for your eyes only. It will be the place I get to talk turkey without men looking over our shoulders. You'll get straightforward, practical, hands-on advice on man-changing without regard to diplomacy or political correctness.

If you're someone who was just about to pull her hair out in frustration, or throw in the proverbial towel, don't do it. You're just pages away from the solutions for which you've been searching. In fact, you've just picked up the book that no woman (in her right mind) will want to be without.

Changing Your Leopard's Spots

In this chapter, I'm going to show how you and you alone can be the impetus for change in your relationship. I know that this notion is counterintuitive because, for one reason, we've been taught that it takes two, not one, to tango; it takes two people who are consciously committed to working things out *together* to untie relationship knots. In fact, most relationship experts believe that without both partners present, chances of relationship reform on any level are fairly bleak. To them, trying to change your relationship alone is like the sound of one hand clapping.

Now, I realize that convincing you that you can change your partner may be putting the cart before the horse. Your doubts about changing your man might run even deeper than simply questioning whether you can do it single-handedly. You might be someone who thinks, "People just don't change." Well, you're wrong. The only man incapable of changing is a dead man.

Change–Defeating Illusions

In order to show you that people, including men, can really change, let's start by exploring some common reasons for your pessimism and why they set you up to be discontented. Believe me, if you hold on to these precepts, you'll stand in the way of change.

"That's just how he is. Personalities don't change."

One of the primary reasons you might feel pessimistic about change is that you believe your partner's irritating behavior is simply a reflection of a deeply ingrained personality characteristic. For example, if your partner gets angry every time you voice your concern about not spending enough time together, you may overgeneralize and start to convince yourself that his anger in those specific situations is actually representative of who he is as a person. Then, you start to look for more evidence to support your hypothesis; that is, you watch him closely and search your memory for other times when he has behaved angrily or callously. Eventually, you have all the evidence against him that you require. Each time he responds in anger, you tell yourself, "No wonder he acts like that, he's just an angry person." But the problem with this thinking is that once you pigeonhole your partner and see him as nothing more than his flawed personality, you fail to notice all the times when his actions defy your "angry person" diagnosis.

For instance, if he responds calmly and lovingly whenever you raise a concern about his handling of the children, do you tell yourself, "He's a patient person"? I wouldn't bet on it. First of all, you probably overlook these moments because they just don't "fit" your image of him. These acts of kindness go by unnoticed, unappreciated. But if you happen to notice his calm reactions, my guess is you rationalize them by saying, "He's probably tired tonight and he doesn't have enough energy to fight with me."

Then, after noticing that he's capable of having a perfectly anger-free conversation with his mother or some other close person about how he spends his time, the very subject sure to set off fireworks between the two of you, do you say to yourself, "Boy, what a calm man I married"? Nah. Admit it. You probably attribute his reasonableness to another negative personality trait: "He's two-faced" or "He must love his mother more than me." In fact, it probably infuriates you that he can tap into a more reasonable side of himself at will, when he won't with you.

So, believing that your partner's annoying behavior is part of his unchangeable personality is dangerous on several counts. (1) You become obsessed with scrutinizing his actions to find evidence to support your theory about him. (2) You fail to notice exceptions. (3) If you do notice exceptions, you explain them away. But that's not all. There's another reason that believing your partner has a personality disorder is ill advised. Sometimes, because you're wearing your "looking for anger" glasses, you may observe a perfectly innocent behavior on his part and cast it in a negative light. For instance, you may be on the phone with him when he's at his office and if he abruptly says, "I have to go," instead of realizing his boss has just entered the room, you think, "There he goes being angry again."

After reading this chapter, I'm going to convince you that labeling or pigeonholing your man is not a productive thing to do, for you or for him. It fools you into thinking his behavior is stagnant and unchanging. It keeps you from recognizing that people act and respond differently in different situations and under different conditions. For instance, have you ever asked your man for a favor when he was tired only to have your head chopped off, but when you approached him later that evening after great sex, he was only too happy to oblige? I'm not saying you have to become a sex kitten to effect change in your man (although most men would agree that you shouldn't rule out this strategy entirely), I'm just suggesting you keep in mind that your man's behavior varies depending on the circumstances. I'm going to teach you how to create the circumstances under which he will feel most inspired to meet your needs. I'm going to show you how to bring out the best in him.

"That's how he grew up."

Another reason you might believe your partner is incapable of real change is that you've convinced yourself that people are merely products of their upbringing. According to this theory, as impressionable children, we observe our parents, how they interact with each other, how they treat us, and we mimic what we see. We learn about life from these early childhood experiences, and the images remain indelibly imprinted on our minds. So, if your father-in-law was angry a lot when your husband was a child, you believe your husband is destined to be an angry person for the rest of his life. If your partner's mother waited on him hand and foot when he was growing up, you tell yourself you can't expect your man to be responsible, he never learned how. In the heat of an argument, how many times have you told him, "The apple doesn't fall far from the tree" or "You're just a chip off the old block"? And although you'd really like him to be different, you truly don't believe in your heart that he can escape the unfathomable hold his past has on him.

Trust me. If what I just said sounds familiar to you, you're not alone. We all believe the "We are a product of our past" theory to some extent. And, I might add, for a very good reason. We are very definitely influenced by how we were raised. However, one of the more interesting developments to surface in the mental health field within the last few decades is a growing body of research on the topic of resilience. Researchers have become fascinated with the question of why it is that some people growing up under extremely adverse conditions such as poverty, overcrowding, violence, drug abuse, and emotional or physical abuse become debilitated by their experiences while others rise above adversity. A growing number of professionals believe that current theories on psychological and emotional development do not fully explain those who beat the odds.

> Broad epidemiological studies, they say, don't explain why one girl, sexually abused by a relative, becomes an unwed mother or a prostitute while another becomes an Oprah Winfrey or a Maya Angelou. Retrospective studies can't explain why one man, raised in a harsh, crowded household in impoverished Richmond, California, becomes addicted to crack cocaine and dies of AIDS, while his younger brother—Christopher Darden—graduates from law school and goes on to prosecute O. J. Simpson. It's time, they say, to see what the Dardens and Winfreys of the world have to teach.[1]

Steven Wolin, a researcher, psychiatrist, and coauthor with Sophie Wolin of *The Resilient Self*, writes that although children from alcoholic families have a higher risk of developing alcoholism than those in the general population, 70 percent of those growing up in these families will not become alcoholic. Seventy percent! Similarly, he comments that growing up in a physically abusive family does not guarantee you will abuse your own children. Far from it. Seventy percent of those who were abused as children *will not* become abusive parents. Clearly, as these extreme examples show, though we're affected by our past, we are not our past. And that's good news because no matter how your man was raised, he can learn new ways to temper the impact of his undoubtedly less-than-perfect childhood.

Think about yourself. No matter what cards you were dealt in terms of your family of origin, you've probably been able to change your life in some significant way that counters your upbringing. Everyone can. That includes your partner.

"Okay, okay," you say. "Maybe people do change, but only if they *want* to change. Other people can't change them." If you believe one person can't change another, it's probably because you've been influenced by conventional wisdom. Just think of all the expressions in our everyday language suggesting people are unmovable. The last time you felt frustrated by a predictable bullheaded response from your partner, did you call a friend and have her console you with the reply "Don't forget, a leopard doesn't change his spots" or something similar? And did you end the conversation thanking her for reminding you to stop beating a dead horse?

Okay, tell the truth. Even if you've never had a conversation like this, haven't you, at one time or another, thought, "You can't teach an old dog new tricks"? What other pet phrases do you have? My mother sent me a button a few years ago that read, "Don't try to teach a cow to sing. It doesn't work and it annoys the cow." Yikes! No wonder you don't have much confidence in your ability to light a fire beneath your partner. We're taught to expect resistance! Well, I'm going to fix that. I'm going to tell you about a situation that occurred a long time ago that changed my thinking forever.

The Ripple Effect

Many years ago, when I was just a rookie therapist, Cathy, a single mother, and her fifteen-year-old son, Jay, sat down in my office. Cathy looked overworked and underappreciated. She was concerned about her son's school performance. His grades were gradually but consistently dropping. Homework was a problem. He procrastinated getting it done until late in the evening and this irked her no end. Some nights he avoided doing his homework altogether. She also noticed that Jay was becoming more reluctant to complete his chores at home.

Above and beyond the issues with Jay, Cathy felt additional challenges stemming from her current living situation. For financial reasons, they were living temporarily with Cathy's mother, who frequently intervened by trying to discipline Jay. As soon as he walked through the door after school, "she'd start in on him," said Cathy. She'd ask, "Do you have any homework? Why don't you start it right now?" Though Cathy knew her mother was only trying to be helpful, she couldn't help but notice that Jay was doing everything he could to rebel. Like most teenagers, he hated being told what to do and proved his independence by not doing what his grandmother requested.

Furthermore, because Cathy's mother was stepping in regularly, Cathy felt that her own efforts to get control of the situation were being undermined. I suggested that Cathy invite her mother to the next session to discuss her concerns, but she didn't think it would be a very good idea. Cathy thought her mother wouldn't understand her need to handle Jay by herself. She believed her mother would feel hurt or insulted if she were asked to back off. I tried to convince Cathy otherwise because I felt that the grandmother was a key player in the scheme of things, but Cathy was resolute in her decision to find a solution on her own. Honoring her decision, I helped Cathy explore other, more effective ways of dealing with her son and ended the session.

Two weeks later, they returned. Cathy reported a marked improvement in her relationship with her son. She said he was more focused on his schoolwork and more responsible at home. She didn't need to nag him about getting things done. Relieved to hear about the improvements with Jay, I asked if she had given more thought to inviting her mother to the session and she replied, "I don't know what happened, but my mother didn't intervene at all in the last two weeks. She didn't even remind Jay about his homework a single time."

At first, I was fairly surprised because no one had confronted Cathy's mother directly about her behavior. As far as I could tell, no one had even said anything to her at all. So I asked myself, "What, then, could account for Grandmother's backing off and allowing Cathy to handle Jay on her own?" Eventually, the answer to my question became apparent.

During the meeting with Cathy, she told me that she had decided to take a stronger stand with Jay. Every night when she returned from work, she reviewed his homework with him. If his homework was incomplete, Jay was denied privileges such as going out with his friends on the weekend. He finally understood that his mother meant business and began to toe the line.

Once Cathy became more effective in handling Jay, and her mother observed these interactions, her mother didn't feel the need to intervene. She saw that Cathy was perfectly capable of handling the situation without her assistance. Cathy changed, her son shaped up, and her mother butted out. End of story.

Cathy and her family taught me a tremendous lesson that day that has stayed with me ever since. Although I once thought that all the people involved in a particular problem must come together to resolve that problem and talk it out thoroughly, I have since learned that this isn't necessarily so. If one person makes a decision to handle things differently, to react in new and more productive ways, this new behavior will trigger new responses in other people. Why is this so?

No Man or Woman Is an Island

To help you understand this principle, envision a mobile. When one piece of the mobile is set in motion, it moves the piece closest to it, which in turn sets off a chain reaction, mobilizing the remaining pieces. Movement in one part of the mobile creates movement throughout the entire mobile. Now imagine that the mobile is a family and that the pieces of the mobile are the members of that family. Can you begin to see how one person's behavior can affect another person's and another's and so on?

For example, have you ever had one of those days when your partner comes home in a bad mood and takes it out on you, which in turn makes you feel grouchy? Then, since you're short of temper, the usual questions emanating from the kids, such as "What's for dinner?" "When will dinner be ready?" "Can I skip dinner and go over to Jason's house to watch a video?" which typically only mildly annoy you, now completely exasperate you. You snap at them loudly, "I don't know what's for dinner and it will be ready when it's ready and no you can't go to Jason's house." "Boy, why are you being so mean?" they ask, and you respond, "I'm just sick and tired of doing everything around here." Ten minutes later, you hear shouting from the living room; your children are arguing over the use of the VCR. The only thing missing is a cat for the kids to taunt (and a hamster for the cat to taunt, and so on).

Now maybe the scene at your house is somewhat different from this, but I think you understand what I'm trying to tell you here. In a family, our actions and reactions are all interconnected. So far, so good. Right? But the plot thickens. My guess is that you could identify with the example above because, if you read it carefully, it makes your partner out to be the culprit. Remember, *he* came home in a bad mood and took it out on you. You can identify with that. But if I were to ask your partner to tell the story from his vantage point, I'm positive I'd hear a completely different version. For instance, he might tell the story like this:

"I came home from work yesterday in a perfectly good mood. I was looking forward to seeing my wife and kids. When I walked through the door, I realized that no one even noticed my presence. Not one single 'Hello.' In the past, after a long day at work, if my wife got home first, I could always tell she was happy to see me by the greeting she gave me at the door. We'd spend a few minutes together, catching up on each other's days before getting dinner together. Now, I come home and I get a big nothing.

"As if that weren't bad enough, she immediately starts talking about chores to be done and bills to be paid. I told her to back off for a few minutes and give me a chance to take off my coat and relax. She snapped back at me and then went on to bark at the kids. Great way to start an evening, eh?"

When you hear the story told this way, it's harder to identify with it, isn't it? That's because from your perspective, it's your partner who starts the evening off on a bad note. But the only reason he appears to be the instigator is that the person doing the judging is you. When communication between you and your partner goes sour, what you notice is how unreasonable, hurtful, and vindictive *he* is. That's because you live inside yourself, and therefore you're very much in touch with your own feelings. You know how his remarks cut to the quick. You're aware of the sinking feeling inside when he disappoints you. You notice your heart breaking when he seems oblivious to your feelings. Feeling violated forces you to pick your head up and take notice, and what you see is him.

Conversely, you're not as aware of how your actions and reactions can have a similar impact on him. When he acts "like a jerk," you're convinced it's due to a bad day at work, his deeply entrenched personality flaws, or that it's merely "coming from left field" and completely uncalled-for. Well, believe it or not, his unreasonable behavior may stem from the fact that he's hurt or angered by something you did earlier. Guys often seem so tough and untouched by our comments or actions, it's hard to imagine that we can inflict pain, especially when that isn't our intention (and most of the time it isn't). Well, we can and we do. Your partner reacts just as strongly to you as you react to him. Blaming him for initiating problems inevitably provokes the classic chicken-or-egg debate: "You started it," followed by "I only did that because of how you treated me earlier," and so on. The problem with believing your partner always initiates the problems between you is that you're failing to recognize the circular nature of your interactions.

The Circular Connection

In intimate relationships, the connection between two people is circular: person A affects person B who in turn affects person A who in turn affects person B and so on. (Or is it person B affects person A who in turn affects person B and so on?) Although the starting point of most relationship problems is arbitrary (depending on the vantage point), couples seem to thrive on identifying the precise moment interactions go downhill.

For example, a few days ago, my husband, Jim, and I were having a conversation. He said something that I considered to be critical, and for a moment I glanced away and looked at the television.

When I turned my head back, he was reading a magazine. Then, since he was reading, I turned toward the television once again. Moments later, he walked out of the family room. I asked, "Why are you leaving?" and he replied, "Because you're watching television." I said, "I'm watching television because you're reading," and he replied, "I'm reading because you're watching television," and I said, "But I told you, I'm watching television because you are reading a magazine," and in a louder voice, he said . . . well, you know the rest. It seems funny in retrospect, but it didn't seem funny at the time.

I was tempted to tell him that the reason I glanced at the television in the first place was that he said something I didn't like. But had I done that, I know exactly what would have happened. He would have explained the reason he said what he did . . . surely it was something I said right before that. You know what I mean? Luckily for both of us, I didn't pursue the conversation and went on to bigger and better things. We both decided that whatever we were arguing about wasn't worth it, regardless of how it started. Sometimes less is more.

So, the point I'm making here is that by blaming your partner and not seeing your own role in your relationship dilemmas, you might inadvertently be pushing his buttons and bringing out the worst in him. Also, you're so focused on his mistreatment of you, you start playing the blame game. You think he's to blame, so you wait for him to change. He's thinks you're to blame, so he waits for you to change. In the meantime, nothing changes.

A while ago, I had another "Which came first, the chicken or the egg" debate. This time, it was with my daughter, Danielle. She and I had been getting along quite well when I started to notice a shift in her behavior; she was acting impatient and being fresh to me. Naturally, this angered me and I confronted her about it. Here's how the conversation went:

> ME: I can't believe how fresh you've been lately.
> DANIELLE: That's because you've been so mean to me.
> ME: I've been mean to you because you've been so fresh to me recently.

DANIELLE: Well, I've been fresh because you've been so mean.

I must admit that we did more than two rounds of this before I said to myself, "Practice what you teach," and stopped. But it became clear to me that over the previous few weeks, her disrespectful manner had prompted me to be harsh with her. My harshness in turn prompted her to be disrespectful to me. I was waiting for her to have more regard for my feelings so that I could be kinder to her, and she was waiting for me to be kinder to her so that she would be more patient and respectful. I was unable to recognize that my harsh manner was actually exacerbating the situation because all I could see was her rude behavior. Does this sound familiar at all?

After I did some soul-searching, I realized that I had been rather busy lately and that it was entirely possible Danielle wasn't getting what she needed from me. I finally figured out that I could wait for her to follow my rules so I could be more loving and attentive, or I could shower her with affection so she would be loving in return. Being the adult, I decided to take the lead. Now, keep in mind, showering someone with affection when they're being fresh to you isn't easy, nor does it come naturally, but doing so reverses the negative momentum. I was loving to her and she reciprocated by being loving and respectful right back, which served as a powerful reinforcer for me to continue being nice to her, and so on. (Besides, a good friend of mine always says, "Kids need hugs the most when they deserve them the least," a philosophy that applies equally well to the men in our lives.)

As I reflect back on both incidents, I feel pleased about the eventual outcomes: Jim and I stopped arguing and started being more pleasant to each other, and Danielle and I started being more loving again. And I feel good about the fact that I was able to decide in both those situations to stop playing the blame game and turn things around. Admittedly, being the "big one" is easier to do with a child—that's your job as a parent. Taking the lead to stop playing the blame game with your man can be a bit more challenging. But the benefits are just as rewarding. Believe me.

So you have a choice. You can sit around figuring out who's to blame and who should change first, or you can start the ball rolling by taking action, regardless of "who started it." That's why I'm putting the ball back into your court. This is not to say that you're at fault. You're not. It's just as much a waste of time blaming yourself as it is blaming your partner. I'm going to help you stop thinking in terms of blame entirely and start thinking about finding solutions. I'm going to help you focus on the parts of your interactions over which you have control. Because if you take charge of yourself in those interactions, the outcome will be much more to your liking. You'll turn your partner into a much nicer person. Let me give you an example of how this works.

Changing Your Steps in the Dance

Joyce was convinced that her husband, Tom, was unable to control his anger when he felt frustrated. Joyce grew up in a family where anger was rarely expressed so when Tom's anger surfaced, she felt extremely uncomfortable and, given her feelings, did what most people in her situation would do. She tried to console, comfort, and reason with Tom. Unfortunately, when she did, his anger only increased, which in turn devastated her because, after all, she was just trying to help. For years, they played out their roles in this dance: Tom gets angry, Joyce tries to console, Tom gets angrier, Joyce becomes despondent, and so on.

One day, Joyce decided to do an experiment. Tom was in their family room working at his computer and beginning to grouse out loud: "I can't believe my boss expects me to do this. I wasn't at the training last week, so how in the world would I know what I'm supposed to do?" She was just about to reassure him that the task probably wasn't as difficult as he thought, but, instead, she bit her tongue, banged her fist on the table, and said loudly, "What was your boss thinking, anyway? I'm really surprised he would expect you to finish this when you don't have a clue as to what to do. That's extremely unrealistic of him."

For a moment, there was dead silence. A few seconds later, a surprised Tom replied in a calm voice, "If I just work at this thing for a while, I'm sure I'll figure it out. No big deal." I'm not certain who was more shocked—Tom, because Joyce didn't comfort him, or Joyce, because of Tom's ability to compose himself so readily. Tom finished his work without incident, and they had a pleasant evening together afterward.

Joyce had spent much of her life blaming Tom, his erratic moods, his boss, or his heavy workload for his impulsive bursts of anger, none of which she could do anything about. Now she realized there was another way to look at the situation: a perspective that offered her considerably more control over the final outcome. She finally saw how *her own actions* were triggering in him the very response she disdained. Instead of calming him, her suggestions and reassurances were actually increasing his anger. Eventually, Joyce realized that her placating Tom made him feel as if she were dismissing or minimizing his feelings, which explains his angry reaction. But to Joyce, even more important than knowing why her placating backfired was the recognition that she could create change in her marriage, and she was eager to investigate other avenues to apply her newfound knowledge.

Joyce learned that once she changed *her* steps in the dance, the dance changed. Tom was expecting her to do the same old thing—be the placater—when he complained about work. He was gearing up to do his same old thing in return—that is, be the irrational, angry, out-of-control husband. When she shocked him by responding differently, it prompted a completely different reaction in him. Joyce's breaking from the script led to Tom's following suit. A change in her led to a change in him. Here's another example:

Ann has been married for ten years to John. Although most of those years have been happy ones, Ann has felt shortchanged lately by John's increased hours at work. He's been working very late several times a week. At first, Ann was understanding, but as months passed and John's late nights continued, her patience wore thin. She felt distant from him and lonely. When Ann expressed her displeasure about his absences, John became defensive and withdrew even further. This hurt Ann tremendously, and she let John know. She felt certain that he would be empathetic and reach out to her in some way. Instead, he got angrier and found himself wanting to spend even less time with her, which in turn enraged Ann. I asked Ann what she wanted to change about her life and she said, "John and I used to love being together. We were always very affectionate and close to one another. Now, I feel as if we're two strangers living under the same roof. I want to spend more time with John, and I want him to be happy to be with me. I feel as if our relationship is a chore for him right now and that really hurts."

I asked Ann how she would act differently with John if he were spending more time with her and doing all those things he used to do to feel close to her. She said, "That's easy. I'd be happier. I'd be more upbeat around him. I would definitely show more interest in what he was doing every day and tell him more about my life. I've completely stopped sharing myself with him these days."

Ann became reflective and added to her list of things she would do differently if John were more attentive.

"I'd be more affectionate to him. We used to touch a lot. Even if we were just watching television, we'd be all over each other. Lately, I haven't even sat down in the same room with him. Also, I know I used to be less serious. I had a sense of humor which is completely gone right now. We don't laugh anymore. I take everything so personally, and my feelings get hurt easily. But if John were more attentive, I guess I'd make more of an effort to be the 'old me.'"

"Perfect," I thought to myself, "a solution in the making." I suggested that Ann try an experiment. I told her to go home and pretend that John had mysteriously decided to be the "old John" and to act as if she were the "old Ann" for several days and watch the results. Two weeks later, Ann returned looking like a "new Ann." I could tell by the smile on her face and her relaxed expression that something positive had happened. She said, "I didn't even have to do the experiment because that very first night after my appointment with you he came home early from work. I was so happy. We went out for dinner, had a great conversation, and came home and made love. It was the first time in a long time and it felt great. I know he enjoyed the evening too. I could tell how happy he was to be with me. It was the weirdest coincidence that he came home early that night because he didn't even know I had an appointment with you."

Although coincidences do happen occasionally, I still wondered if in fact Ann had done something to lay the groundwork for John's response. I said to her, "Think back. What did you do after leaving here that day that might have made a difference to John?" Initially, she recalled nothing, but shortly thereafter . . . epiphany! "You know," she commented, "I completely forgot that I called him at work and told him I loved him at the end of our conversation. I haven't been calling him or telling him 'I love you' lately. I suppose that was pretty different for me. I hadn't thought about my call until now. That's strange. I thought he just had had a change of heart."

I asked Ann to tell me what else she had been doing to be like the "old Ann" since our last meeting. She said, "Well, after that first night, being more involved with John came naturally to me. I didn't have to pretend. I called him several times at work just to say hello, and asked him how his day was going. On two or three occasions, I took the time to make him his favorite meal. We went out together on Saturday night and had a great time. John would probably say that I was livelier and more fun to be with. On the few nights when he worked late, instead of grousing or keeping to myself, I waited up for him and greeted him with a glass of wine. He seemed to very much appreciate my being there for him."

At that point, I was curious as to the differences she noticed in John over the past two weeks. She said, "He was really back to his old self: happier, more playful, more interested in me, more involved. He only worked late a few times since then. I was surprised. I couldn't believe he had changed so quickly. It's almost too good to be true. I don't quite trust it completely yet, but I'm really enjoying it.

"These two weeks made me realize how miserable I had been, not only because John was so unavailable to me, but because I had been holding back being affectionate toward him. I don't like *myself* as much when I hold back from being a loving person. I feel freer and more spontaneous now. Though I knew I'd love it when John came back to me emotionally, it was an added bonus to learn how much more I like myself too."

Sound too good to be true? It isn't. I've seen it happen countless times. In fact, I expect "miracles" like this to occur and am taken by surprise when they don't. Let's take a closer look at Ann's situation and why it turned out the way it did.

Isn't it interesting that Ann attributed the change in their relationship to John? Despite the fact that she placed a very loving call to him, she still only remembered his coming home early. That's because, as I said before, we're so much more sensitive to and focused on the effect our partners have on us than we are on the effect we have on our partners. Though Ann could write a treatise on how John's affection impacted her over the past two weeks, she probably paid little attention to the ways in which her calling him more frequently, cooking his favorite meals, and being more animated in his presence affected him. Her efforts to please him made pleasing her a top priority for John. There's something to that old expression "I'll scratch your back if you scratch mine," isn't there?

Also, Ann may have overlooked her small but significant act of goodwill because in having already made the decision to do something positive about her problems with John (by seeking counseling *and* by agreeing to act differently toward him immediately), making a phone call to him didn't strike her as being anything extraordinary. It was a logical extension of her decision to change. No biggie. Yet, to John, who was unaware of her new resolution and who up until that point had been feeling attacked, Ann's call was quite remarkable and out of character. It felt like a peace offering. Eager for more tranquillity in their relationship, John seized the opportunity to show Ann his appreciation and did so by surprising her and coming home early.

Like Ann, it's not unusual for people to think that solutions to relationship problems arise when their partners finally get with the program and change. Sometimes it works that way. But, more often than not, giving your partner all the credit for things going well is just as shortsighted as assigning all the blame to him when the relationship is floundering. Chances are, if your partner changes, you've probably been doing something different to get his attention. Even if you're not aware of it, you've probably taken some subtle action to make it more conducive for him to respond favorably to you.

Helping Ann see her own role in the positive changes between John and her made her realize how much influence she truly had on John. Realizing this, she knew she had a choice: she could either influence John by sulking and pushing him away or she could influence him by showing her affection and pulling him toward her. Her choice was obvious.

Change Leaks All Over

In my work with couples, I often notice how one small act of kindness sparks another and another and so on. A minor gesture of a positive nature, such as Ann's phone call to John, can be the start of a solution avalanche. For example, if a couple who argue a great deal over money learn better ways of handling their disagreements, the benefits to their relationship go far beyond their improved financial planning. The tension and hard feelings that have permeated the relationship will disappear. Over time, they'll probably like each other more and feel better about themselves as individuals; as a result, they're likely to experience improved communication in general. Because the relationship feels more loving, they might have a greater desire to make love. And because they feel more serenity, they might treat their children with more patience and understanding. An improved home life might enable this couple to concentrate better and be more productive at work. The possibilities are infinite. Improvements in one area of your life lead to improvements in other areas as well. Solutions know no bounds.

You may think I'm exaggerating the benefits of taking that first step, and you're having trouble envisioning how a minor shift in your actions can transform your relationship. Well, think about it in another, perhaps somewhat less optimistic context. Have you ever been troubled by how quickly and completely a good time between you and your partner can disintegrate? You might be having a perfectly wonderful dinner together, and all of a sudden, one minor negative comment turns into World War III, right before your very eyes. Sometimes, you don't even know what hit you. Well, the force creating the speedy downward spiral happens to be bidirectional; that is, its energy can be harnessed to create sudden upward spirals just as easily.

Yes, But . . .

Okay. Everything I'm saying makes sense, but there may be a part of you that wonders whether all this stuff applies to you. Despite my optimism, you may have some questions and lingering skepticism. Here are some of the most common questions women ask.

Q. "You talk about how people are connected and how they affect each other, but my husband and I are two ships passing in the night. Will he even notice if I try something new?"

A. If things between you and your man are stormy at the moment, you might feel distant and detached from him. You start to believe you're worlds apart and that nothing connects you. You need to know that this is really just an illusion. Everything is connected.

When you're in a relationship, whether it's a relationship with your partner, children, parents, coworkers, or friends, you are connected to them in very powerful ways. What you do affects them. What they do affects you. It is unavoidable. Even silence or apparent disinterest speaks loudly and often triggers strong reactions in others. A sarcastic glance can turn an entire evening upside down. We act and react to people around us whether we're blissfully in love or desperately at odds with them. So don't be fooled by your feelings of distance or detachment from your man. He's watching you through the corner of his eyes. Count on it.

Q. "Why do I always have to be the one to change?"

A. This is a common reaction. But I want to make something perfectly clear. I am not suggesting that you change because you're wrong or because you're the source of the problems between you. I am not suggesting you change in order for you to become a better or more enlightened person. I am not suggesting you change to please your man. The *only* reason I'm suggesting you make a change is that I know you will get more of your needs met. When you change how you're approaching your partner, he will change. He'll become more the person you want him to be, and you'll be happier as a result. Remember, this book is entitled *Getting Through to the Man You Love*. I'm writing this book for *you* to get more out of life and more satisfaction out of your relationship. If what I'm suggesting doesn't yield the results you're hoping for, quit doing it! But I'm confident that when you start seeing your frog turn into a prince, you'll feel that your tipping over the first domino was well worth it. Do it for you.

But maybe you're still thinking, "Why do women always have to be the ones to take the lead in relationship improvement? Why doesn't he ever suggest talking together about our marriage, reading a self-help book together, or going to a relationship seminar?" If you're guided by this kind of thinking, you're doomed, because, as I said in the last chapter, a lot of men aren't too keen on taking the time to strengthen and tone their relationships by way of structured activities. It's just not their thing. (I saw a cartoon of a knight in full armor with a long spear in his hand who says to his wife, "I'm ready for that talk now.")

Or maybe your man is willing to work on your relationship conjointly in theory, but your schedules never seem to coincide. You want to talk at night when your work is done, but he's ready to go to sleep. He's willing to talk over dinner, but you don't want to open Pandora's box at the same time you're trying to digest your meal. You both set aside an afternoon to hash things out and his beeper goes off, he's gotta go. It's like playing telephone tag without the telephone.

Here are a few important pointers to keep in mind about all this. Number one: If your man is less than enthusiastic about working on the relationship with you, *don't take it personally*. It doesn't necessarily mean he doesn't love you or that he isn't committed to making the relationship more satisfying. It just means he's not going to do it your way. And although I'm certain you believe that *your* way is best, it's not *how* you get there that counts. Getting there, regardless of the route, is what matters. So don't forget that.

Pointer number two: If you spend time worrying about his level of commitment to resolve the differences between you, or trying to convince him to join you in your efforts, *you're wasting time and expending valuable energy that you'll need later.* So stop trying to persuade him. Stop feeling sorry for yourself that he's not like Michael, your best friend's husband. Don't fritter away another moment wondering what it would be like to be married to a more communicative kind of guy. Take the bull by the horns and change your man by yourself.

Q. "Isn't it manipulative to try to change him?"

A. Sometimes women wonder if they are being manipulative when they begin using the methods described in this book because they learn to become strategic about how they approach their partners, instead of just allowing emotions to guide them and doing "what comes naturally." But when you're in a relationship, you want that relationship to be the best it can possibly be, and you want to do whatever it takes to get there. There's nothing wrong with that. And you're not an evil person because you want your partner to be more sensitive to your needs. No matter what he tells you, he wants the same consideration from you. Sometimes it seems that we women ask more of men than they ask of us, but that's simply because we're much more verbal about our requests for change than they are. Don't be fooled for a moment: men want to shape their partners, too (even if all they want is for you to stop trying to change them!).

So, remember, whether you do it effectively or ineffectively, when you ask your partner to do things differently, you are trying to change him. When you ask him to rinse the dishes before putting them into the dishwasher, pick his dirty socks up off the floor, stop smoking, stop snoring, or say "I love you" more often, you're trying to influence him to change. Furthermore, if you spend a lot of time trying to change him with ineffective methods, you will start resenting him because he's not bending and he doesn't exactly appreciate you either. In fact, he gets downright mad. So, if you are going to try to reform your partner in any way, big or small, why not use a method that's sure to minimize resistance and feelings of indignation and hostility? Why not do what works? The methods in this book will teach you to be more results-oriented in your problem-solving—and any male will appreciate that.

Q. "Even if he does change, will it last?"

A. There is an entire chapter devoted to helping you help your man make the changes stick. But let me give you the Cliff Notes version here. Your partner's changes will have been prompted by the changes in you. As with weight loss, as long as you continue eating healthfully and exercising, the weight will stay off. Pig out and become a slug, and you'll get pudgy again. No mystery here. The same is true with changing your man. By remaining solution-focused in your responses to him and avoiding, as best you can, old knee-jerk reactions, you'll continue to enjoy the man of your dreams. It's up to you.

You need to keep in mind that one other reason he'll stay on track is that when you're happier, he'll be happier. You'll have stopped nagging. You'll be smiling more. You might even be more affectionate. He'll like the changes in you. So when you change, he'll change, then you'll change in return, which will make him a happy camper, and happy campers keep camping.

Q. "Why should I believe that he can change when nothing I've ever done before has worked?"

A. It's easy to believe that our goals are unachievable when we don't get the results we want. Especially when we've worked at it for a while. But stop for a minute. Think of how many times you were finally able to reach a goal despite many disappointments along the way. What if you had concluded that success wasn't possible because the going was rough? Where would you be now? In his book *Unlimited Power*, Anthony Robbins writes about the importance of viewing failure as nothing more than another rung on the ladder of success.

> There's a famous story about Thomas Edison. After he'd tried 9,999 times to perfect the light bulb and hadn't succeeded, someone asked him, "Are you going to have ten thousand failures?" He answered, "I

didn't fail. I just discovered another way not to invent the electric light bulb."[2]

So just think: the longer nothing's worked and the more you know about what not to do, the closer you are to a solution! In the next chapter, I'll help you figure out what makes your man tick so you can get him to tock. And like Edison's lightbulbs, I know you'll find the information illuminating. I promise.

CHAPTER THREE

Testosterone Simplified

*G*etting Through to the Man You Love embodies two fundamental principles: that one person can be the catalyst for change in another and, more specifically, that a *woman* can *get through to a man.* Perhaps the last chapter convinced you that you can trigger change in other people, but you're still fairly certain that your man isn't one of them. I'll admit that most men stubbornly resist women's attempts to change them, but despite John Gray's advice to women, "The best way to help a man grow is to let go of trying to change him in any way,"[1] men *can* be changed. Even your man.

However, the secret to successful man-changing lies in the strategies you choose. But before we talk "strategies," let's talk "men." To start, you first need to know what you're up against. As I mentioned earlier, part of the reason we have so much difficulty influencing our partners is that we make the mistake of approaching our men as if they're just like us. We don't take into account the now well-accepted fact that men and women are different. Our brains and bodies are wired differently. We think differently. We react to situations differently. We have different needs and ambitions. What we want from our partners is different.

Trying to persuade or influence a man by doing what comes naturally to woman is like trying to send information from one computer to another completely incompatible computer. It simply doesn't work. In order for you to improve your odds at changing his mind, or at least changing his actions, you've first got to get a better handle on what makes him tick. You have to be able to see the world through his eyes so that you can approach him in a way that will make sense to *him*. Only then can you begin to speak his language, so to speak. So, before we get into specific strategies for changing your testosterone-laden partner, I'm going to help make him user-friendly. Since you need to study the lay of the land before you set out on the road to change, this chapter will give you a road map for understanding your man. And while it's true that the map is not the territory itself, it's still damn handy to have one when you're lost. (Especially when your man won't stop to ask for directions.)

You're about to learn the five most common things men do that drive women nuts. Some of these annoying habits will be instantly recognizable to you. On the other hand, some of the other items on this list may not apply to your guy. That's because no two men are exactly alike. Don't get sidetracked by this. Just pay particular attention to the sections that scream out your man's name and skim through the other parts.

Additionally, with each complaint, you'll find an explanation for why your partner acts the way he does. And, no, it's not because he's intentionally annoying. I realize that if your partner is in the doghouse as you're reading this, you may not agree with me, but I'm convinced that men don't stay up late at night dreaming up ways to make us miserable. (It just comes naturally to them.) With the exception of extremely pathological men, most guys want their partners to be happy. They really do. So, here's a list of women's beefs along with that long-awaited explanation of why, if not for the reason of purposefully antagonizing us, men do what they do.

Beef #1: "He never wants to talk. And on those rare times when he does talk to me, he never shares his feelings."

If you're like most women, I know there have been times in your relationship when you've felt frustrated—no, exasperated—because the man in your life seems to have little (or nothing) to say. To us, nothing is more satisfying than deeply personal conversations with people we love. Lunch with our girlfriends, long conversations over the phone with relatives, tête-à-têtes with our kids, catching up on every detail with an old friend; conversation is the mainstay of our emotional well-being. Talking to others intensifies our experiences. Words make things real. Words are our lifeline.

Now, one might assume that the topic of a woman's conversation is irrelevant, just as long as she's talking. But this is definitely incorrect. Women have preferences. We know the difference between good conversations and meaningless chatter. Good conversations are about feelings—deeply personal, soul-baring feelings. The more personal, the better. In them, we reveal our feelings about our partners (and their latest transgressions), our love or disdain for other family members, friends and neighbors, our current emotional crises, our fears, fantasies, insecurities, and last, but not always least, our joys.

On the other end of the spectrum, we're experts on identifying meaningless chatter. We can spot it in an instant. You know exactly what I mean. Here's the equation: meaningless chatter = what men talk about. We can't believe they waste their time on such superficial, cotton candy topics as business, sports, cars, politics, and how frequently they have sex. What lightweights. How shallow. And to think that they call women bimbos!

From a woman's perspective, men have two modes. They're either engaging in meaningless chatter or they're actively avoiding conversation, and it's generally the latter. In his show about gender differences, *Defending the Caveman*, comedian Rob Becker says that women speak approximately ten thousand words a day while men speak a meager two thousand words. That explains why when men are done talking about business, how to make more money, close more deals, and outsmart their competitors, they come home and have nothing to say. Apparently, they've used up all their words.

And there's more. Maybe you've noticed that when you have something you want to talk about, there never seems to be a good time to talk. Mornings are too rushed. Evenings are for unwinding or sleeping. Weekends, he's too busy watching television, playing sports, or reading. You can't talk before dinner because he doesn't want to ruin his meal. You can't talk after dinner because he has work to do on his computer. On sunny days, it's too nice outside to waste the day talking. On rainy days, he has to pay bills. Face it, girl. He's not a talker.

Now, if any of this sounds familiar, I know how you've been feeling, and I can also predict what goes on at your house. You've been feeling hurt and angry that he never shares himself with you. You've been wishing he would ask you about your day or seem more interested in what you do. You've been irate that he doesn't make the time to hash out the things that are important to you. Most of all, you've been blaming him. Blaming him for withholding emotionally. Blaming him for being with you in body but not in spirit. Blaming him for being punitive with his silence and withdrawal. Blaming him for bailing out on you as a partner. Have I forgotten anything?

Well, the truth is, while men generally don't love to talk as much as we do (to say the least), their apparent lack of interest in verbal communication is not due to their being withholding, disinterested, punitive, or emotionally thwarted. It has to do with their being guys. Guys are just different. Their brains are different. Here's how. The human brain consists of two hemispheres, the left and the right. Each hemisphere controls certain functions. The left hemisphere is responsible for rational, factual thought and logic. The right hemisphere is responsible for abstract thinking, communication skills and spatial perception, feelings and emotions. Males predominantly depend on the left hemisphere. Women, on the other hand, use both sides. That's because the corpus callosum, the delicate fibers connecting the left side of the brain to the right side, is 40 percent larger in women than men. Our brains are better able to send messages back and forth between hemispheres. Therefore, verbal ability, comprehension, and other language skills—all right-brain functions—simply come more naturally to women.[2]

From a personal perspective, while I realize that two is not a very large sample, I don't have to look any further than my own two children to see the impact gender has on communication style. Last fall, when I was driving my then fifteen-year-old daughter, Danielle, and ten-year-old son, Zachary, to school, we had an interesting conversation. Danielle was sitting in the front with me, and Zach sat in the back. Danielle said with a sigh, "Mom, I can't believe how much I have on my mind lately. I have sooo much to think about." I responded, "Me, too. I can't believe how much I have on my mind." Several seconds later, Zach pipes up from the backseat, "And my mind is completely empty."

Similarly, I recently asked Zach about a friend of his I hadn't seen in a while. "How's Mike doing?" I asked. Zach replied, "I don't know." Since they are in different classes this year, I asked, "Don't you see Mike in school?" "Yes," he said. "Don't you play with him at recess?" I asked. "Yeah, Mom," he said with annoyance, "I *play* with him at recess, but I don't ask him how he's doing."

You know, in some ways, guys had it easier back in the fifties. No one expected them to talk a whole lot. That was back in the days when men were breadwinners, protectors, and not much more. That was when the strong, silent Marlboro man was something to aspire to. But the sixties and the seventies placed an entirely new set of expectations on men. It was then that we were told that behavior is learned and not biologically determined. So we dragged men to sensitivity-training groups and told them to express their feelings. We expected them to be successful warriors by day and vulnerable confidants by night. We wanted them to go shopping with us and enjoy it. We assumed they'd ooh and ahh over our neighbors' newborn babies. We wanted them to really care about the pattern on the new kitchen wallpaper. But after twenty to thirty years of working at this unisex thing, it just didn't happen. Guys apparently do the guy thing a whole lot better than they do anything else. And, after all, they should. They're guys. It's not a bad thing.

You might think it's a bad thing because you think your way of seeing the world—your love of communicating, for example—is the right way to be, the only way to be. And for a while, we almost had guys convinced of this, too . . . but not quite. Guys like being guys. They don't think they're broken. They figured out that being different from us isn't equal to being wrong. And although it wouldn't have been politically correct to openly admit this in the eighties, lately men appreciating men is cutting-edge stuff. Lots of people are doing it. There appears to be a growing consensus that men aren't always wrong and that they may actually have some redeeming qualities. How could this be?

Well, in the last few years, the topic of gender differences has received a tremendous amount of attention. The trials and tribulations of dealing with the opposite sex have been the focus of many books, popular magazine articles, stand-up comedy routines, and seminars. Instead of pointing fingers of blame, we began to lighten up and start laughing at ourselves. Yes, most men leave the toilet seat up. Most men will have nothing more than a nagging feeling that something is different about you when you bleach your hair from deep, dark brown to platinum blond. In regards to men's dependence on women to locate their belongings, Roseanne Barr claims, "Men seem to think that the uterus is a homing device." Laughter is good medicine.

As laughter took the place of tears or defensiveness, men started to feel more self-acceptance and even view their masculine traits as strengths as opposed to character flaws. Here's what men noticed about themselves. We're right, they don't get the same charge out of conversations that we do. They'll do it if they have to, but generally their conversations are, like many other things in their lives, goal-oriented. For us, talking is an end in itself because it brings us closer to other people, but it's not that way for men. It's not that men don't want or need to feel close to other people, it's just that they do it in different ways.

For example, if your man wants to feel close to his male buddy, a being more like himself, is he likely to call him on the phone just to chat? Probably not. He's much more likely to ask him to play tennis, golf, baseball, or go fishing. Men are more action-oriented. They feel connected to people through activity. They don't have to talk. They don't want to talk. Doing things together breeds connection.

I was once working with a couple who were hoping to improve their relationship. At the start of a particular session, I asked how things were going, and the wife related a story about a hike they had taken in a national park. After hiking for a period of time one incredibly beautiful fall day, she said to her husband, "Paul, what are you thinking about?" to which he responded, "Nothing." She turned to me and said angrily, "Michele, how can a person be thinking of nothing? It's obviously a sign that he just doesn't want to be close to me." He quickly came to his own defense, stating, "I don't know what she's talking about. There we were on a beautiful trail. The sun was shining. The leaves had turned to the most amazing fall colors. I was just soaking in nature, and I felt so close to Sue that I didn't feel the need to talk." This story, I think, says it all.

"Okay, okay," you say, "even if he doesn't like to talk as much as I do, why is he allergic to talking about feelings or other personal matters?" Because while we like to share our woes with others and "be there" for our friends when they hit emotional walls, men pride themselves at solving their own problems. They believe it's a sign of weakness to rely on others for answers to the quandaries in their lives. Appearing confused or uncertain to others is tantamount to failing. Sometimes when men are silent, they're working something out internally. They become reflective and turn inward as opposed to looking for support from the women in their lives. This is not a comment on women or the nature of their relationships. It's simply how most men deal with ambiguity and other uncomfortable feelings. They do it solo. So, even though you may think you're being gracious and loving by extending yourself to your partner when he looks down in the dumps, he may not interpret your actions that way. He may even get pissed. That's because he wants to soothe himself by himself.

Men don't excel at discussing personal matters for another reason. They're less focused on that kind of stuff than they are on other things. For example, Rob Becker talks about going to a party with his wife and by the end of the party she will have collected enormous amounts of information about the personal lives of the people she talked to. She knows who's getting divorced, which couples are having problems with their kids, who's depressed, and so on. Conversely, after spending two hours alone with his buddy out in the garage, Rob learns nothing more than the fact that his buddy just purchased a brand-new saw. And that's okay with him. It's all he needs to know.

Now you may be asking yourself, "How does knowing that real men don't talk help me?" First of all, it's good to know that you're not alone. It's not just *your* partner who's chat-phobic; most men are. Knowing this will help you to stop blaming him. And that's a good thing, because if you think you're right and he's wrong about the role verbal communication should play in your lives, you can't help but be angry at him. You can't help but take his silences personally. If you're constantly angry at him, it clouds your thinking. You do things that aren't productive. And remember the circular connection—if you behave hostilely to him, he will toward you, and so on. . . . Besides, being angry at your man for being less verbal than you is like getting mad at your dog for rolling in bad-smelling dead things. We may not like it, but it's part and parcel of the species.

However, don't take this to mean that you need to acquiesce and accept the status quo. I'm not saying "Don't worry, be happy" that your man doesn't talk. I realize that you want him to be more communicative, and I'm going to teach you how to lure him out of his world of action and into your world of words. But, I'm warning you, he'll only be a visitor to your world. He won't take up permanent residence there. Yet despite the fact he'll probably never feel the same love of conversation that you do, you can teach him how to take better care of your needs in that area. Men may not be verbal, but they are trainable.

Conversely, I want to teach you how to visit *his* world so that you learn your way around. If men are action-oriented, then I'll teach you to go where the action is, where the boys are. You need to internalize that we have to approach men differently from the way we would our female friends if we want to get through to them. We need to talk less and act more.

With this in mind, I find it very ironic that although relationship experts acknowledge this difference between men and women, most relationship programs still focus primarily on teaching verbal communication skills. No wonder women get frustrated! They learn new communication techniques that have little appeal to their partners. For instance, I recently read an article in a popular women's magazine stating that some expert advice should come with the warning label "Do not try this at home." In particular, the author was referring to a technique taught in communication classes called "reflective listening." Reflective listening means that a person reiterates in her own words what she thinks her partner is saying. This is intended to decrease misunderstanding and invite further discussion. After several minutes of the author's trying her hand at being a reflective listener with her husband, he turned to her and said in a huff, "Why in the world are you repeating everything I say?"

So, woman, save your breath and get your feet moving. You'll be surprised how quickly your man will get your message. And since his world of action may be totally new to you, I'll teach you everything you need to know to navigate. Once you see the power you have through action, you'll agree that when it comes to men, it's oftentimes easier done than said.

Beef #2: "Our relationship is last on his list of priorities. Everything seems to be more important to him than us."

Guys just don't get it, do they? They think that relationships run on automatic pilot, that it isn't necessary to spend time together, go places, do things, show interest in each other's lives. To them, relationships are just supposed to happen. Love conquers all. Oh, yes, they realize the importance of dedication, time, and energy when it comes to anything else in life—such as excelling at sports or in their careers—but not when it comes to the people they supposedly love.

Take careers, for example. Men spend inordinate amounts of time working, and when they're not working, they're thinking about work. Sometimes, when we talk to the men in our lives, we know nobody's home. Men often have that glazed-over look in their eyes, revealing even to the most unperceptive that they're not hearing a word we're saying. Their bodies return home but their minds are still at work. Plus, to add insult to injury, they tell us that they're working for us, for the family. Hah. Whom do they think they're fooling? We know they're workaholics. We know what really matters to them. Why don't they just come clean and admit it?

Okay, maybe some men aren't workaholics. Then they're sportsaholics. When they're not playing 'em, they're watching 'em on TV. And whether it's eighteen holes of golf, a set of tennis, fishing, baseball—these things take time. Plus, the socializing thing. Guys don't come home after the eighteenth hole or the ninth inning. They go out for a beer with their buddies to relive the game. This takes even more time. And it's time away from us.

And if it's not their careers or sports, it's that other diversion from the relationship, hobbies—working on cars, boats, motorcycles, having affairs with their computers, playing with electronic toys or their tools, and collecting stuff. Days seem to pass without so much as a sign of life when they're in the garage, basement, den, or wherever they do their things. When they're into their hobbies, we might as well be on another planet. They get so absorbed in what they're doing, we evaporate.

Whether it's working, playing sports, doing hobbies, memorizing every word in the newspaper, watching television for hours on end, tinkering in the garage, or sitting on the toilet for an ungodly amount of time, one thing is certain—men crave time without us. They must be avoiding something. Intimacy, maybe? Responsibilities, perhaps? It's hard to understand why, with the little time that's available, men so often choose to exclude us from their plans. Don't they ever think about the relationship?

We're different. We know what really counts. We measure our success in terms of how we're getting along with our loved ones. We know what's important in life even if our partners lose sight of it. We know it's our job to remind them of what's up. After all, if we don't do it, who will? And when we impart our wisdom to the men in our lives, do they appreciate it? When we voice our disappointment about being apart so often, do they stop what they're doing and lavish attention on us? Do they show us gratitude for setting them straight? Nooo. They get angry. They tell us we're trying to control them. They go fishing even if they really don't feel like it—just to make a point.

So we feel hurt and rejected. We get tired of their expecting us to be satisfied with the few emotional crumbs thrown our way. Resentment starts to build, and we begin to notice other ways men tell us they're not thinking of us. They leave their socks around the house. They don't do dishes. They act as if there's a gene for doing housework—women have it, men don't.

So we share our resentment and they tell us we're nagging. They tell us to get off their backs. They go deeper into their shells and withdraw. It seems the more we want to be with them, to be close to them, the more they retreat. Something is wrong with this picture. Men can't possibly be this insensitive, can they? Why do they have a knack for doing everything but what we want them to do? Why don't we matter to them the way they matter to us?

Believe it or not, men may not be as sinister as we make them out to be. In fact, there are some good reasons they behave as they do. In the same way that you feel incomplete without meaningful conversation and connection to others, men feel inadequate unless they achieve. In his book *Men Are from Mars, Women Are from Venus,* John Gray writes that a man "can come close to understanding a woman's experience of sharing and relating by comparing it to the satisfaction he feels when he wins a race, achieves a goal or solves a problem."

It's not that men don't value people or relationships. They do. But men judge themselves by their ability to set and accomplish goals. Achievement allows them to feel competent, powerful, knowing. Conversely, lack of achievement leaves men feeling ineffectual and impotent. Without goals, men feel lost. Men must have something to aim for.

In order to feel good about themselves, many men climb the ladder of success in terms of their careers. They become determined to make lots of money, get promoted, receive recognition and awards, or be the best at whatever they decide to do. And once the goal is set, men become single-minded about getting there. Men's intense focus on their goals often blinds them to anything else going on around them, including the women they love. They don't neglect us intentionally. The lack of attention we feel is simply a by-product of their desire to do well.

But there's something else to consider. Many men tell me that they work hard not simply to achieve personal goals, but also to be good providers for their families. They truly believe they must burn the midnight oil to care for the people they love—and they do it without distraction.

But when you think about it, you'll realize that this goal-orientation, this single-mindedness, is not limited to career aspirations. It permeates men's lives. It affects almost everything they do.

For example, have you ever noticed that, despite the fact that you can talk on the phone, write a note, signal to your kids, and answer the door all at the same time, your partner can do only one activity at a time? It's that focus thing. When he's watching TV or reading and you're talking to him, does he hear a word you're saying? Does he even know you're talking? If he's preoccupied and you tell him something specific, doesn't he swear later on that you never said anything about it in the first place? Even worse, doesn't he have amnesia concerning your entire conversation?

When I'm having a conversation with Jim, things go along swimmingly unless one of our kids walks into the room or the dog begs for food. Even if the kids walk past in silence, Jim stops dead in his tracks because they've broken his concentration. He forgets what he's talking about. I used to think his distractibility was due to attention deficit disorder, but now I know it's due to the fact he's a guy. Guys can only do one thing at a time. Everything else fades into the background. (That's why when they're driving and they get lost, they have to turn down the radio.)

Men are kind of like cats. If you've ever had a cat, you know how single-minded they are about going after moving objects. Anything that wiggles becomes the intense focus of a cat's undivided attention. Try as you may to distract your cat, nothing will deter it from its goal. That's just how cats are wired. Doesn't this tunnel vision sound familiar?

Just think about going on outings with your man. Have you ever taken a car trip together and suggested making an unplanned stop at an art fair or an interesting little town filled with antiques? What are your chances of having him pull over? Are they nil? Stopping or slowing down on the way to your destination gets you off track from the goal. To men, this is a bad thing. They feel out of sorts taking detours. They've got their eyes on the wiggling object—the hotel where you'll spend the night. Exploring for the sake of exploration is simply unnatural. You have to get to your destination directly and expeditiously. You have to relax on schedule.

Or how about those times you're telling your man about your day and share a feeling of sadness, anger, disappointment, or confusion. I can just predict how those conversations unfold. You confide your innermost feelings and you want him to listen. You want empathy, evidence of his caring for you, his understanding. But that's not what you get, is it? Nope. In all likelihood, he interrupts your heartfelt disclosure to give you instructions. He starts telling you what to do. Or, even worse, he tells you how you mishandled the situation, something you can do nothing about.

What we have here is a failure to communicate. Our wires are crossed. Despite the fact that we feel shortchanged and misunderstood, believe it or not, men are really trying to help. They're not out to get us. To your partner, conversations, like everything else in his life, have to be goal-oriented. If you present what he hears as a problem, he simply has to fix it. Your problem becomes the wiggling thing, and he must pounce on it at once.

So although you tell him about the hurdles in your life because you want him to say, "Boy, it sounds like you had a rough day," or "I can't believe your supervisor acted that way. What a blockhead!" he doesn't understand your way of thinking. If he believes something in your life is "broken," he assumes you want him to fix it. Otherwise, he asks himself, why in the world would you be discussing it?

Where does his one-track-mindedness come from, anyway? One explanation has to do with the way men use their brains. (They do, trust me.) As you learned in the previous section, men predominantly use the left side of the brain. They can access the right side of the brain but do so by shifting back and forth between sides rather than using both sides concurrently, as women do. So when a man uses the right side of his brain, his left side is temporarily out of commission, so to speak. Since each hemisphere is responsible for specific functions, when he's doing one thing, he can't do another. Not only that, it takes energy and effort for men to shift gears.

For example, if your partner is working on his car—a task that requires spatial thinking—he might be oblivious to the fact you're talking to him—which requires verbal thinking. To truly hear you, he must stop what he's doing and reorient himself. That's why he sometimes seems annoyed when you want his attention. It's work for him to shift gears.

In addition to men's achievement and goal orientations, there's another reason relationships don't appear to be a top priority for them. Men seem to require more time alone than we do, to decompress or simply veg out. In fact, though women in my practice typically complain that men are emotionally unavailable, men complain of feeling smothered or suffocated. This discrepancy in itself is not a problem. Partners are bound to have different needs in relationships. However, problems arise when a man's need to retreat or a woman's desire to connect gets misconstrued.

For instance, though men feel smothered and suffocated, do you think women intend for their partners to feel that way? Do you believe women go out of their way to make men feel trapped? Of course we don't. You know your intention is pure when you suggest spending time together. You're certain you have no interest in invading his space or making him feel uncomfortable, you simply want to feel closer to him.

Well, the same is true in reverse. When he picks up the paper at the breakfast table, he's not trying to hurt you. He's not avoiding intimacy. He hasn't fallen out of love with you. If you've been thinking these things to yourself, or saying them to him, quit it. You're reading way too much into things. You're hurting yourself. You're annoying him. And if you've been criticizing him for holding back when he's been needing some space, I am 100 percent confident that he's been pulling away from you even more. And instead of considering the fact that he might be reacting to you when he withdraws, you've probably condemned him for being even more unavailable.

How much do you like it when he tells you you're needy or dependent because you want to be together? How much do you appreciate being thought of as a person with a major character flaw because you value togetherness? What does it feel like when he angrily demands that you leave him alone and go get a life? The answer to these questions is self-evident. You hate it. His lack of understanding and appreciation of your need for closeness is one of the most isolating feelings you ever have.

Well, guess what. He feels the same way you do. He wishes you could be more compassionate about his need to go inside himself and refuel. We energize ourselves by connecting with those we love; guys go inside themselves or they zone out. In fact, in her book *The Alchemy of Love and Lust*, Dr. Theresa Crenshaw posits that the tendency in men to require more alone time may actually be hormonally related. She writes, "This 'loner profile' of testosterone is absolutely crucial to understanding what men are all about. . . . Testosterone motivates the male to strive for separateness in ways a woman is not designed to comprehend. He wants to be alone!"[3] And we thought they were just being selfish and obstinate!

Look, we may not like their style of recharging their batteries and they may not like ours, but that's life. That's what is. Members of Alcoholics Anonymous have a wonderful saying that bears repeating here: "God grant me the serenity to accept the things I cannot change, courage to change the things I can, and the wisdom to know the difference."

So what's changeable here and what isn't? That's the question. Let's start with what isn't changeable. The sooner you get used to the idea that your partner may never feel exactly the same way you do about time together and time apart, the better off you'll be. You need to stop analyzing things to death and attributing malevolent intention every time he initiates time alone; otherwise things will deteriorate rapidly, if they haven't already.

If you believe your partner is intentionally avoiding you, you start to feel abandoned. Then, one of two things happens—you get angry or you get depressed. Either way, you're doomed to failure. Anger will prompt you to act in ways that are self-sabotaging. You'll push your partner away with your criticism—the more you complain, the more he works. The more he works, the more you complain. Eventually, you will become estranged from your partner and your relationship will falter. Not a good idea.

Some women don't get angry, they get depressed. After repeated failed attempts at more closeness, these women start feeling helpless and hopeless. And instead of finding more productive ways of handling the situation, they surrender. They stop fighting for their relationships. Then there's peace. But it's peace with a price. A sadness begins to creep into every nook and cranny of their existence. They take Prozac. They show up in therapists' offices not with the intention of improving their relationships, but rather to talk about the zest that's gone out of their lives. They search for potential causes for their rotten moods—their jobs, their weight, their parents, the size of their breasts, their kids, you name it. So they change their jobs, take aerobics classes, forgive their parents, get bigger breasts, get along better with their kids . . . but they're still in anguish. That's because the real problem—a life sentence in a passionless relationship—goes both undetected and unaddressed.

If you've been feeling depressed about your man's priorities, you've got to get hold of yourself. Depression slows you down. It zaps your energy. It takes all of your frustration and turns it inward. And if you've been inside your head, you can't possibly muster the resolve, strength, and creativity you'll need to make things better. If your man has been preoccupied and aloof, the last thing you need to do is lie down and roll over. Pick yourself up, woman, and dust yourself off. I've got plans for you. The first step in moving beyond anger or depression is to stop blaming your man for being a man. Allow him to be different. When you begin to accept his quirks and idiosyncracies, you won't be so reactive. You won't feel hurt. In fact, you might even feel stronger. You'll be more clear-headed. Then, and only then, can you start to focus on what *is* changeable about him. There's a lot you can do to move yourself up several notches on his list of priorities. For starters, when you give him the space he needs without judgment, he'll be more interested in being with you. And when he's with you, he'll be less judgmental of your desire to be with him. His acceptance will feel good. But that's only a beginning.

Even though he will always think differently from you about the place togetherness has in your relationship, you *can* get him to spend more time with you. You *can* get him to leave work at work. You *can* even get him to stop reading at the table from time to time. Not by coercing him, not by making him feel guilty, not by pouting, but by using new and improved strategies that act as a billboard directing his attention to you. And in the technique chapters that follow I'll give you lots of new ideas to make him realize how very important you are. And, no, you won't have to greet him at the door stark naked, wrapped in cellophane. (But you can if you want.)

Beef #3: "Why do men always have to have a one-track mind? Why can't they think of anything besides sex?"

Do you remember that commercial a few years ago featuring a bulldog marching down a busy sidewalk with dispatch saying to himself, "Kibbles 'N Bits. Kibbles 'N Bits. I've got to get me some Kibbles 'N Bits." Everyone could tell that this hound was on a mission. Nothing could distract him from finding and eating his Kibbles 'N Bits. Kind of reminiscent of guys. Guys and sex. Only they'd be walking down the street thinking, "Boobies and Tits. Boobies and Tits. Boobies and Tits."

Why does it seem that at any given time men are no more than a nanosecond away from having their next sexual thought? Talk about your day, it reminds them of sex. Make dinner, it reminds them of sex. Brush by them in the kitchen, it reminds them of sex. Breathe, it reminds them of sex. If life were a Rorschach test, every abstract ink blot would be a pair of boobs, a nice ass, or some sort of phallic symbol. Doesn't it ever get tiring? Apparently not. They're like those relighting birthday candles that never extinguish regardless of how hard you blow.

Plus, it's really amazing. Other than being alive, they don't have to be in any particular state of mind before having sex. Any mood will do. A heated argument in the afternoon won't deter them. They can be grouchy, angry, down in the dumps. They can even be feeling under the weather. Rain, sleet, or hail, the male must go through. And men are great at putting everything else out of their minds—the kids knocking at the bedroom door, the work needing to be done around the house, the talk they promised to have with you a week ago—and switching gears. They're masters at tuning out the world and tuning in to their penises. (Or are they antennas?)

We're not like that. We have to be in the right mood. Feeling good about our partners is a prerequisite for our wanting to be intimate. Isn't it odd? We want to feel close emotionally before we make love. Distance and hostility are not exactly aphrodisiacs for us. But men don't understand our disinterest in jumping in the sack right after being criticized or seeing their clothes lying all over the house. They don't comprehend that we don't desire them when they're mean-spirited or sarcastic. A heated argument in the afternoon won't deter them from wanting sex. As far as they're concerned, quibbles are quibbles and sex is sex, and never the twain shall meet.

What is it with guys, anyway? They're so shallow. To them, having sex is like scratching an itch. They don't need to feel connected to us to want it. They don't need to feel anything at all. Women make love, men have sex, and there's a big difference. We like to cuddle, caress, embrace, kiss, and explore. We like to take our time. But men have to hurry up so that they can get ready for their next orgasm. Think about it. You know those back rubs you give your man because you think it turns him on? Wrong. If he's honest, he'll tell you that you're wasting your time. You should direct your rubs ten inches below his waist. So much for love, passion, and bonding together. What gives here?

For starters, no chapter entitled "Testosterone Simplified" would be complete without at least a brief explanation of the ways in which testosterone affects your partner's behavior. It does, particularly when it comes to sex. Testosterone is one of the hormones responsible for our sex drive. Among other things, it increases sexual desire, sexual thoughts, and fantasies. Both men and women have testosterone, but men have *twenty to forty times* more of it than women. This in part explains why men seem so obsessed with sex. Furthermore, research shows that the more people think about sex and are sexually active, the more testosterone their bodies produce. That explains why your man never seems satisfied. The more sex you have, the more he wants. It's not that he's perverted, it's just that he's pumped with a chemical that draws him to his genitals in the same way that insects are drawn to lightbulbs. Men are genital-tropic.

Interestingly enough, men don't think they're oversexed. They think we're undersexed, and they complain about it all the time. They complain to us and to their male buddies. Maybe they get sympathy from the guys. One day I was teasing my husband and told him that under certain conditions I could imagine having less sex than we were currently having. His response? "Michele, that would be a physics problem. We'd be getting into antimatter." We laughed. And then there was another occasion when he was complaining and I was telling him that he was overreacting. "Jim," I said, "there really are only two times when I'm not into sex." And before I could finish my sentence, he finished it for me, saying, "Yeah, whenever I want to and every other time." We laughed then, too.

You see, it's not unusual that Jim and I have different sex drives. What is unusual is that we can laugh at it sometimes. Many couples don't laugh. Ever. In my practice, so many couples experience serious relationship problems not because of the discrepancies in their sexual appetites, but because of the ways in which they handle these differences. Generally, they blame each other big-time. She condemns him for being a sex addict, and he's convinced she should have been a nun. They lose sight of the fact that everything is relative. Instead of understanding and finding peace with gender-related differences, both partners stop feeling loved.

Women question their partners' love because, after all, men's intense need for sex appears to have little to do with us. The fact that men don't seem interested in plain old affection outside of the bedroom makes us feel as if we're just a means to an end. Holding hands, snuggling on the couch, gentle touching, and asexual hugs are not tops on their agendas. Guys can't hug without their hands sliding down our butts or across our breasts. It simply isn't possible.

We don't understand this. We take this personally. We want our sexual relationships to be outgrowths of the physical, emotional, and spiritual bonds we feel with our partners. We want our partners to realize that you can't have great sex without a loving, intimate connection, a connection stemming from spending time together, talking, and sharing your souls. Women believe that if we were more important to men, men would feel this way, too.

But women are wrong about this. Men share women's need to feel connected and close to their partners. They yearn to feel accepted, loved, and appreciated. Men show us their love and affection, but they do it differently. They do it through sex. They feel more loving toward us and loved by us during the sexual act and when their sexual needs are met. Guys feel appreciated and cherished when we acknowledge them as sexual beings. Believe it or not, they're not just getting their rocks off when they have sex. They're not just scratching an insatiable itch. Men are more in touch with their feelings during sex. Their defenses are gone. Their hearts are open. They're much more emotional with their pants down. Women don't understand this all that well.

Men say that women also don't understand how much it hurts their feelings when we aren't interested in sex. It makes them feel unattractive and unloved. They wonder what's wrong with them. They wonder what's wrong with the relationship. They wonder what's wrong with us. Most men derive great satisfaction from pleasing a woman sexually. It makes them feel competent and powerful. Relationship expert Ellen Kriedman tells women that contrary to what they may believe, it's not just lust men are after. She says that a man falls in love with a woman based on how he feels about himself when he's in her presence. And when he's adding up his virtues, his ability to satisfy his partner sexually is high on his list of priorities. So when a woman's disinterest in sex prevents him from shining in this way, he feels deflated.

Arnie, a very close friend of mine who happens to be a man and a therapist, had an interesting reaction when I told him that I was going to write a book entitled *Getting Through to the Man You Love.* He said, "That's going to be a very short book. Just one chapter, I imagine." In case you haven't figured out his cryptic comment, let me explain. Arnie was suggesting that you could get through to your man, you could have him eating out of the palm of your hand, if you paid a little more attention to him sexually. And, despite the fact Arnie's a guy, there's some merit to what he has to say.

Folklore has it that the way to a man's heart is through his stomach. That's one way. But there's another, more obvious route. Men are really very simple. Make sure they don't get hungry. (They get grouchy when deprived of food.) And have sex often. They'll be much nicer to be around. Many women have told me about a curious observation. Their partners do more housework, are better fathers, and even communicate better when they're satisfied sexually. It's hard to keep this in mind when we see things so differently from guys.

Here's the Catch-22. We need to feel good about our relationships in order to desire sex or to want to please men. Men need sex in order to feel good about their relationships or for them to want to please us. We know part A by heart. We forget part B. I'm just reminding you. Do with it what you wish. Just remember that one key to transforming your guy lies in your hands. No pun intended.

Beef #4: "Why doesn't he do a damn thing around the house? He's blind to the mess, he doesn't see dirt, he doesn't even notice the kids."

Rare is the man who believes housework is something he's supposed to do. Somewhere along the line, men got this idea that housework is an exclusively female activity. Somehow, we're the ones who are supposed to be responsible for cooking, cleaning, doing laundry, grocery shopping, running errands, chauffeuring, and making sure our toddlers don't stick metal objects into electrical sockets or drown in toilet bowls.

If we're full-time homemakers, by the time our partners come home, we're looking for a little relief. Forget companionship, we need help! But what happens if we turn to our partners and ask for some assistance? We get "I've been working all day. What do you do all day, anyway?" What an idiotic question. We stay home, watch talk shows and soap operas, and eat bonbons. We've got it made. What fun we have! While the guys are off slaving away, we perfect the art of relaxing. Never mind the kids and the housework and the three square meals every day. These things just take care of themselves.

Those of us who work full-time out of our homes have it a lot better. Our partners recognize how hard we work, so when we get home, we split the housework fifty-fifty. Just testing. I wanted to see if you were paying attention. Split the housework fifty-fifty? Not on your life. That's when we have two full-time jobs. And we wouldn't mind the housework so much if it weren't for the fact that guys are so inconsiderate. You can tell exactly what they've been doing at home by noticing the trail they leave behind them. Comes from reading "Hansel and Gretel" too many times as kids. If nothing else, why can't they take responsibility for themselves? Why do we always feel like their maids or their mothers? Why can't they just be fair?

We understand that relationships were different generations ago. Guys weren't expected to do housework. Women were the Supermoms and Superwives while men faced the outside world. If you're too young to believe me or too old (or too smart) to remember, read the following excerpt from a 1950s high school home economics textbook about how to be a good wife:

> Prepare yourself. Take 15 minutes to rest so that you will be refreshed when he arrives [home from work]. Touch up your makeup, put a ribbon in your hair and be fresh looking. . . .
>
> Clear away the clutter . . . just before your hus-

band arrives. . . . Your husband will feel he has reached a haven of rest and order, and it will give you a lift too. . . .

Don't complain if he is late for dinner. . . . Make him comfortable. . . . Have a cool or warm drink ready for him. Arrange his pillow and offer to take off his shoes. . . . Allow him to relax and unwind.

All right, already. We understand that life was different back then. But, guys, hello! Wake up! Do we have to drag you kicking and screaming into the twenty-first century? We don't want to do it all anymore. We want partners. We want a little more equality. Slavery ended a few years ago, remember?

In all fairness, some guys help. But that's just the point. They "help." Whom, may I ask, are they helping? Oh, that's right. This housework stuff is our domain, so they're helping us. We should be thankful. They're extending themselves to help us with our jobs. What's worse is that this "helping" attitude isn't restricted to housework either. Have you ever noticed that men don't parent? They baby-sit. We parent. They baby-sit. And—wait, this is a good one—they expect us to be extremely grateful for the hours they put in baby-sitting.

But back to this helping thing. There are problems with men helping. First of all, why do we need to tell them what needs to be done around the house? Don't they know? Haven't they lived there just as long as we have? Don't they realize that automation hasn't advanced to the point that clean houses, clean clothes, and clean children just materialize? Why do we have to spell out everything that needs to be done? Don't they have eyes?

Then, when we lay out our expectations, one of three things happens. The first two are familiar. (1) Men say, "Get off my back. Stop nagging." (2) Men say, "Yeah, I'll do it later." Now, a very important point is about to be made, so get out your pen and paper and commit this to memory. The responses "Get off my back" or "Yeah, I'll do it later," while different on the surface, can both be roughly translated to mean "Not in this lifetime, hon." At least you have to give the guy who tells you to get off his back credit for being honest.

There is a third response, however. This guy actually pitches in. He does the laundry. He puts the kids to bed. He watches the kids on Saturday so you can meet your friend for lunch. He does some cleaning around the house. He breaks through the gender barrier to do what's asked of him. Yet, you can't help but notice your size ten shirt has shrunk small enough to fit a Barbie doll, or that your six-year-old has stayed up to watch *The Tonight Show* on television on a school night, or the gray film on the sliding glass doors and windows throughout the house because he washed them without changing the water even once. He's into conservation. Brother!

No wonder we feel angry. No wonder we nag and criticize. What else can we do? Nothing we say or do makes a difference. So we live with this low-grade resentment that lurks just below the surface. It slowly corrodes the love we feel for our partners. We can't help but take their actions, or lack of actions, personally. We feel unappreciated and alone. So we shut down emotionally. Sex becomes the last thing on our minds. It's hard to make love to someone who seems to have so little regard for our feelings. Who would ever have thought that arguments over housework could be so divisive?

What if I were to tell you that a man's aversion to housework has anthropological underpinnings? You know, men were hunters and women did more of the nesting things around the cave. Not impressed? Okay. What if I were to tell you that in most societies and cultures, women are more involved with home-oriented tasks and activities than men. Still not impressed? Me neither.

Probably the best explanation of why men sneak out of the room when cleaning time is imminent is that housework avoidance is a learned behavior. They learn it as kids growing up. Guys observe their mothers doing the lion's share of the housework. They grow up thinking this arrangement is normal. They don't question it. It seems okay to them. And when they visit friends' houses, in all likelihood things are pretty much the same. Moms cook and clean while dads do other things—usually outside their homes. It's no wonder men so often believe that caring for others, tending to their needs and nourishing them, is "women's work." That's what their mothers did. And that's what their father's didn't do. Plus, in many families, boys aren't expected to do housework and, as a result, never really learn how to do it. It feels alien to them. Little girls play house. Little boys don't. Some things don't change.

But I have some news for you. If your man is chore-phobic, your in-laws and our culture may not be the only reasons he's like that. Believe it or not, one of the reasons your partner may not be as responsible as you would like him to be just may have something to do with you. I'm not saying it's your fault, I'm saying that you may have inadvertently trained him to skirt around any sort of home improvement. I see it happen all the time. So here's what I'm going to do. I'm going to tell you the five most common ways women turn men off to being more involved at home. See if any of these sound familiar to you. And be honest with yourself.

1. You Take Over

Most women tell me that in the early years of their relationships, things were better; their partners were more involved. Responsibilities were more equally divided. Then somehow, gradually and mysteriously, things changed. When I help them retrace their steps, these women inevitably point to a time when they started doing more and their men backed off. And, then, the more men backed off, the harder these women worked. They had to! Who else would if they didn't? That's what they tell me, anyway. But there's a catch.

I'm going to explain more about this later, but relationships are like seesaws. The more one person does of something, the less the other person does of it. This holds true for just about everything. If you put the kids to bed every night, your partner won't. If you're a tidiness freak, your partner is probably a slob. If your partner plans family vacations, you probably take a backseat to doing that. If you're the nurturing one with the kids, he's probably stricter. We balance each other out. Just like a seesaw.

So the more we do, the less they do. We get into roles with each other. Some habits die hard, particularly if one person really likes his role and doesn't want to give it up. Know anybody like this? Naturally, you say, that describes your man to a tee. He doesn't want to give up being catered to. That's probably true, but there's a flip side to all of this, too. Even though we hate feeling overworked and underappreciated, I can't tell you how many times women reject their partners when they offer to do something around the house! "Never mind, I'll do it," women say. Can you believe it? Back off, girl. Let him do it. Remember the seesaw.

2. You Critique

Guys tell me that every time they do something around the house, whether it's the dishes, making beds, vacuuming, or taking care of the kids, they receive unsolicited instructions about how to do it "right." Based on their need to feel competent, a matter covered previously, men don't appreciate being corrected and feeling incompetent. Furthermore, they tell me, they are not thoroughly convinced there's only one way to do a particular thing. So when we lecture them about their feeding the kids ice cream *before* their sandwiches, they get angry and plan their revenge. And guess what they have up their sleeves. That's right. It's the revenge of the couch potato. "If you don't like the way I do it," they chant, "then do it yourself." And then they cease and desist. Some guys are more open to instruction. However, when we calculate the time it takes to explain things properly versus the time it takes to do the job ourselves, we opt for the latter.

There are pros and cons to everything in life, and though it's definitely a disadvantage to be responsible for most of the work required around your home, when you do it, at least you do it your way. You have control. The job's done to your specification. If he does it, he'll do it his way. And unless you're willing to retreat, he won't do the work very long. He doesn't like feeling criticized or henpecked. You have to decide what's more important: his active participation—even if it isn't perfect—or everything done just the way you like it. The choice is yours.

3. You Nag

When someone asks a woman to do something, because she values cooperation, she'll probably do it. We mistakenly believe that men think this way, too. But men value self-determination and often resist being told what to do. Then, when women notice that men fail to take action, women repeat their requests because they think that men probably didn't understand the request in the first place. For if they had, certainly they would have obliged. Right? Not necessarily.

Men seem to have radar for anything that smacks of being controlled. They don't like it one bit. So, even if they agree that the job needs to get done, either they won't do it, or they'll do it when they're good and ready, on their own terms. Given this tendency to be oppositional, many women make their own situations worse by digging their heels in even further when what they're doing isn't working. Guys will go for days without clean clothes or clean dishes just to prove a point. They're not going to do what you want, when you want it. So there.

Now, not all guys have that mentality. (Just most.) But if you're one of the lucky ones who is living with a man destined to resist any suggestion you make, even a good one, then you have to stop what you're doing and get smarter. I'll tell you how to do that later, but for now, you have to make a promise to yourself. If your partner has ever said, "Quit nagging about the house. I'm sick and tired of hearing you complain," that's exactly what you have to do. Thankfully, once you've read this book, you'll see how many other, more productive things you can do besides begging him to help out. Nagging just makes him angry at you and, more than ever, makes him determined not to give in. Don't give him that out.

4. You Keep Score

When it comes to arguments about housework and kids, one of the ways women squelch even a minute desire in men to be more co-operative is by keeping score of who does what. Women are really good scorekeepers. We're aware of the deposits men make into our emotional banks, but we're absolute experts on keeping detailed track of their withdrawals. We remember that although they might have taken the kids to their piano lessons last week, they didn't help them with their homework on the past three Tuesday evenings as planned. We recall that although they mowed the grass four times this month, they only took the garbage out once in six weeks. Boy, we're good. We've got photographic memories. Nothing escapes us, does it?

And when we keep score, we're guided by a standard we picked up somewhere along the line that says when it comes to care of the family and of our home, things must be split fifty-fifty. Right down the middle. If not, life is unjust, our relationships are imbalanced, and our partners are slime. There are some problems with this sort of thinking. For one thing, men often complain that when women tally up the score, they don't factor in some of men's contributions. Anything inside the house counts. Anything outside doesn't. So guys feel shortchanged. Plus, even if you account for every task fairly and accurately, this scorekeeping thing is bad for the health of your relationship. It pits you against your teammate. Good relationships don't work that way. They're based on flexibility and mutual respect.

Second, who ever said that things have to be fifty-fifty all the time? At the risk of being politically incorrect, I say life doesn't work that way. Not in relationships, anyway. In some ways and on some days, you carry more than your fair share, and he does the same at other times, in other ways. And that's okay. There's nothing wrong with your relationship if things aren't always perfectly balanced. I know many good marriages where the women do more than half the housework and half of the child care, and they feel okay about it. They feel that their partners more than make up for their housekeeping shortcomings in other ways.

So if you're a scorekeeper, make absolutely certain that you're looking at the bigger picture when you're adding things up. Stop thinking you're weak or unassertive if your man isn't the Martha Stewart of men. I suggest that you change what you can about his willingness to be responsible—and I'll help you jump-start this process—and, for God's sake, quit memorizing who does what. Leave that to the feminists.

5. You Ignore His Needs

Many women tell me that their relationships seem to go better when their partners pitch in. We're happy when there's teamwork. And when we're happy, we're nicer. We're nicer to everyone, especially our men. They're being considerate, and we're loving them back. Our relationships thrive.

However, when I talk to men in these happy relationships, they tell the story differently. They don't see their actions as the cause of things going smoothly. They give their women the credit. They say they became more active around their homes because their women were being more loving, more considerate, more tuned in to their needs: "She gave me more space to go out with my friends. I really appreciated that," or "She initiated sex for a change. That felt great to me," or "I've been asking her to host a dinner for my colleagues, and she finally said okay."

Have you ever heard the expression "You scratch my back and I'll scratch yours"? It's a basic law in relationships. If you're nice to me, I'm nice to you. But what does this have to do with housework? Right or wrong, since men know how important teamwork is to us, if they're angry or resentful for some reason, they'll stop pitching in. They'll "express" their feelings through action. (Remember? They're action-oriented.) Their actions are saying, "You don't care about me, so I won't care about you." Is this fair? No. Is this right? No. Doing housework shouldn't be considered doing something "for us." But whether we like it or not, that's how guys look at it sometimes. It just is.

So, if it's true that a man may be expressing his feelings through his actions, the question is: What's going on when he checks out? Now, I'm certain that when your man does nothing around your house, you're convinced there's only one explanation—he's an insensitive lout. You may be right, but I'd like you to consider an alternative explanation as well.

His holding back may be a symptom of an underlying resentment or disappointment. Indirectly (and unproductively, I might add), he may be telling you he's hurt or angry. He may be feeling overlooked in some way. Has he been asking you for something about which you've been unresponsive? Have you been ignoring him lately? Has he been complaining about something you've refused to acknowledge? Now might be a good time to reconsider. Look, I know that you shouldn't have to be nice to your man for him to be responsible, but I'm being pragmatic. I'm telling you that he's just much more likely to do what you want when he's feeling good about you. Even the least domestically oriented guy is a smidgen more helpful when he feels loving.

One more pointer. Some women tell me that the housework haranguing stopped when they put themselves into their partners' shoes for a while. Yes, equality around the house is a fair and reasonable expectation. Yes, it's true that men don't always take their responsibilities seriously. But it's also true that they often have to reverse years of indoctrination to become better partners at home. This isn't always easy. On a very deep level, lots of guys equate being cared for by their women with being loved. Becoming more independent on the home front, while an absolutely essential goal, may still feel like a major loss to a man who's been socialized to think love means never having to push a vacuum. So, woman, even though your man doesn't deserve it, acknowledge improvement, however small. It will make your life a lot easier.

Beef #5: "Why does he have to be so damn controlling? He's always telling me what to do. He always has to be right."

Why in the world do guys think that they know everything? They're always telling us what to do and when and how it should be done. What makes *them* so smart? We'd really like to know why men consider themselves experts on everything in life. If you ask men, they'll tell you that they're better drivers, they pack boxes into small spaces more efficiently than we do, they know more about child-rearing, they're more knowledgeable about how dishes should be loaded into the dishwasher (even though they don't do it themselves), how food should be arranged in the refrigerator, how free time should be spent, which channels are worth watching on television, and . . . well, the list is endless, but I think you get the point. And because they think they're so much better at doing all these things and so much smarter, they're always giving us directions. Face it, men like to be in control.

We don't mind their input on things because, after all, that's what a partnership is all about, teamwork. But it's hard to have a team when the only players on the team are the coach and the water boy. It's so frustrating to feel that it's a constant fight to have an equal vote on important issues that arise in relationships. Well, never mind important issues, we're willing to start off with having an equal vote on the unimportant issues such as which movies we see, the temperature the thermostat should be set on, the position of the toilet seat lid, the route we should take when we're driving, and so on. Then we could graduate to having equal say about the big things: how money is spent, where we live, whose career we follow, whose obligations take precedence, and so on. That would be nice, wouldn't it? Instead, guys seem to have a running commentary on everything we do. It really gets tiring having someone criticizing you all the time and thinking he's doing you a favor. Actually, it's exasperating.

We're much better at understanding that there's more than one Correct way to do things. We're better team players because we don't have to be in control of everything we do. We know that two heads are often better than one. Plus, we weren't absent from school when kids were taught about sharing. We don't hog the remote control; we'll take a consensus. We don't mind sharing our razor blades. We don't get mad if they forget to reset the driver's seat in the car back to our favorite position. We don't always have to be right. We ask people's opinions about things. We actually feel we can learn from the differences between people. We try to put ourselves in other people's shoes rather than immediately assume they're buffoons for disagreeing with us.

If all this sounds familiar to you, you should feel comforted because, although you might have thought your man's need to be in control is unique to him, it isn't. It's a guy thing. Your man doesn't critique you or bark orders at you because of something you're doing wrong. He thinks he's supposed to do that. Most guys feel it's their job to take charge, make decisions, give directions, and handle things. But why? What makes them think that?

For starters, you don't need to look a whole lot farther than the animal kingdom to realize that males in many species are the dominant sex. (Male rhesus monkeys insist on hogging the remote control, too.) Testosterone, the hormone with which males are well endowed, is responsible in part for aggressive behavior. Males in most species are wired to be on top of the pecking order and will do what they must to get there and stay there. So, when your man takes over, he's just doing what his biochemistry instructs him to do—he's being the leader.

Testosterone is also responsible for competitive behavior. Men must win whether at war, at work, at home, with their buddies, on the road, or even when playing a game of checkers with their young sons. To them, winning isn't everything, it's the only thing. Losing is for losers. That's why discussions become competitions. They have to be right. That's why, when you play a game together, you have to remind him a thousand times that "it's just a game." That's why when a driver cuts in front of your man on the road, he doesn't calmly move over. He puts the pedal to the metal to mark his territory. And don't even think of telling him to calm down unless you want to get snapped at.

But biochemistry isn't the only thing affecting your man's controlling attitude and behavior. Your man is who he is because of how he was socialized. Boys are trained to be decisive, to take charge of situations. As men, they're expected to be aggressive and take control at work. If they don't, they won't succeed. The decision-makers are the guys at the top. They have to be tough and hard. They have to call the shots. They need to make the rules and fire people. In short, they need to have all the answers. The buck stops with them.

And these are the same guys who come home at night. Lots of guys have a really hard time switching gears. Some don't even know how. For example, I've worked with many professional pilots and their wives who struggle with these issues in their relationships. These men are responsible for the lives of hundreds of people every day. A bad decision can be fatal. No wonder some of these guys still have their captain's cap on when they return to their families. No wonder they have difficulty taking a backseat on family matters.

Plus, many years ago, if a man was dominant in a relationship, his behavior wasn't considered sinister. In fact, women expected their men to take charge. Men made decisions and women felt protected and cared for. That's why most men feel that they're actually helping us when they tell us what to do and how to do it. They believe we need their guidance. But now things have changed. We expect different things from men than we used to. We don't want dictators; we want collaborators. We want our men strong but open to suggestion. We want men who don't equate being wrong with being weak. We want to be appreciated and valued as people.

We want men who want equal relationships. We want to work the remote sometimes, too.

So, no wonder men are slow to change. When you consider their physiology and the lessons they learned as kids, they have a lot of programming to overcome to be better team players. Given the challenge, I think we have to be more patient. Guys were raised to believe "real men have all the answers," and now we're telling them that's wrong. They just need a little time to catch up with us and a little prodding along the way. But it all depends on how you prod. The worst thing you can do to a control freak is challenge him head-on. That's why you're about to learn lots of backdoor techniques that will enable you to change your man *without his even knowing it.*

Now What?

Perhaps as you read through the above traits, you realized that your man doesn't quite fit the mold. Many don't. Unlike other guys, your guy may talk *too much.* Maybe you wish he'd quit gabbing once in a while. Or perhaps losing sight of the importance of your relationship isn't his problem. He might be *too* possessive of your time. And unlike most oversexed men, maybe you wish your guy would chase after you more often, since sex seems to be the farthest thing from his mind. And, finally, perhaps he does lots and lots of housework, but he's so compulsive that he drives you nuts.

Or maybe your pet peeve hasn't even made it on to this list. Maybe you can't believe that he always thinks what he's doing is more important than what you're doing. (When Jim and I are cleaning up after dinner and he's rinsing a dish, if I reach over to the faucet to moisten a rag to wipe the counter, he gives me a dirty look as if to say, "Can't you see I'm doing something?") Even if your particular peeve isn't mainstream, don't worry about it. I haven't forgotten about you. Know that the man-changing methods you'll learn are diverse enough to zero in on all kinds of men, regardless of their unique eccentricities. And speaking of zeroing in, that's exactly what's next on our agenda—goal-setting. In the following chapter, I'm going to help you pinpoint exactly what you want to change about your man and your relationship. I'll help you define a goal so clear, you'll almost taste it. *Bon appétit!*

PART TWO

AIM

CHAPTER FOUR

So Many Changes, So Little Time: Where to Begin

Obstacles are those frightful things you see when you take your eyes off your goal.

—Henry Ford

Irecently heard a motivational speaker speculate how professional tennis players managed to keep their focus when they played against the boisterously theatrical John McEnroe. With his ranting and raving at the judges and cursing up a storm, it would be easy to see how a person could have lost one's concentration and therefore lost the game. "Not so," said the speaker. "Pros learn that the only thing that matters is the ball coming over the net. As long as they keep totally focused on that ball, potential distractions [like John McEnroe] will not threaten their game."

In regard to relationship change, a man's undesirable behavior is the moving target. That's where our eyes must be glued. But I'm forewarning you that you'll get sidetracked by all kinds of things unless the target of change is in sharp focus. You must know *exactly* what it is about your man that needs changing. Although you may think you've always known what your relationship goals are, trust me, they're probably not as well defined as they ought to be.

For example, saying that you want more closeness or you want him to be a better listener, or that he needs to be less angry, won't get you what you want because these goals are only half-baked.

Well-defined goals offer action plans, blueprints for change. Aiming at fuzzy goals is like aiming at nothing at all. And I've heard it said that if you aim at nothing, you'll hit it every time. So, this is the chapter where I'll help you bring your vision of your metamorphosed man into clearer view. Get out your zoom lens—we're moving in.

But before I tell you the mechanics of developing solution-driven goals, I want to tell you why this process is so important. If I don't, I know you'll be tempted to skip this chapter and get right into the how-tos. I would do the same thing. But I've learned the hard way that there are distinct advantages in having clear-cut goals before you dive into this man-changing business, and I want you to know what they are.

If I were writing this book for men, I wouldn't bother explaining the virtues of goal-setting. As I said in the last chapter, for better or for worse, guys are just natural goal-setters. They need to know where they're going and how they're going to get there before they take off. For instance, have you ever tried rearranging furniture with your partner? You want to move things around and see how things look once in place. He, on the other hand, wants you to have a plan or a goal before he puts any effort into the project. Like the sculptor who has a vision in his mind's eye of the finished product as he chisels away, men need to see the end before they can begin.

Sometimes we hate this quality in men because we want them to be more spontaneous. We want them just to go with the flow, relax, lighten up. And, undoubtedly, there are times they would do well to heed our advice. But before we throw the baby out with the bathwater, let's take a closer look at the possible virtues of being so results-oriented. It ain't all bad, honey.

Being able to envision exactly what you're after helps you to get there.

Are you one of those people who loves to watch the Olympics to witness world-class athletes at their best? I know I am. Do you know that in addition to all the physical training athletes do for their particular sport, they're often required to do something referred to as "armchair rehearsal"? Athletes are asked to sit down and visualize themselves during their peak performances. They're encouraged to recall what their bodies were doing, how their muscles were moving, what they were thinking and feeling, the sounds around them, and so on. They recall in amazing detail that incredible moment as they crossed the finish line or passed their opponents. They're asked to re-create in their minds the physical, emotional, mental, and spiritual experience of achieving their goals. Armchair rehearsal, research tells us, actually improves athletes' performances. Hard to believe? Keep reading.

A group of basketball players were asked to shoot baskets to determine their skill level at throwing free throws. After the initial testing was completed, the players were divided into three groups. The first group was told to spend an hour each day practicing free throws. The second group was told to set aside some time each day to imagine themselves getting the ball into the basket every time. They were supposed to recall the position of their bodies as they threw the ball, note the feeling inside them as the ball hit its mark, imagine the sound of the ball going through the net, and the cheer of the crowd in its wake. The third group was told not to practice at all, just to forget about basketball for a couple of weeks.

Several weeks later, the players were retested. The first group, the players who practiced on the court, improved the rate of their successful free throws by 23 percent. The guys who didn't practice on the court but imagined themselves shooting well improved by 22 percent. The percentages of free throws made by the players who were asked to put basketball on the back burner remained exactly the same two weeks later. Apparently, envisioning yourself stepping into a highly detailed picture of your desired outcome simulates what it takes to get there. It helps turn fantasy into reality.

Maybe you can appreciate how an athlete might improve his or her performance by envisioning all the elements involved in winning, but you're having a bit of trouble applying this notion to relationship enhancement. For years, I've helped couples transform their troubled relationships—almost overnight—by prompting them to paint a detailed picture of themselves in love again through a series of questions I pose to them. In responding to my questions, they begin to visualize themselves as committed partners, passionate lovers, loyal friends, steady companions, and trustworthy confidants. At once, it seems they know just what they need to do to recapture positive feelings. Later in this chapter, I'll ask you these very same questions, which will enable you to envision your dream-come-true relationship in full Technicolor. All you'll need is popcorn.

Being specific about your goals lowers your partner's resistance to change.

I know you may not believe this, but some of your man's opposition to change may very well be due to the fact that you have not been specific enough with him about what you want. If you're absolutely convinced you've spelled out your needs in black and white and it's never made a difference before, perhaps you're right. If so, I'll teach you other ways to overcome his resistance to change. But, maybe, after reading this chapter, you'll see that I'm right—that your partner is much more willing to accommodate your wishes when he knows exactly what you want from him.

You see, guys are terrible mind readers. If you're vague at all or leave anything out, they're not good at filling in the blanks. They try sometimes, and when they miss the mark and we don't load them with praise, they give up. They think we're too demanding. Women are better at filling in the blanks because we spend a lot of time attending to the needs of others. We're decent second-guessers. In fact, we're damn good at it.

Guys have to have everything laid out for them in excruciating detail if we expect them to get it right. They're slow learners. You may not like this quality in them, but . . . oh well. Stop wasting time wishing he were different and start being concrete. When young children try their hand at bowling, bumper guards are placed in the gutters so that they can't throw gutter balls. No failures. A winner every time. Being specific with your partner is like surrounding him with bumper guards that ricochet him back in the right direction when he gets off track. Not a bad idea, right?

Solution-oriented goals offer action plans.

Some time ago, my husband asked me what I'd like to be doing professionally five years down the line. I was tempted to tell him the truth, which was "Who in the world knows what I'll be doing five years from now when I can hardly figure out what I'd like to eat for dinner tonight?"—but I restrained myself. I remember telling him that I would want to be teaching more seminars, writing another book, and seeing more clients. I thought I answered his question really well, but judging by the look on his face, I could tell it wasn't the answer he was looking for.

So he explained to me what he does when he constructs his five- and ten-year plans for his business, which happens to be real estate development. First, since being financially successful is important to him, he determines how much money he expects/hopes to be earning; then, knowing how much profit he makes from each home he builds, he calculates how many homes he'll need to build and sell to meet his goals. Then he outlines precisely the tasks he'll need to accomplish each month, week, and day to build and sell those homes. He's got it down to a science. My mind just doesn't work like that. He's goal-oriented and I'm fly-by-the-seat-of-my-pants-oriented. But, I must admit, there have been times when he's forced me to put pencil to paper, and I've found it to be incredibly productive.

For instance, I remember the first time I got a book contract. I was so excited, my feet barely touched down on earth. Several days later, that feeling disappeared and a feeling of dread swiftly took its place. After days of staring at my computer and asking myself what I had done to my life, Jim encouraged me to sit down and set some goals. He asked that I calculate the approximate number of writing days available to me in the upcoming year, given my busy travel schedule and my days in the office seeing clients. Then he asked the total number of pages I needed to write. Being the math whiz that he is, he divided the number of pages required of me by the number of available writing days and, *voilà*, a goal! It turned out that I needed to write only two pages a day to complete my book by the deadline.

Two pages a day! Anyone could do that, I thought. Even me. So with this specific goal in mind, on each writing day, I knew I couldn't leave my computer until I had at least two pages completed. I bet I don't have to tell you what really happened, though. Some say that the hardest part about running is putting on your running shoes. And, then, even if you tell yourself that you don't have to run too far that day, once you have your shoes on and you're running, why stop? As it turned out, I wrote a lot more than two pages on most days, and sometimes I didn't write at all. In any case, it all worked out. I got the book done before its deadline. The lesson I learned? Knowing exactly what I had to do each time I faced my computer made the task seem doable. Goal-setting tamed the inertia monster living inside me.

Now back to you. Whether you want to change something about yourself—such as responding unproductively to your partner—or you simply want your partner to shape up, after you go through the goal-setting exercises outlined in this chapter, you'll see instantly how being specific makes your goals feel more achievable. Believing that you can do what it takes to make your goals happen recharges your problem-solving batteries. You'll keep going and going and going.

Goal-setting forces you to take yourself seriously.

I just told you a story about Jim and how he establishes five- and ten-year goals for his business. I shared with you how amazing it is to me that he can think that far into the future. But there's something else that he does that I find noteworthy. When he sets his financial goals, it means that he takes himself and his desires seriously. He dares to dream and, even more impressive than that, he pushes himself to construct the formulas he will need to achieve those dreams. He believes in himself. He knows he's capable of winning. He exudes this confidence in everything he does. And apparently, so I've learned, goal-setting and goal-getting have a lot to do with this quality in him.

Let's face it. It takes a fair amount of confidence to be able to say to yourself that you expect your partner and your relationship to change. And I'm not referring to those times when you're mad at your man and, with your hands on your hips, you inform him, "Things are going to change, or else." That's bitching. It's easy to bitch when your relationship has gone flat or if he's being obnoxious—anyone can do that. But sitting down and devising an action plan to move him in your direction takes a little more chutzpah. It means you truly believe you deserve more from your partner. It means you're convinced you'll do what it takes to make that happen.

Guys are better than we are at taking themselves and their goals seriously. Women have to work at it. When it comes to formulating what *we* really want and need, and then feeling justified in taking the time to follow through, we fall flat on our faces. I know a woman who very much wanted to lose weight and get in shape. She knew what she had to do to get more fit, but since she had a busy career, she felt she needed to spend all of her spare time with her two children. Going to her health club for a few hours each week— even though she enjoyed it tremendously and her husband encouraged her to do it—made her feel too guilty.

I know this story sounds familiar to you. I'm convinced you know someone (maybe even you) who fails to follow her dreams because it's too time-consuming, too costly, too inconvenient for others, too unreasonable. . . . So many women burn themselves out taking care of everyone else, making sure everyone around them is happy. But when we're so busy caring for others and ignoring ourselves, we fail to notice our own unhappiness. And if we're unhappy, look out. We're not good mothers, partners, friends, daughters, or anything else, for that matter.

Have you ever noticed that men aren't plagued by guilt when they take care of themselves and pursue their goals? Many women express bewilderment over how the men in their lives can be so guilt-free, so egocentric. I think this is a subject worth exploring. Feeling justified about feeling good is not something to scoff at. Yes, men *should* be more concerned about other people's feelings when they prioritize how they spend their time, but we should take a lesson from them. We should take better care of ourselves. We should take our needs more seriously. We should live our lives by design rather than by default. We deserve it.

Besides the fact that we're on the bottom of our own to-do list, there's another reason we don't take our goals as seriously as we should. We don't believe in ourselves. Just think of how many of your New Year's resolutions have died on the vine because, in your heart of hearts, you really didn't believe you could achieve them. Oh, yes, you were *wishing* they would happen. You were hoping against hope you'd lose weight, he'd talk more, or you'd take better care of yourself, but that's not good enough. To turn New Year's resolutions into lifelong habits, you need an action plan. And what kept you from creating that plan wasn't laziness or lack of will-power. You didn't develop a plan because you were reluctant to believe you could actually make your goals happen. That's what kept you at arm's length from achieving those goals.

And that, my friend, is why goal-setting is so important. It's the first step in believing change is possible and that you have the resources to create this change. Goal-setting helps you to start taking yourself and your aspirations seriously. It forces you to make promises to yourself. It allows you to entertain the possibility that what you want for yourself might actually happen someday.

The power of believing in positive outcomes is hardly a new subject. Take, for example, author Deepak Chopra, M.D., who strongly believes that expectations create reality. He explains how many people are actually able to rid themselves of serious illnesses simply by expecting to be cured. He cites medical studies in which patients are given placebos (sugar pills) and are told that the medication will stop pain, reduce gastric excretions in ulcer patients, lower blood pressure, or fight tumors. Although the pills have absolutely no active ingredients, pain is lessened, ulcers disappear, blood pressure drops, and tumors shrink.

Norman Cousins, a prolific writer on the topic of the effect positive beliefs have on healing, once met an elderly woman who many years before had been advised by her doctor that she had only six months to live. Impressed by her longevity, Cousins commented, "When your doctor told you that you only had six months to live, you must have been shocked. What did you say?" In a strictly matter-of-fact tone, the woman replied, "I told him to go fuck himself."

Examples of people achieving near-miraculous goals because of their positive expectations can be found in almost every walk of life. How about sports? Aside from his truly amazing basketball skills, I'm fairly convinced that what sets people like Michael Jordan apart from the rest of the world are the unrelenting expectations he has of himself. Michael Jordan expects to win and, for that matter, he does most of the time.

Even if you're not a basketball fan, you have probably heard about the 1997 championship finals where, in one particular game, Jordan was so ill with the flu and a high fever that he had to be carried out on a stretcher. Everyone could see the incredible pain in his eyes as he raced up and down the court. Yet, in true Jordan style, he carried his team to victory, scoring most of the winning points.

If positive expectations can cure cancer, shrink tumors, eliminate physical pain, and make people winners instead of whiners, just imagine the powerful impact these expectations can have on your relationship. Motivating your partner to be more responsive, more cooperative, more loving is child's play when compared with curing oneself of a terminal illness or winning a championship. Right? Once you harness the power a solid belief in change unleashes, you'll be amazed at what you discover. The possibilities are endless. So let's start setting some goals right now. Okay?

The first thing I want you to do is get out a pen and a piece of paper. I want you to commit your goals to writing. I know, I know, it's a strange thing to do, especially if you're not used to it. But I'm telling you, it really makes a difference. I also realize you're busy and that there are a million other things you could be doing with your time, but I also know that you picked up this book for a reason. You want guidance to change your man. So, take the time to write down your goals. You'll be glad you did. For another thing, imagine how much fun it will be several weeks down the road when you look back at what you wrote and see how far you've come.

Goal–Setting 101

Rule #1: Focus on what you want, not what you don't want.

The very first question you must ask yourself is "What am I hoping to change about my man?" You probably think this is an obvious question with a simple answer, but it isn't quite as simple as you think. Most of the time when I ask women, "What are you hoping to change?" they don't answer that question. They tell me what they're unhappy about. They say things like "I wish he wouldn't be so nasty," or "I would really like it if he were less critical," or "He never seems to be interested in sex anymore." Then, when I ask, "When he stops being nasty, what will he be doing instead?" or "When he starts being less critical, what kinds of things will he be saying or doing?" I usually get a blank stare. These questions are more difficult to answer. We're experts on what makes us miserable and novices at what we would like to have happen instead.

The problem with negative goals such as "I want him to be less critical" is that in order to assess whether he's making progress, you must keep a vigilant eye out for those times when he's being critical toward you and hope that he's doing it less often than usual. You're still focused on his negative behavior. Although you're hoping he'll cut back somewhat, you're still expecting him to act in ways that are hurtful to you. Not exactly solution-oriented.

My husband frequently tells me that I drive him crazy when I critique his choices instead of offering my own options. For instance, when we're trying to figure out which restaurants we'd like to eat at, he'll come up with several suggestions. I like to veto them. I'm good at that. Then he'll say, "Fine, Michele, where would you like to go instead?" Hmm. Good question. I really hadn't gotten that far. I just knew the flaws inherent in his plan. Well, I try to practice what I preach, but obviously I don't always succeed. It's annoying to have your partner tell you what doesn't work or what is unsatisfactory without offering what he or she wants instead. So when you think about what you would like to change in your partner, for starters, make sure you're envisioning positive behavior rather than what bothers you about him.

If, when you responded to my question "What are you hoping to change about your man?" you wrote, "I want him to be less critical," don't worry about it. It's simple to translate a negative goal into a positive one. Ask yourself, "When he starts being less critical, what will he be doing differently? What will he do instead?" Watch what happens when you answer these questions. You might respond, "He'll give me more compliments," or "He'll tell me I did a good job." When you think of positive goals, you start looking for the times that he lives up to your positive expectations. You're eager to hear compliments, both big and small. Anticipating compliments is a far cry from keeping track of those times when he's being critical. Once you start focusing on solutions (supportive behavior) rather than problems (criticalness), you'll notice a difference right away, and so will he.

Rule #2: Make certain your goals are action-oriented.

Earlier in this chapter, I mentioned that one of the reasons your partner may not do what you ask him to do is that you haven't been specific enough about what you want. Even if you're skeptical about this, please make sure you're as concrete as possible. You owe it to him to give him the benefit of the doubt before you condemn him for being resistant. Also, throughout this book, I've been impressing upon you how action-oriented men really are. When you are specific about the *actions* he can take to please you, you'll be talking his language. Here's what you need to do to be as explicit as possible.

Ask yourself, "What will my partner be *doing* when he's more the person I want him to be?" If you responded, "We'll have better communication," or "He'll show me more respect and affection," or "He'll help more around the house," you aren't being clear enough. You see, these phrases or goals probably mean a lot to you, but they might mean something entirely different to your partner. If you don't define your terms by identifying exactly what you expect your partner *to do* differently, he might think you think the way he thinks. Know what I mean?

For instance, I remember the time Julia told Nick that she wanted to feel more connected to him. Great, he thought, that's exactly what he wanted, too. The next time I saw them, I asked, "How was your week?" In unison, he said, "Great," and she said, "Lousy." Perplexed by this, I asked for clarification. Julia explained, "Right after I told him about my needs, I thought he really cared. Instead, we went home and he suggested renting a video. I thought to myself, 'Okay, we can snuggle on the couch and talk about the movie.' Instead, we sat there across the room from one another and didn't say a word. Some evening!"

Then it was Nick's turn. He looked completely confused. He said that they agreed to rent a movie and picked it out together. In the midst of watching the movie, he realized that he felt so close to

Julia that he didn't feel the need to talk. He really appreciated that and assumed she felt the same way. Surprise, surprise. Sorry, Nick, no go.

You see, Julia never told Nick, "I need you to talk to me after we watch the movie," or "Let's sit next to each other on the couch instead of sitting in separate chairs," or "I'd like it if we would hold hands while we watch the video together. That would make me feel closer to you." Knowing this couple, I can tell you that had Julia been more specific, Nick definitely would have responded. Despite relatively good intentions, he was clueless. And when he heard Julia's disappointment, he became defensive, which, in turn, angered Julia. Very messy indeed. But easy to undo. Here's how.

When you write down your goals, make absolutely certain that your goals are *action-oriented*. Tell yourself what your partner will be doing or saying when he's hit the mark. Make sure you're thinking about behaviors or actions, things you and he can see or hear. Let me give you another example.

Georgia told me that she wanted her husband, Ben, to be a better listener. Well, maybe you think what Georgia wanted is obvious, but I'm a stickler for details. I had her spell it out. I asked, "What will he be doing when he's a better listener?" Her first stabs at responding to my question weren't so hot. She said, "He'll really hear what I have to say," and "He'll show more interest in what I'm talking about." So I pushed up my sleeves and started to help Georgia talk about her needs in action language.

"Georgia, how will you know that Ben has become a better listener? What exactly will he be doing differently then?" Finally, she caught on to what I was asking of her. She said, "To begin with, when I talk to him, he'll turn off the television, or at least he'll turn down the sound. I always feel that I'm competing with the TV. Then, it would really be nice if he made eye contact with me once in a while. When he's looking at the newspaper or somewhere else in the room, I don't feel as if he hears me." When I asked her, "What else?" she added, "I would die of shock if he initiated conversation by asking me about my day. That would make me feel he was interested in me, and I would really appreciate that." Finally, she said, "When I talk to him, he usually says very little in return.

If he would comment about the things I'm discussing or even ask me a question about these things, I would feel that he's with me."

Okay, now we're on to something. Now Georgia has a blueprint for change. She knows exactly what she wants Ben to do to be a better listener. Here's his "to-do" list:

1. Turn off the TV.
2. Make eye contact.
3. Ask about Georgia's day.
4. Comment or ask questions about what Georgia is saying.

Georgia admitted that before this goal-setting exercise, she was uncertain as to what she really meant when she told Ben to be a better listener. That's why he wasn't so good at it. Ben hadn't learned Georgia's rules for being a good listener. And if you haven't noticed, men like having rules and parameters. That's one reason they love sports. Every sport has lots of rules and everyone knows exactly what happens if the rules are broken. That's because there are rules about breaking rules. Men like that. So if you want your man to take better care of your needs, define the rules. Spell things out. You'll score more points that way.

Being specific with your partner is so important that I just want to make sure I've given you all the information you need to help you become as explicit as possible. I want to give you a few more examples of how you can translate vague goals into action-oriented ones.

Vague Goal	Action-Oriented Goal
I want you to be more affectionate.	Please hold my hand or hug me once in a while.
Be more involved with the kids.	Put the kids to bed three times a week and help them with their homework at night.

Show me your feelings.	Say, "I love you." Ask me out on a date. Call me from work once a day.
Stop being so inconsiderate.	Turn the television lower when I'm trying to sleep. Close the cabinet doors in the kitchen quietly. Put the bottle caps back on the soda bottles.

Do you get the picture? Now go back to your own goals. Are they specific enough? Do they pass the Michele test? If your goals are vague, such as "He'll be happier around the house," don't despair. That's a good first step. But then you must ask yourself, "What will he be *doing* differently when he's happier?" How will his behavior change when he's a happier human being? And, remember, actions, actions, actions. If you haven't distilled your goals down to the specific behaviors you'll notice when he's changing, you still have work to do on your goals. The magic question is "What will he be doing when he starts being more_____?" (Fill in the blank with your goal.) Do yourself and your partner a great big favor: don't do anything else until you answer these questions.

Rule #3: Break your goals into minigoals.

One of the secrets to successful goal-setting is to set goals you can actually accomplish in a short period of time. There's nothing more uplifting than the feeling you get from seeing yourself reach your target quickly. You become your own biggest fan, and you feel encouraged to keep going. Too often, people make the mistake of not breaking their grand goals down into small, achievable steps. It makes getting there unlikely. For instance, I remember a very depressed woman who when asked, "What are you hoping to change about your life?" responded, "I want to become a rock star." Unaware of any method for becoming an overnight success as a rock star, I asked her, "What will be *the very first sign* that you're starting to be on track to your goal of becoming a professional singer?" "That's easy," she said. "For months I've been wanting to perform during amateur night at some local night clubs. I haven't done that yet. I'm going to do it soon, though, and when I do, I'll know I'm on track." Perfect, I thought; she identified something she can do the moment she leaves my office that will help her feel better. You see, your goals need to be achievable in the here and now, sooner rather than later.

So look at your goals. Are they realistic and doable? Are they distilled down to steps you or your partner can take within the next week or two? If you're not absolutely certain, ask yourself, "What will be the very first sign that I'm moving in the direction of my goal? What will be the first thing I notice [about him, about you, or about your situation] as things start to improve?" Again, be sure the mileposts you choose are achievable within a short period of time. If you set megagoals without breaking them into these smaller steps, you'll get frustrated because you won't feel the rhythm of progress. You'll want to give up because it will seem as if nothing is changing. The key to making megachanges in your life is training yourself to notice and rejoice in the small steps forward. Even if you don't get to your ultimate goal quickly, you'll be certain to get there eventually.

I remember a feeling of despair recently when I went into my basement and looked at the mess. I told myself that my basement was beyond repair. It was so disorganized, it could never be fixed. It would be messy forever. But then I recalled the importance of taking small steps, a mind-set I endeavor to teach others, and applied this thinking to my own situation. As a result, I made minigoals for myself. I made a commitment to go into my dungeon every Tuesday—garbage day—and throw away one box worth of junk. Just one box and no more. Though it would be months before I could even see a dent in the disarray, I knew that I would have a spanking-clean basement someday if I just kept it up. Once I established these minigoals, I can't tell you how good I felt about myself with each trip down my driveway, box in hand.

Similarly, I worked with a woman who had divorced but wanted to consider reconciliation with her willing ex-spouse. She wasn't certain whether this was a good idea or not. One of the primary reasons their marriage ended was that he had had several affairs and they never worked through these issues in their relationship. When she told me that she wasn't completely certain whether she wanted to work things out with her ex-husband again, I asked, "How will you know if you're making the right decision?" and she said, "I will feel complete trust in him again."

Well, let's face it. In a perfect world, over time and after a lot of work on the relationship, feeling complete trust may be something she can look forward to someday. Maybe. But not now. Not soon. Feeling complete trust was not a reasonable goal given their situation. So I asked, "What will be the very first sign that you're starting to be on the right track?" and she said, "We really haven't talked about the affairs very much at all. If we are able to discuss them and he's willing to examine why they occurred, I know it won't be easy, but at least I'll feel as if we're making progress. As long as he's willing to talk about what drove us apart, I'll feel a little more confident that he'll do what it takes to build trust in our relationship again." Thankfully, she identified a much more practical goal.

So take a lesson from my messy basement and from the woman wanting to believe in her husband. No matter how involved your end goal might be, aim at something within range. Start small. Be patient. Remember, romance wasn't built in a day.

Aside from the three simple goal-setting rules—describe what you want instead of what irks you, think action, and break big goals into smaller chunks—there is one more thing you need to know. Once you get a picture in your mind's eye of your goal—exactly what your man will be doing differently when things improve—don't lose sight of it. Memorize it. Let that image be your guiding light. Remind yourself that that's what you're after. Don't let your man distract you. You see, sometimes when you try really hard to change a man, he puts up a good fight. He argues. He complains. He pouts. He defends himself. He goes on the offensive. He gives you the silent treatment. None of this really matters. Honey, let him do his thing. In fact, let him do all of his things. Don't respond. Don't let him push your buttons. Don't defend your position. Just continue to watch him very, very carefully. If you remain focused on the ball coming over the net, you just might notice that despite his gurgling and grumbling, he's doing exactly what you've asked him to do! All's well that ends well!!

By now, you should have a pretty clear idea of what you want to change about your man. Good for you. That means you know where you're headed, and that's a great start. There's an old English proverb that says, "Of a good beginning, cometh a good end," and I wholeheartedly agree. The next question is what's the best route for getting to your destination. You're about to discover something glorious about change. There are many, many different paths you can take to get there. In fact, once you eliminate dead ends or cul-de-sacs, almost any other road will do. You can take a scenic route, back roads, or the superhighway. The choice is yours. But first things first. I want to make sure you know where *not to go* so you don't waste another minute spinning your wheels. The next chapter will help you detour around your all-too-familiar dead ends.

....

CHAPTER FIVE

Don't Even Go There, Girlfriend

Have you ever been smack-dab in the middle of a heated argument when all at once you have this gnawing feeling inside that you've been there, done that? I mean déjà vu, big time. In fact, you've been there so many times, you have the script down. You've memorized your lines. You even know his. If he got sick, you could be his understudy. And, for that matter, he could be yours, too. Every time your buttons get pushed, the skit begins. The only things missing are the applause and the talent scouts.

What's your favorite skit? Is it the too much, too little sex skit? The too harsh, too lenient parenting skit? The too cheap, too extravagant with money skit? The too little, too much talking skit? The too neat, too messy household skit? The too much, too little time with me skit? The "You're just like your mother/father" skit? The "You're so selfish. Oh, *I'm* the one who's selfish" skit? The too critical, too sensitive skit? Do you have an altogether different favorite or is it all of the above?

Even though it may feel as if I'm picking on you, I'm not. Really, I'm not. You're not the only one with scripts. Everyone has them. Everyone does them. I have several of my own, thank you. My personal favorite is the too harsh, too lenient parenting skit. I accuse Jim of being too harsh with the kids, and he accuses me of having no backbone. He defends his behavior and gets even harsher, which, in turn, prompts me to intervene in his parenting style even more. Enter Mother to the rescue. Father becomes enraged. And so on and so on and so on. The skit ends, the curtain goes down, but we hardly even notice.

Later in this chapter I'm going to help you determine the spots where you and your partner go round and round endlessly. And while it's true that the skits would have happier endings if your man would just wake up and see the light, apparently it's not working out that way. So since you're the one reading this book, I'm going to focus on you. I'm going to help you eliminate these go-nowhere dialogues by offering you a lead role in changing your relationship. I'll help you set the stage for real change in your life. Before I do, I want you to know why changing your role in these unproductive interactions is so crucial.

When you read about the idea of having scripts in your life, my guess is that you chuckled with recognition. But, in reality, these skits are no laughing matter. They really do damage to your relationship and move you farther away from getting what you want from your man. They make things worse. Here's how.

When "More of the Same" Leads to More of the Same . . .

When difficulties arise in your relationship, you do something to resolve them. If what you do works, life goes on and you're happy. If what you do doesn't work, instead of telling yourself, "That didn't work, I should try something entirely different," in all likelihood you just end up doing more of what hasn't been working. You think, "He probably didn't hear me," so you repeat your message louder and more emphatically. Once again, with feeling. Well, guess what happens when you do more of what hasn't been working. You continue to get poor results. Worse yet, not only don't things improve, they actually get worse! The very thing you do to solve the problem becomes the problem. Here's a classic example.

Parents discover their teenager is sneaky, so what do they do? They spy on him. The kid discovers that the parents have been spying, so what does he do? He gets better at being sneaky. Alas, the parents notice that what they're doing isn't working. So guess what they do. Do they switch gears and try a different approach? No. They become more intent on surveying him, trapping him in his lies. The more they spy, the better he gets at eluding them. Unwittingly, they're actually training him to be more devious. Their solution—espionage—is actually creating more of a problem with their son. Want another example?

Hank was depressed because his career hadn't been going as well as he had hoped. His wife, Leann, felt that Hank was no longer the same person she'd married ten years before. An outgoing, fun-loving person by nature, Hank was no longer interested in spending time with her on weekends or participating in projects around their home. Hank used to enjoy gardening and woodworking and had built many beautiful pieces of furniture for their family. Recently, Hank spent hours watching television or staring off into space.

Out of concern, Leann often gave Hank pep talks, hoping to cheer him up. Initially, Hank was appreciative of her interest in him, but nothing changed; he continued to mope around day after day. When she realized her cheerleading wasn't working, she upped the ante. Now she offered frequent suggestions as to what Hank could do to improve his mental state. "Take a class," "Go out with your buddies," "Talk to a shrink." Her never-ending but well-meaning advice impacted little on Hank's outlook or behavior. In fact, Leann started to notice a disturbing trend. When she showered him with concern, he became angry, telling her to back off, to leave him alone. And following each outburst, Hank appeared even more depressed.

Instead of signaling the need for a brand-new approach to Hank's sullenness, Leann interpreted Hank's sinking farther into depression as a louder cry for help. His anger and withdrawal prompted her to make a more emotional plea for Hank to take hold of his life. The more she encouraged, the worse Hank felt.

On the surface of things, Hank *shouldn't* have responded as he did to Leann's efforts to reach out to him. He *should* have felt a sense of relief. However, that's not what happened. Each time Leann offered him a "snap out of it, there's a silver lining behind every cloud" sermon, he felt she couldn't possibly understand the depth of his anguish. He felt misunderstood and alone, which made him more depressed. Furthermore, the longer Leann's words of encouragement were ineffective in helping Hank feel better, the more he wondered about the severity of his condition. "She thinks I should be over this and I'm not. There must be something dreadfully wrong with me," he regularly told himself. Leann's cheering Hank up had the paradoxical effect of bringing him down.

When I accuse Jim of being too harsh with the kids, when the parents spy on their sneaky kid, when Leann tells Hank, "Don't worry, be happy," we all have something in common. We're doing what's referred to as "more of the same." Unfortunately, more of the same leads to more of the same.

This is such a simple, commonsense idea, and yet the truth is that people do more of the same with surprising regularity. Some couples have the same argument every time they put up the lights on the Christmas tree. Others quarrel each time the in-laws visit. Some people find themselves bickering every evening after work. Other couples notice the uncanny similarities in their arguments when they broach the topic of sex, money, the children, or how free time is spent. One woman I know mentioned that she and her husband fight every time they go to a particular restaurant for dinner. Yet, we seldom say to ourselves, "The last time I was in this situation, things didn't work out so well. I want to plan how I can handle it differently next time to get better results." Instead, we plunge headfirst into doing the usual.

Perhaps you're asking yourself, "Why in the world do people do more of the same if the results are so disastrous?" Are we basically masochistic? Definitely not. I don't believe we derive pleasure from going in circles. In fact, we hate it. But we do it anyway. Why? Well, there are a few reasons.

We forget to keep our eyes on the cheese.

Remember the rats in the beginning of the book? Sometimes, when we are at odds with our partners, we become so intent on getting them to agree with us that we lose sight of what it is we want from them. We become totally oblivious to the fact that our actions are unproductive. When being "right" becomes paramount, we keep our feet firmly planted and say the same things over and over.

We hope that someday our partners will snap out of their deluded worlds. We aren't deterred by their total disregard of our wisdom because we trust that eventually they'll come to their senses and change. We'd rather be right than happy.

Well, there's nothing wrong with being right, but it's hell being unhappy. And if your guy is someone who refuses to see things your way (the right way, of course), it's time to reconsider what's really important. Throughout this book, I'm going to urge you to pay a whole lot more attention to how your man *is* responding to you versus how you think he *should be* responding. Even if ten out of ten people would agree that your man is off base in how he acts, the fact is, that's still how he acts. Face it and get smart.

The point is, I want you to become more results-oriented—to notice the impact you're really having on your man. If what you're doing works, by all means keep doing it. But if what you're doing isn't working, honey, abandon ship. Even if you're thoroughly convinced your reasoning is unblemished, set out for higher ground.

Though ineffective, more of the same is the logical thing to do.

When we experience difficulties in our relationships, how do we decide what to do about them? How we handle these problems depends in part on our assessment of our situation. In other words, when we're unhappy about something, we try to figure out what's causing the problem, and on the basis of this diagnosis, we take action. For example, if your husband has lost interest in sex, what you do about it will hinge on your interpretation of why it is happening. Here are three plausible explanations:

1. He's angry at you.
2. He's overworked, overwhelmed, or his feelings are hurt about something.
3. He's got a medical condition.

Although each of these explanations may be perfectly valid, which one you choose determines your course of action. Let's say you believe that your partner's avoiding sex because he's angry at you. Imagine how you feel inside when you think this. Your stomach starts to tighten because you can't believe he's being so vindictive. You can't believe that he would stoop so low to withhold sex because he's angry at something you did. How immature! How evil! And as you work yourself up into a frenzy, your mind starts to work in equally vengeful ways. You begin to envision creative ways of getting back at him, at hurting his feelings. "Okay, the next time he asks me to go out with the people from his work, I'm going to tell him, 'Drop dead.'" Or maybe you think, "Just wait till the next time he wants sex, I'll say, 'Sorry, Charley, you should have thought about this three weeks ago.'" Or maybe instead of dreaming of the perfect retaliation, you simply let him have it. You angrily confront him about his insensitivity and lack of interest in you.

However, if you believe that his lack of interest in sex is not due to anger at you but due to his feeling overwhelmed at work, you'd undoubtedly consider a kinder and gentler approach to the problem. You might feel inclined to cater to him a bit, lighten his load at home, make him his favorite meal, ask him out on a date, or give him a back rub at the end of a long day. You'd be more loving, more forgiving. Similarly, if you believed he was hurt by something you said or did, you might approach him tenderly, asking him to share his feelings with you. You'd exude compassion and caring. Clearly, this loving response is a far cry from how you'd respond if you believed he was being vindictive.

Let's take this one step farther. What if you thought his low sexual drive was due to a physical condition. Would you angrily attack him or dream up ways to get back at him? No. Would you make him his favorite meal or ask him to share feelings? Probably not. In all likelihood, you'd make a doctor's appointment pronto or convince him to seek professional advice. You'd want him to address this condition immediately to get the proper medical treatment and to make sure everything is all right.

So how you diagnose your partner's undesirable behavior dictates, to some degree, the path you will take to modify it. Explanation number 1 suggests solution number 1. Explanation number 2 suggests solution number 2, and so on. Once you opt for a particular approach, despite the fact your strategy might not be effective, you're not crazy for persisting. You're not masochistic. You're simply doing the most rational thing you could do based on your thinking at the moment. But if your approach doesn't work, rather than question your original hypothesis about his behavior, which would be a good idea, you pull out bigger guns, which is a bad idea.

It's essential to keep in mind that for any given problem in your relationship there are many, many different, equally plausible explanations for your partner's actions. As long as you don't get glued to your favorite interpretation, one often made in haste, you'll be surprised how much more creative you can be when things are at a stalemate.

But one final note about this. Even if you can't bring yourself to believe that there may be more than one explanation for your man's annoying habits, force yourself to stop reacting the same way to him. The bottom line is that regardless of *why* he does what he does and *why* you react as you do, doing more of the same is futile. Spare yourself the aggravation.

If *he* weren't so stubborn . . .

Another reason we do more of the same is that we're so focused on our partner's stubbornness that we fail to even notice our own obstinacy. For example, Lena's husband, Barry, loved to golf, and every Saturday morning, he would urge Lena to golf with him. Because she was of the opinion that people should get their work done before they play, she would insist they do housework first. He would get angry at her for being such a stick-in-the-mud and thwarting his plan to golf. They'd end up fighting all day. Lena told me that she couldn't believe, for the life of her, how stubborn Barry was being about putting golf before housework on Saturdays. She was outraged that he would allow this issue to ruin their day. What's wrong with this picture? Can you see that the same thing could be said of Lena?

If you ever say to yourself or one of your friends, "I can't believe how stubborn he is. I can't understand why he keeps doing the same thing over and over," do yourself a favor and stop dead in your tracks. That should be a red flag. I'll bet you anything that you're in the throes of doing more of the same. Stop blaming him and start paying attention to what you're doing that brings out the worst in him.

Perhaps you're thinking that you're clueless about what you do that's more of the same. Well, I'm going to help you figure it out. First, I want to tell you about two common "more of the same" methods women use when they try to change their men. Keep in mind that these are only two out of an infinite number of ways women do more of the same with their partners. If either of these approaches sounds familiar to you, switch gears at once. If they don't ring a bell, ask yourself the questions that follow. They'll help you determine your unique brand of doing the ineffective.

More of the Same Method #1: Women Who Talk Too Much

Some of us are really good at expressing our feelings. Anytime we are disappointed, uncertain, afraid, angry, or joyful, we talk about it. We say what's on our minds. We share ourselves openly with our men. We're not afraid to make our needs known. We address issues rather than sweep them under the carpet. We're direct.

Having honest and open communication in relationships is extremely important. Relationships don't survive without truthfulness, no doubt about it. Real intimacy stems from candor and genuineness in our interactions. Having said that, there's an exception. Sometimes, as I've said before, when difficulties arise in relationships, talking things out is not always the best method for getting through to our partners. That's because men are good at tuning out words. They press the mute button. They don't hear us anymore. I can't tell you how often I've seen a man become overloaded in conversation and completely disregard what his woman was saying. No matter how she phrases things, no matter how diplomatic she becomes, he just isn't listening. Sound familiar?

As we discussed in chapter 3, if your man has refused to be influenced by what you've been *saying* to him, chances are that that won't change, no matter how well you explain your feelings. That's why you have to stop talking. You need to take an action. Men listen better when you have their attention, and action makes them sit up and take notice. Let me give you one of my own examples.

Many, many years ago, Jim and I used to support ourselves by building wooden planters and selling them at craft fairs. The planters were wonderful, and we were quite successful at selling them. Not only did we earn decent money, we thoroughly enjoyed our artsy lifestyle. No bosses breathing down our necks, interesting travel, meeting new people, and the challenges of being entrepreneurs. We loved it.

Then, one summer, Jim decided he didn't want to do it anymore. I was upset because I needed money to help pay for my graduate school program, and the thought of a traditional nine-to-five job wasn't very appealing to me. For weeks, I tried talking him out of his decision. I said everything I could think of, but nothing worked. He simply wanted out. Since I couldn't come up with any new angle to present to him, I gave up.

Soon after, I realized that just because Jim was no longer interested in the business didn't mean that I had to stop doing it. I called a friend who also needed employment and asked if she would be interested in being my partner. I agreed to teach her everything she needed to know to make the business work. She was absolutely delighted and, with her parents' permission, offered their basement as a work space. We were both excited about the prospects of working together. I told Jim of my new plans, and all I can say is that he had a funny expression on his face.

A week or two later, in the middle of our workday, in walks Jim. "Just checking. Wanted to see how you both are doing." He looked around, made a few suggestions, and left. Several days later, he made another guest appearance. That evening, he approached me with the idea of the three of us doing the business together. Hmmm. "That's interesting," I thought to myself. I talked and talked and talked about wanting him to work with me, but nothing I said made a difference. However, when I took action, that clinched the deal. I tucked this story away in my memory bank, and it has proven to be an invaluable lesson for me. If I want Jim to do something he's hesitant to do, he's much more likely to do it if I stop talking about it and take action. This is true about many things in our relationship. (Oops. I have to make sure Jim doesn't read this chapter.)

There are other ways that too much talk turns men off, and I'll discuss that in the chapter entitled "Smart Talk: How to Talk So Men Will Listen." For now, though, if you're someone who's had a hard time getting through to your man despite all the talking you do, stop wasting your breath. Zip it for a while. Take action. It's time to speak *men's* language for a change. The technique sections that follow will give you plenty of ideas of what you can *do* to motivate your man to change.

More of the Same Method #2: Women Who Say Too Little

Perhaps you're not a woman who talks too much. You may even be someone who lets things slide whenever you feel upset. If your partner does something that bothers you, you hold it inside. You stuff it. If this is your pattern, chances are you feel pretty crappy sometimes. In fact, you probably feel a lot of resentment. Long-standing feelings of resentment are extremely detrimental to your relationship over the long run, not to mention your health. You might start feeling depressed, have sleepless nights, experience panic attacks, lose loving feelings for your partner, and so on.

When you bottle up unresolved emotions day after day, eventually you blow, and when you do, all hell breaks loose. The people in your family think you're screwy. They have no idea why you're acting like such a raving maniac. Since you've been storing everything inside, no one knows how upset you've been, and when you explode—usually over some small, irritating thing—they don't really understand your reaction. For you, it's just the straw that broke the camel's back.

Your bewildered partner probably attributes your rage to something other than him, anything other than him, as a matter of fact. He might ask you if it's "that time of month" or if you're going through menopause. His lack of empathy makes you even angrier, which confirms his worst suspicion—you're losing it. Not a good thing.

If you're one of these women who keep things to yourself, it's possible that you don't get angry. Instead, you feel depressed. You tell yourself that you'll never get what you want from your partner. You resign yourself to living a bleak existence. You try to accept less than what you dreamed of for yourself. Sometimes, you're okay with things, but every once in a while, you notice that you've started to feel numb. This is also not a good thing.

If keeping things in is hazardous to one's health and happiness, why do women hold back? Our reasons vary. Some of us do so because we fear our partners will get angry. We don't want to rock the boat. Although we don't like the feeling of resentment, the by-product of stuffing things inside, we like conflict even less. We tell ourselves, "It's not worth the argument," or "He wouldn't understand anyway," and we just keep moving along.

Others of us say nothing because we have a hard time asking for what we really want and need in our relationships. We're not convinced it's okay to request that our partners put themselves out to meet our needs. We're so practiced at tending to everyone else's desires that when it comes to tending to our own needs, we're just babes in the woods. We're not even novices.

Finally, one more reason women clam up is that they think, "After all these years, he should just know how I feel. I shouldn't have to tell him." Brother, is that ever wrong. As I told you earlier, men are terrible, terrible mind readers. You have to remember that. If you want something from him, you have to tell him. You have to spell it out. Don't blame him for not being clairvoyant. It isn't in his genes. Memorize this rule and live by it. It will spare you a lot of hardship.

If you're someone who hasn't been particularly forthcoming in your relationship, it doesn't mean that there's something wrong with you. Maybe you were raised that way. Maybe you saw your mother devoting herself to making the men in her life happy and ignoring her own needs. Whatever the reason, I'm going to drag you kicking and screaming into the twenty-first century. It's time for you to evolve. Squelching your thoughts on a regular basis allows your man to become selfish. You're teaching your children (if you have them) how to become martyrs. You're showing them that relationships are one-sided (which they're not). Devoting yourself to keeping peace or making your partner happy is wonderful and noble as long as your partner feels the same way that you do. You deserve peace and happiness, too.

But more than anything else, if you keep stifling your thoughts, you're doing more of the same, and since your partner doesn't have a clue as to what you really want from him, he'll keep doing more of the same, too. Imagine how you'd feel five years from now if you're still keeping things to yourself and he's still driving you crazy. Scary thought, isn't it? If you're afraid you'd be risking things by disclosing your feelings, don't be. The real risk is in not changing. Let him in on the secret to your happiness. If you don't, you might end up being like the Walkaway Wives I described in chapter 1.

What Is Your "More of the Same" Behavior?

Okay. Have I thoroughly confused you? On one hand, I'm saying sometimes women are ineffective at bringing about change because they talk too much and sometimes it's because they talk too little. "Well, Michele," you're wondering, "which is it, too much or too little?" It depends. What you need to change about your particular strategies depends on what you've been doing that hasn't been working. And since everyone is different, only you really know what you need to change. You're the expert on yourself.

You see, I don't know you personally, and unlike other experts who offer one-size-fits-all, generic solutions to relationship challenges, I think that's a gigantic mistake. I know that your style of interacting with your partner may be completely different from your best friend's. I know that what feels comfortable or works for your neighbor and her mate may not appeal to you. Any single approach (such as expressing one's feelings) may be one woman's salvation and another's demise. That's why I want to help you know *yourself* better. I'm writing this guide for you. I want you to be able to identify which methods bring you closer to your goals and which ones you should avoid like the plague. Below are several questions you should ask yourself before moving on to the next chapter. Answering these questions will put into black and white the circular skits you keep enacting, and what your role is in them—what your "more of the same" behavior is. And, most important, answering these questions will help you remember what you need to do to prevent that "been there, done that" feeling in the future.

Which issues in your relationship seem to resurface frequently? List them.

_____

_____

_____

What arguments do you have on a regular basis?

_____

_____

_____

How do you approach your partner on these matters?

_____

_____

_____

If you're having difficulty identifying your more-of-the-same, here's another question that might help.

If I were to ask your partner, "In regard to your heated issues, what does she do that drives you nuts?" what would he say?

_____

_____

Keep in mind, you don't have to agree with him. Just answer the question. If your man thinks you nag constantly, you have to stop doing what he considers to be nagging in order to have him respond differently. If he thinks you've been sullen, you have to perk up a bit. If he accuses you of being too demanding, figure out what he means by that and quit doing it. Otherwise, you won't have his attention.

Stopping what isn't working is the very first step you need to take in order to make things better between you. That's because at least you've stopped making things worse. More important, when you stop doing more of the same, you'll like yourself better. It's no fun going in circles, particularly when you *know* you're going in circles. It's dizzying. Once you stop doing the usual, you'll feel more in control of your life, and, I promise you, that feels good.

The second step in improving things between you and your mate is knowing what to do *instead* of the same old thing, and, at last, that's what you're about to learn. The following chapters are about solutions. I know you're probably eager to get some more new ideas under your belt. After all, you most likely noticed that while you've been reading this book, your man hasn't been reforming himself. He still needs a little training. The next chapter will teach you everything you need to know about the basic principles involved in training your man when the going gets "ruff."

CHAPTER SIX

Basic Training: Sit, Stay, Come

S ue, an attractive woman in her mid-thirties, told me that her primary issue with her husband, Mike, was their vastly different parenting styles. Although she thought he was an extremely involved father and that their four children loved him very much, he was too quick to anger and often said cruel and hurtful things. She cringed each time he criticized one of them. Sue described a recent incident that really bothered her.

The family had just returned home after watching their son Jason play on his soccer team. Uncharacteristically, Jason played quite poorly that day. Since Mike spent a great deal of time practicing soccer skills with Jason, he was very disappointed in his performance. When they got home, instead of realizing that Jason was upset, Mike laid into him, saying, "Where was your head? What were you thinking about? Obviously, it wasn't the game." Jason ran upstairs to his room and slammed the door. Incensed by Mike's insensitivity, Sue let him have it. "I can't believe you're criticizing Jason. What's wrong with you? Don't you see how bad he feels? You are really something else. Now you've hurt his feelings. Good job." Mike defended his position and left the room.

A short while later, Sue noticed that Mike was heading upstairs to Jason's room. About fifteen minutes after that, both Mike and Jason came downstairs together, appearing rather calm. When Jason was out of earshot, Sue asked Mike what had happened. Mike said, "I told Jason I was sorry about what I had said. I told him it was crummy of me to have done that, especially since he was feeling bad enough already. I assured him that he was a great soccer player and that everybody has an off day once in a while. I asked for forgiveness for being such a louse, and he smiled and said, 'Okay, that's a deal.' We hugged and it's over now."

Knowing that this sort of apology was unusual for Mike, I asked Sue what happened next, and she said, "Nothing. I nodded and left the room." Surprised by her unemotional reaction, I said, "I'm confused. What did you say when Mike told you about his loving actions with Jason?" "I didn't say anything," she replied. "Besides," she said, catching on to the reason I was grilling her, "why should I be complimenting him when he shouldn't have said anything negative in the first place?" At once, I knew I had my work cut out for me. Sue's "no news is good news" mentality had to go. Pronto.

I asked Sue if she had a dog, and she told me she did. I asked her whether she was the person responsible for housebreaking the dog when it was young, and she told me she was. "Tell me what you recall about the process," I said. Since their dog was only eight months old, the process of housebreaking was still relatively fresh in her mind.

"I tried to spend a lot of time with our puppy and watch for signs that she had to go out. If she started sniffing around, I would pick her up and take her outside. When she peed or pooped, I would lavish her with praise, pet her, and take her back inside the house. If she had an accident, I wouldn't make a big deal of it. I would just take her outside and see if she still had to go and praise her if she did. She was trained very quickly."

I asked Sue why she made a very big deal about positive behavior and basically ignored the accidents. She said, "Puppies learn faster by being positively rewarded for good behavior." I chuckled to myself and told her, "Tonight I want you to go home and pretend your husband is a puppy." She laughed but completely understood my message: "Men learn faster with positive rewards for good behavior, too."

I must admit, I was somewhat surprised with Sue's unfamiliarity with the importance of catching her husband in the act of getting it right instead of rubbing his face in his mistakes. But when I did some more soul-searching about this, I realized that Sue was not alone; many, many people are completely unacquainted with the very basic principles of behavior modification—a well-accepted theory about behavior change . So that's what this chapter is about, Behavior Mod 101, the magic behind Lassie, Toto, and Rin Tin Tin. And what you will undoubtedly discover is that what works with dogs also works with men.

If you've been angry with your man, you might be thinking, "Great, a dog-training manual for men. We're finally getting into some good male-bashing material." Wrong. In case you haven't noticed, I'm really not into male-bashing. In fact, I like men a lot. I compare dog-training with man-training for two reasons. The first is that dog-training techniques—behavior modification— really do work with men. But truth be told, behavior modification techniques work equally well with women, too. In fact, they work with everybody. But this isn't a book about changing everybody, this is a book about changing men.

The second reason I compare dog-training to man-training is to put a smile on your face. When it comes to changing men, we get so damn serious. We need to lighten up a bit. So I thought I'd give you some worthwhile things to think about and make you chuckle at the same time. The principles of behavior modification and a good sense of humor should definitely be part of your man-changing repertoire.

In its most basic form, the goal of behavior modification is to in-crease desirable behaviors and eliminate undesirable ones. A dog owner might use behavior modification techniques to get her hound to be more obedient outside, stop annoying the neighbors with incessant barking, or to teach him tricks. You might use these techniques for a variety of reasons: to prompt your partner to be more helpful around the house, to get him to talk more, to teach him to be more romantic about birthdays and celebrations, or to get him to stop being tactless with your mother when she visits. If you're familiar with some of the techniques you're about to read, consider this a refresher course and let it serve as a reminder to put these principles into practice when shaping your man's behavior.

Dog-Training Principle #1: Emphasize the Positive

"Millions of words have been written in the last couple of decades on the theories of dog training. I'm going to sum it up a little more simply: Dog training is a carrot-and-stick endeavor which in recent years has become a whole lot more carrot and a lot less stick."[1]

"Dogs that are complimented for a job well done, rather than condemned for a few mistakes along the way, will progress faster and more happily."[2]

"Praise that's well timed and appropriate is essential to your dog's learning process. If all you ever do is tell your dog no, your relationship isn't going to be a very good one."[3]

Researchers have long observed that when animals are rewarded for certain behaviors, those behaviors will increase. If you pet your dog affectionately or give him a dog biscuit each time he holds out his paw to "shake" your hand, you'll soon have a "shaking" dog. Without a doubt, positive reinforcement is the most effective training method. Furthermore, research shows that it is considerably more effective than punishment when your dog behaves badly.

This principle holds true for people, too. For example, if your kid throws temper tantrums, you'll cure him of it more quickly by rewarding him—complimenting him, giving him an ice cream cone, hugging him—when he's behaving appropriately than by screaming at him or grounding him when he's acting out.

Yet, oddly enough, it is not uncommon for women to make a much bigger deal about the times their partners let them down versus the times their partners toe the line. We expect guys to get it right, so when they do, we say nothing. When they screw up, we nail them. We let them know that we're unhappy, why we're unhappy, and how they should have done better. We're hopeful that they'll heed our reprimands and, once and for all, shape up. Rarely do we say things like "You know, hon, when you helped me put the kids to bed last night, it really made a difference. I appreciate it a lot." After all, we tell ourselves, "They *should* be more responsible with the kids. Why should *we* be the only ones putting kids to bed? Aren't they parents, too?"

Yes, yes. You're absolutely right. We shouldn't have to fawn over men simply because they're doing their jobs. Men should be active parents. Men should put kids to bed at night. Men should do this, they should do that, but what if they don't? What should we do then? Complaining feels good when we're angry. We're getting things off our chests. We're letting men know how we feel. Isn't that right? Shouldn't we always tell our partners what we think, even if it's negative? To beef or not to beef. That is the question.

And here is the answer. Like it or not, rewarding your man when he's doing what you expect or want is the most effective way to get your message through. Catch him in the act of getting it right, no matter how infrequently—or even unintentionally—it occurs, and underline it. Make a big deal about it. Act appreciative. Let him know how grateful you are. Do something he'll like that will cement in his mind how important his actions are to you. Watch a football game with him. Initiate sex. Call him at work just to let him know you're thinking about him. Even if you think what he's doing is part of his job description as a partner, bring on the fanfare anyway. Remember, what you focus on expands.

I recall an incident that took place many years ago. I was talking to Arnie, my friend and colleague, on a plane ride home after several days away at a conference. I was sharing my annoyance about the fact that Jim complained about being Mister Mom in my absence. Arnie asked me how I responded after hearing Jim's gripes, and I said, "I told him, 'Well, now you know how it feels to work and have responsibility for the kids. It isn't easy, is it?'" Not exactly the world's most empathic response. Arnie asked why I hadn't thanked him for his support and hard work at home. "Simple," I said, "he doesn't deserve it. I'm always expected to do what he's been doing this weekend, and no one thanks *me*. What's so special about him?"

Arnie agreed with me and acknowledged my feelings, but added, "You're right. Jim doesn't deserve to be thanked, but what if thanking him would make him want to be Mister Mom more often? What if showing your appreciation would make him feel more loving toward you? What if acknowledging the effort he put into the family recently would make him feel good about his time with the kids and less infringed upon the next time you leave town? Would it be worth it?"

As much as I hated to admit it, Arnie was right. Jim wasn't trying to make me feel bad about being away. He was just saying that he felt overworked. I can fully understand that feeling. I've been there many times myself. So instead of giving him the cold shoulder when I returned, I took my friend's advice. I thanked Jim even though he didn't deserve it. And you know what? He really appreciated my appreciating him. And since that conference, there have been dozens more just like that one, and Jim holds down the fort each time. He supports my work and never complains about his responsibilities when I'm gone. Being positive pays.

So, again, rule number one is that it's far more efficient to praise than scold, to reward than punish. It's important that you remember this because it often feels so much more natural to grumble when things go wrong. It's almost a knee-jerk reaction. But the lesson I want you to learn throughout this book is that you must always keep your eye on the cheese. Your griping will only make your man annoyed and annoying. Become more goal-oriented. Emphasize your man's strengths and lay off his shortcomings a bit.

Dog-Training Principle #2: Rewards Must Be Rewarding

Some dogs learn new behaviors quickly when their owners praise them verbally. "Good dog" is all it takes. Other dogs do better when the trainers pet them affectionately. For certain dogs, especially hungry ones, dog biscuits or small pieces of food do the job best. All dogs are different. What's reinforcing or rewarding to one dog may not work at all with another. People are like that, too.

Since Sam was making more of an effort to please his wife, Ella, by staying home with their children so she could go out with her friends, she wanted to show her appreciation. She decided to surprise him and plan a night out after work for just the two of them. When she apprised him of her plan, he seemed less than enthusiastic. She said, "You seem so unmoved by my being nice to you. I don't understand you." He responded, "If you want to be nice to me, let's stay home. I just want to relax. Going out is your idea of fun, not mine."

Ella loves going out, so she assumed that Sam would see her invitation as a gift of sorts. Unfortunately, Sam is more of a recluse. He loves staying home. So Ella's plan, as exciting as it might be for

Ella, was not exactly up Sam's alley. And if it's not up his alley, it's not reinforcing.

Ella's confusion comes from the fact that we tend to give to others that which we would like to receive. If you love back rubs when you're stressed out, you probably think that back rubs will also work for your partner during harried times. If you reward yourself for a job well done by giving yourself permission to eat a pint of ice cream, you might buy your mate a box of chocolates when he's had a success. The problem is, your partner might be neutral about back rubs and hate chocolate. So the bottom line is that a reward must be rewarding to *him*, not necessarily to you. You've got to do something that's right up his alley or it won't have the impact you desire. It won't say, "Good job."

In the early years of my marriage, I thought that Jim was the luckiest man on earth because he had a therapist-in-residence. I could help him self-actualize, evolve, become insightful and verbally expressive. I could offer him my gifts as a helper. What a lucky guy! But soon after, I learned a long, hard lesson. He wasn't particularly interested in receiving my gifts. I got "return to sender, no such address" messages from him all the time. I thought I was giving and he thought I was a pest. In time, I figured Jim out. If he's sexually satisfied and well fed, he's pretty happy. A romantic evening or a Julia Child meal goes a lot further in terms of saying "You're on track" than a Hallmark card, bouquet of flowers, or tickets for a great show. (Jim tells me that I don't put my knowledge about what works with him to use nearly often enough.)

So your challenge is to figure out exactly what you want your partner to change, and when he does it, do something that's rewarding to him. Think about your man. You know him better than anyone else. What do you do that makes him feel appreciated by you? Is it when you tell him you love him? Is it when you tell him how much you like it when he _____ (fill in the blank)? Does he love it when you give him a hug, buy him a shirt, or make him his favorite dinner? How about an X-rated video and a bottle of wine? Will that do the trick? The point is, do what he likes, not what you think he should like.

Dog-Training Principle #3: Timely Consequences Work Best

If a dog is particularly well behaved one day and you give it a dog biscuit a week later, it won't ever make the association between good behavior and yummy dog biscuits. In order for the dog to understand that you like something he or she did, the reward has to be immediate. In other words, if you tell your dog to sit and it does, give it a dog biscuit when its butt hits the floor, not an hour later.

Your man is like that, too. If you want to positively reinforce something he's done—cleaned the kitchen spotlessly, spent long hours playing lovingly with the kids, or tried his hand at making lasagna—you have to reward him as soon as you notice (or shortly thereafter) for maximum benefit. Then he'll link good behavior with the positive feeling he'll get from your reward. Simple, but effective. So don't dillydally. Give him his *Good Housekeeping* seal of approval promptly.

Dog-Training Principle #4: Reward Progress Toward the Goal

If you've ever seen a circus dog get up on its hind legs and start dancing, twirling in circles to the beat of the music, you can't help but wonder how it learned to do that trick. After all, it's a rather complex action. Dog trainers teach dogs complex behaviors by rewarding each small step toward the goal.

For example, to train the circus dog to dance, the trainer would first teach it to get up on its hind legs. The dog might be given dog biscuits for jumping up. Once that behavior is learned, the dog might be rewarded for balancing itself for longer periods of time. With that lesson in place, the next reward might come as the dog makes a quarter turn when on its hind legs. Following that, a half turn and a full turn, and then a reward would be withheld until the dog made several turns in a row. Once it does . . . dog biscuits! In other words, training is done in chunks, reinforcing progress along the way.

Now let's go to man-training. They learn best in chunks, too. If you want your partner to change something about himself, you need to reinforce the small steps he takes toward your end goal. For instance, if your man is someone who rarely helps around the house and you've decided that his laziness just has to go, pick a well-defined goal for starters. Let's say you decide that you'd like after-dinner dishes to be his responsibility. So what if your end goal is clean dinner dishes as well as a spotless kitchen. So be it.

Now here's one of the biggest mistakes women make when training their men. They have their end goal in mind and withhold praise or positive reinforcement until the end goal is achieved. The baby steps toward the goal are either ignored or, worse yet, they're criticized. So for the chore-phobic man, his wife might say nothing, or she might condemn him for a less-than-perfect kitchen or less-than-perfect dishes. Though her frustration might be entirely understandable, her tactic undermines her end goal—to shape up her husband's helping behavior. That's because when he feels unappreciated, he gets defensive and stops trying.

I've seen women make this man-changing error so many times. We want our husbands to take more prominent roles with the kids, and when they do, we tell them they're doing it the wrong way. We ask for more help around the house, and when they oblige, we lecture them on the right way to clean a counter or toilet bowl. We ask for more romanticism, and we complain that we don't like the fragrance of the perfume they bought us. We lose sight of the big picture. We forget that we have to shape behavior in chunks.

So here's what our frustrated friend should do instead of nailing her husband for his lack of attention to details in the kitchen. She could offer some well-timed compliments about the fact that he's taking her feelings into consideration and making an effort to help more around the house. That would serve her needs better in the long run. Then, several days later, she could ask if he would consider fine-tuning his dish-washing or kitchen-cleaning technique and reward him when he does. The most efficient way to take a giant step in your relationship is to acknowledge baby steps, no matter how small.

In chapter 4, I helped you to become clearer and more concise about your relationship goals. Part of the process included answering the question "What will be the very first sign that things are moving in the right direction?" Your response to that question is your partner's first baby step, a step that requires positive reinforcement of some kind. After you've achieved the first step toward the goal, you can continue to ask yourself, "What will be the very next sign that things are continuing in the right direction?" Your responses will guide you as to which of your partner's actions merit your positive input. Remember, a journey of a thousand miles begins with one small step.

Dog-Training Principle #5: Keep It Simple

"To give your dog a chance to please you, it is necessary that you use a system of communication that is simple and clear."[4]

One of the first things you'll notice about dog trainers is that they usually use one-word commands. Think about it. They'll tell their dogs, "Sit," "Stay," "Come," "Down," "Fetch," "Shake," "No," and so on. There's a reason for this. When it comes to making requests of dogs, the simpler the better. Longer sentences are confusing and easier for the dog to tune out. I'm telling you, girl, there's a lesson here for you.

Because of our love for verbal communication, when women ask their partners to do something, we sometimes get long-winded. We beat around the bush. We explain our rationale for asking our partners to change. We go off on tangents. We talk about our feelings. By the time we're done, our guys are lost. They've stopped paying attention. Between you and me, there's nothing wrong with us for being this way, but if our goal is to change men, women have to keep in mind that men are more like dogs. Your requests should be short but sweet.

I knew a woman who, facing being an empty nester within several months, desperately wanted a closer relationship with her husband. She tried telling him. She talked about wanting more closeness, more connection, and spent several hours explaining why this was important to her. By the time she was done with her soliloquy, her husband felt discombobulated. He didn't have a clue as to what she wanted from him. (And, by the way, I'm not convinced she knew exactly what she wanted at that point either. She just felt a void.)

After reading the goal-setting chapter, she decided to become more concrete about her expectations. The following day, she spelled things out in a language even dogs could understand. She told her husband, "I need you to kiss me good morning when you wake up and kiss me when you get home from work every day." "No problem," he thought, "I can do that," and he did. Obviously, this act alone didn't win them the couple of the year award, but the good feelings it engendered and the changes that it invoked at least got them nominated. For men, simple is sublime.

Dog-Training Principle #6: Don't Reward the Incorrect Behavior Inadvertently

If you ever brought home a seven- or eight-week-old puppy, you know that the first night—or the first few nights—are hell. Separated from its mom and littermates for the first time, in completely strange surroundings, this little creature is scared to death. If you put the puppy in a crate at night or lock it in a laundry room, it undoubtedly howls the loudest howl you've ever heard in your life. It's hard to believe how such a piercing sound can be emitted from such a small, sweet puppy. It tugs on your heartstrings.

If the pressure gets too great, you tell yourself, "This puppy is going to wake up the whole family. I'll let it out of the crate . . . just this once." Famous last words. All the puppy knows is that when it yelped long enough and loud enough, you opened the crate door. Although this rescue behavior on your part is totally understandable (I've done it a million times myself), in essence, you're teaching the puppy, "If you make enough of a nuisance out of yourself, you'll get love." This is a doggone bad idea. You're actually training the dog to be a pest. Dog trainers will tell you that if you really must let the dog out of the crate, wait until it calms itself down for a while and then let it out. That way, the puppy will be rewarded for quiet behavior.

What does this have to do with men? Has your partner ever asked you to do something and for a variety of reasons you put it off? Then after he throws a tantrum or gets really pissed off, you start doing what he asked you to do? Although your heart may be in the right place, lady, you are actually rewarding irrational behavior. He will associate achieving his ends with his angry outburst.

You're training him to throw fits. Is that what you want? If you agree that it's important to do what he's asking of you, then the alternative is to wait until he stops whining and starts acting civilly—and then do it. Rewarding calm behavior is a much better idea.

Dog-Training Principle #7: Ignore Undesirable Behavior

Dog-training principle #6 described the importance of letting the whining puppy whine it out before responding. In other words, you must resist the temptation to react to the undesirable behavior. If you do, you're giving the puppy attention, and even if the attention isn't positive—scolding, for example—the puppy may prefer negative attention to not being noticed at all. In other words, any attention, good or bad, may be reinforcing. According to dog trainers, the best way to combat this is to completely ignore the undesirable behavior because, if it's not reinforced, eventually the dog will stop doing it.

In relationships, sometimes the smartest thing you can do if you want to extinguish your partner's irritating behavior is to let it roll off your back. Act as if he's having no effect on you whatsoever. If he expects to push your buttons and you surprise him by appearing unfazed, he won't get the reinforcement he's expecting. Ignoring negative behavior won't necessarily eliminate it instantly because your partner will keep testing you to see if he can hit a nerve—or maybe just because his actions have become habitual. (Remember your skits?) But if you persist and fail to react to the provocation consistently, eventually he'll stop doing it, or at least he'll do it less often.

I knew a woman whose husband often felt very pressured by his high-intensity career. Frequently, he would come home in a bad mood. Her approach to his irritability varied: on some nights, she would be empathetic and urge him to open up and tell her what was bothering him. Talking about his hard day was the last thing he wanted to do so he rejected her offer and kept to himself. She pursued him further and they ended up fighting. On other nights, she felt incensed by his self-absorption and would let him have it: "I'm sick and tired of your long face when you get home. I'm fed up with being single. Get a grip on yourself." What would your best guess be as to his response? Let's just say that he didn't like it all that much. He yelled back at her, and they retreated into their own worlds.

Then one day I made a suggestion. I asked her what she thought would happen if, when he came home grumpy, she just ignored it. She hadn't even considered it. I asked her to review what happened when she demonstrated her concern by asking him to share his day or giving him a "shape up or ship out" lecture. She was smart enough to realize that the results weren't sterling. So I instructed her to do an experiment: "When he returns home disgruntled, pretend you don't notice him at all. Just go about your business as usual." Several days later, she reported to have nipped his moodiness in the bud. He was back to his old self. Ignoring is bliss.

Dog-Training Principle #8: Be Fair with Corrections

Although positive reinforcement and ignoring are the most efficient ways to train your dog, sometimes dogs do need correcting. Dog trainers will tell you that corrections should not be excessive. In other words, let your dog know that you're displeased, and move on. If after your correction your dog shows appropriate behavior, turn the negative into a positive by rewarding him or her. If a dog jumps up on people, a dog trainer might knee him quickly and firmly, saying "Down" loudly. But the trainer won't keep scolding the dog. And if the dog then behaves obediently, the trainer will end the training session with tons of praise.

Sometimes your partner does something that rankles you. You can try to ignore it in the same way you might ignore the whining of a young puppy, but occasionally it's important to set him straight. You can do it through words—by letting your man know you are disappointed or unhappy about something he did—and if that doesn't work, you can do it through action. The key here is to avoid holding grudges or seeking revenge. Holding grudges and becoming vengeful generally don't work very well. The problem with both approaches is that you make it too easy for your man to focus on *your* behavior and stop examining his own. It prevents him from learning the lesson you're trying to teach. So correct if you must, my dear, but be clear, swift, and forgiving.

Dog-Training Principle #9: Expect Prompt Compliance

If you want to teach a dog to sit, you give the command "Sit." If the dog sits, you reward it. If the dog doesn't sit, you can repeat the command once, but if it still doesn't sit, you have to take action. You have to push its butt down and say, "Good dog." Novice dog trainers often give their dogs commands seven or eight times in a row, waiting for the dog to comply. Even if the dog eventually complies, waiting until the dog is ready to respond is a very, very bad idea. You see, if you allow the dog to hear seven or eight requests before it responds, in essence, you're teaching the dog that it doesn't need to listen to you until it wants to, that you don't really mean what you say the first time.

For many years, I worked as a family therapist with teenagers and their parents. Inconsistency gets a lot of parents in trouble. Frequently, parents instruct their children to do something and the kids completely ignore their parents' wishes. Then parents reiterate their expectations, often repeating word for word what they said in their previous sermon. Nonetheless, the children seem unfazed. Sometimes, this kind of interaction goes on for months before parents finally figure out that it's time to do something, to take action, to show that they really mean what they say. Once they do, children are much more responsive. Unwittingly, parents often teach children that they don't expect their children to respond promptly.

When I worked with these parents, I often used an interesting technique with them. I assigned a homework task a colleague of mine called "After twice, there's a price." It went like this. The parents could make a request of their children—one time. If the children didn't comply, the parents could say, "This is the second reminder." If the children still didn't comply and the parents offered a third reminder, the parents had to pay the children a predetermined amount of money. Remember, after twice, there's a price. However, the parents were told that after the second reminder, anything but a verbal reminder is fair play. The kids were told that it was their job to try to get their parents to remind them as often as they could. We'd laugh and off they'd go. Generally, the parents returned with wonderfully creative stories about the actions they took to get their points across. They were highly motivated to avoid the embarrassment of shelling out money to their kids for being disobedient.

Expecting prompt compliance is a good thing with men, too. For example, if you detest lateness and you make it absolutely clear to him that you want him to be prompt from now on, when he arrives at the movie fifteen minutes late or shows up at a friend's house an hour later than promised, you need to do something other than complain or express your feelings again. If you take no other action, the lesson you're teaching your man is that your words are meaningless.

So what should you do if you have a tardy husband? Anything *other* than repeating yourself! Leave the movie theater before he arrives. Be late for your next date together. Tell him to meet you twenty minutes earlier than he really needs to be there. Refuse to make plans with him the next time he wants to go somewhere. The possibilities are endless, and that's what the rest of this book is about. But the most important point to remember is that if you repeat yourself, you're training your man to think it's okay to ignore you.

Okay. Now you've had a crash course in Dog-Training 101. I hope it unleashes your determination to stop chasing your tail and do more of what works in your life. And speaking of doing what works, that's exactly what the next chapter is all about.

PART THREE

FIRE

CHAPTER SEVEN

Becoming a Solution Detective

If you have school-age children or you've ever been around them, you are undoubtedly familiar with *Magic Eye* illustrations. Stare into these colorful pictures using techniques outlined by the developers, and something magical happens: images begin to appear to be three-dimensional! It's quite the rage. My son, Zach, sees the 3-D images hidden in the picture almost instantly, and so, by the way, do most of his friends. My daughter and husband take a few seconds longer, but, hocus-pocus, the images jump out at them, too. It seemed that everyone could see these images. Everyone, that is, except me.

Knowing that these images existed, but were imperceptible to me, drove me nuts. So I became a woman obsessed. I practiced for hours, and finally, one wonderful day, I joined the throngs of people who could see! Technique, practice, and patience bought me a ticket to the third dimension.

Well, I'm about to tell you of another world that's imperceptible to the untrained eye. A world of solutions. Simple, straightforward solutions lying just beneath the surface of seemingly intractable relationship problems. So close, in fact, they're right under your nose. But unless you know how to bring them into focus, you're guaranteed to miss them. And that's what this chapter is all about. I'm going to help you become a solution detective. I'm going to assist you in finding all the clues you'll need to solve the mystery of man-changing. I'll teach you to see beyond the distracting, sometimes even blinding, unproductive interactions between you and your partner in order to unearth the hidden keys to loving each other more. Get out your magnifying glass, Sherlock, we're moving in.

The Illusion of All-or-Nothing Thinking

Has your partner ever said, "You *never* want to relax on weekends," or "You *always* want to talk," or "Why can't you *ever* take my feelings into consideration?" If he has, and he probably has, my guess is that you didn't like it very much. As a matter of fact, you hate when he generalizes and exaggerates, when he overlooks your efforts to please him. It frustrates you no end that all he ever seems to notice is the bad times. You get no credit for getting things right. Sound familiar?

Most couples play the all-or-nothing game from time to time. And when you're on the receiving end, it's exasperating. That's because you know nothing happens all the time. Nothing. For example, if he accuses you of wanting to talk all the time, you know that that's absurd. Even if you love to talk, there are countless times when talking's the last thing on earth you feel like doing. Times when you're busy, when you're meditative, when you feel like taking a hot bath and being left alone; times when you just want to sit next to your partner and savor the moment. I know that. You know that. But, for some reason, your partner experiences you as having an insatiable, never-ending need to gab.

Conversely, perhaps you accuse your partner of acting a certain way all the time. You tell him, "You're *always* angry," or "You *constantly* criticize me. Why do you *always* think you're right and I'm wrong?" or "You *never* talk about your feelings." Now, admit it. You've played the all-or-nothing game, too. Haven't you? Sure you have. That's because when he's angry, his anger feels all-pervasive. When he's critical or uncommunicative, it *feels* as if the only time he opens his mouth is to put you down. That feeling is normal. Normal . . . but distorted.

Since nothing happens all the time, there are times when the so-called angry person responds with tranquillity. There are times when the critical person expresses approval. There are times when the controlling person seems less invested in a particular outcome. In short, for every problem people experience, there are problem-free times; occasions when, for some reason, things go more smoothly than others. I refer to these problem-free times as "exceptions."

Exceptions usually go unnoticed and unappreciated. The problem with overlooking problem-free times is that the seeds of solution are planted there. Let me give you an example. A number of years ago, I started feeling an imbalance in my relationship with Jim. I talked to him *all the time* about my work, and he *never* did. So I sat him down and complained. Basically, he informed me that he had no need to rehash his day once he was home, and that was that. I felt at a loss. I appreciated his interest in my life, but I wanted more from him. I wasn't sure what to do next, since talking to him about it didn't turn out to be the panacea I had hoped for.

Sometimes, when I feel stuck, I play therapist with myself and ask myself the same questions I ask my clients in similar situations. For example, I might ask someone in my situation, "What's different about the times when he does talk to you about his day?" And when I asked myself that question, I recalled a few situations when Jim was quite open. In thinking about these situations, I noticed a pattern. Jim was considerably more likely to talk to me about the details of his life when there were no distractions—no kids tugging at my sleeve, no phones ringing off the wall, no doorbells. In fact, the most revealing conversations we've had occurred when we were out of the house, eating dinner at a restaurant, in the car alone, or taking a walk together. Jim would share more of his life with me when we were alone.

So although I had been down in the dumps because I almost convinced myself that Jim shared nothing with me, focusing on the exceptions made me much more optimistic. Once I became aware of this solution, I consciously created times we could be alone. If we couldn't go out, I'd talk to him in the privacy of our bedroom instead of the Grand Central Station we call the living room. I became smarter, and Jim became the communicative man of my dreams. Well . . . maybe that's an exaggeration, but you get what I mean.

Instead of sitting around feeling bad about Jim's tendency to hold things in, I focused on the exceptions—his talkative times. And once I ferreted out the common denominator evident during these times, I realized I didn't have to feel bad anymore. I could turn an exception into a rule. Instead of dissecting problems, I could dissect solutions. Let me give you another example.

I knew a couple whose marriage was on shaky grounds. He was a pilot and she a homemaker. Although she thought she knew what she was getting herself into when she married him, she had no idea how difficult it would be for her to handle his long absences from home once their four children were born. She complained constantly. As a result, her husband dreaded coming home and felt as if he were walking on eggshells much of the time. Although he hated the situation, he didn't have a clue as to what he might do to rectify things. He imagined that the only solution would be for him to pursue an entirely different career, one that entailed no travel, and he was not about to do that.

When I met with them, I asked his wife, "What's different about the times when you don't feel unhappy about his being gone?" After a few moments of contemplation, she replied, "Every now and then I feel somewhat more comfortable about his being away." Excited by the slight scent of a possible solution, I urged her to reflect on what was different about those times. She said, "Those are the times when he calls me more often. If he calls home every night when he's flying, I feel less agitated about his time away."

Since he was a practical man, eager to put an end to his wife's complaints, his response to my obvious suggestion, "Why not call her more often?" was predictable. He agreed to do it. As it turned out, she appreciated his calls and was considerably happier when he returned home. He was somewhat surprised by the simplicity of the solution because he believed that nothing short of a career change would suffice. But he was wrong. The best solutions are often the simplest.

Perhaps you're thinking that identifying the exceptions seems so simple. Why don't we do it all the time when we encounter roadblocks? There are several reasons we fail to focus on exceptions. Here are a few of them.

People Often Focus on What's Wrong Rather Than on What's Right

Ever hear this joke? A elderly woman buys her grown son a gift of two shirts, a blue one and green one. He immediately changes into the green shirt. Upon seeing him, the woman says, "What's the matter, don't you like the blue one?"

This woman's glass is half empty, no doubt. And although you can laugh at her response to her son, you probably wouldn't laugh if she were your mom. Is she your mom? Is she like someone you know? I know some people who have advanced degrees in pessimism. They're highly skilled at overlooking anything remotely positive and at transforming any blaring, undeniable virtue into a deficit through misinterpretation.

Have you ever slaved all day long to get your home spick-and-span and your partner walks in only to notice the one item out of place? Or perhaps you turned over a new leaf and started pampering your husband sexually, yet all he remembers is the one time you were too tired to have sex that week. Or despite the fact that you've made a huge effort not to talk on the phone at night because you know it bothers him, he points to the one time your mother called and you talked with her for twenty minutes. Doesn't it infuriate you that his perception is so lopsided?

Well, he's not necessarily evil. He's just human. We all tend to focus on what's wrong rather than on what's right. We're the Fault Police, closely watching . . . monitoring meticulously for screwups. Good stuff is nice, but bad stuff really makes us stand up and take notice. We're titillated by wrongdoings, not virtue. Just think about the news or talk shows. Our fascination with the dark side of life hypnotizes us into being a captive audience for stories of murder, rape, theft, political indiscretion, and so on. Problems capture our attention. Imagine what it would be like to wake up one morning, turn on the news, and discover that all the news is good news, human interest stories. Hard to imagine, isn't it?

Well, our relationships don't have to be subjected to this negative mentality. We can train ourselves to "see" and "think" positives and exceptions. We can learn to notice the breaks in the pattern. We can become astute observers of what works and what's good in our lives. We can sift through the rubble and discover the treasures. It takes some doing, but it can be done.

Connie wanted her husband, Bob, to have a better relationship with their son, Joey. She said that Bob "never" talked to or spent time with Joey. This upset Connie because she had a very close relationship with her father and recalled many wonderful childhood memories involving him. She tried talking to Bob about her concern, but he just got defensive.

Since I knew it was unlikely that Bob *never* spent time with Joey, I asked Connie to tell me about the times they spent together. She said that the only thing they did together was play soccer. In fact, Bob took Joey to all of his soccer games and practices. Connie hadn't thought of this exception before because she was yearning for the two of them to talk more, and soccer didn't quite fit the bill. However, I pointed out that guys often bond through sports and that their time together might be very special to Joey. She agreed that it was a possibility.

Having identified this exception, Connie decided to ask Joey if he wanted to play on a Little League team. He did and so she signed him up. Truth be told, she had an ulterior motive. She knew Bob would get involved and he did. As a matter of fact, after every game, Bob and Joey went out for ice cream together and often lingered longer than Connie thought they would. Apparently, they were having a great time.

In the weeks that followed, Connie noticed Bob and Joey interacting more. In fact, one night, instead of asking Connie for help on his homework as he usually did, Joey went directly to Bob. Connie was shocked. Joey had always acted as if Bob weren't even present when he needed something. Now he had two parents. By focusing on what Bob was doing right, Connie was able to set the groundwork for greater change.

When Things Go Wrong, We Lose Perspective

Another reason we overlook exceptions is that when things go wrong, we lose perspective. We become pessimistic and tell ourselves that whatever's annoying us about our partners at the moment has always annoyed us in the past and will probably continue to annoy us in the future. If our partners are mean-spirited for a few days, we immerse ourselves in memories of their every mean-spirited deed and convince ourselves that things will never change. As I said in chapter 2, once we brainwash ourselves into believing that our partners are immovable, we've put blinders on. We fail to notice anything that doesn't fit our theories about them. When mean-spirited guys act lovingly, we overlook it or explain it away, saying to ourselves, "This couldn't have anything to do with our relationship; he must have had a good day at work," or "He probably wants sex," or "He must be feeling guilty," or . . . you get the picture? We don't give credit where credit is due. We don't see the exceptions for what they really are.

Although there are many reasons for this shortsightedness, I'll explain one of them. Research shows that your current mood state—how you're feeling at the moment—creates the lens through which you view your life. If someone asks you about your childhood and you're feeling depressed, you will recall and emphasize unhappy memories. Conversely, if you're feeling happy, you'll recall fond memories. So when you're angry at your mate, all that you think about are his bad traits. Given this perspective, no wonder you think you'd come up empty-handed if you scanned your memory for times when your partner acts the way you desire.

Bad Times Get Superglued Together

I've noticed something very curious about the way couples perceive their relationships. If a couple has an argument in the beginning of the month but not again until the end of that month, they will nonetheless report that they fight "all the time." That's because they unconsciously link one disappointment to another. They fail to notice the three and a half weeks in between that are argument-free. My theory about this is that, for them, the bad times simply carry more weight than the positive times. The effects of three weeks' worth of purely positive interactions can evaporate in an instant following one sarcastic, hurtful comment. Perception is a funny thing.

When I encourage the "We fight all the time" couples to really think about and discuss their peaceful times, they always seem a bit surprised by the end of our conversation. They'll say, "You know, now that we're talking about it, things are considerably better than I thought." The point here is that our discussing their week together changed absolutely nothing about how they actually interacted. It simply shifted their focus. But shifting one's focus, emphasizing strengths rather than weaknesses, can make all the difference in the world. Instead of seeing themselves as a couple riddled with conflict, they began to define their relationship more optimistically.

By now, I'm sure it is easy to see the value in identifying exceptions. Once you know what works, even a little, you know what you need to do more of. When you do more of what works, the good times begin to crowd out the bad times—a formula for success.

So now it's your turn. It's time to start detecting solutions in your life. Here's how. Go back to chapter 4, the goal-setting chapter. It's there that I helped you define what you want to change about your man. Refer to that goal as you search for solutions, following the steps below.

Clue #1: Think about times when your partner responds the way you want him to.

It's helpful to recall recent experiences first. These events will be most vivid in your mind. You'll have an easier time following the remaining clues if the exception you recall happened within the last few days or weeks. Even if it was short-lived or, in your opinion, a fluke, it doesn't matter. It's still an important clue.

If you're having trouble recalling a recent example, keep pushing yourself, but if you're still drawing a blank, think about times past. If you have to, you can go as far back as the beginning of your relationship. That's okay. I'll help jostle your memory in order for you to reconstruct what might have been working back then. Once you recall some positive times, write them down:

_____

_____

_____

_____

Clue #2: Note anything that's different about the times your partner responds the way you want him to.

I'm well aware that it isn't always that easy to identify why something is working. Oftentimes, we're so close to the situation, we can't see the forest for the trees. Here, following, are some places to look for solutions.

Your Own Actions

Ask yourself, "When I get a better response from my partner, what am I doing differently?"

Even if you think your behavior doesn't trigger your partner's behavior (it does), answer the question anyway. It's tempting to assume that your partner's positive actions have nothing to do with you and everything to do with his job, his personality disorder, his midlife crisis, but don't do that. It won't help much. Force yourself to think how you might be treating your man differently those times when you end up getting the results you want. Even the pilot admitted that frequent calls home turned an alleged shrew into a near siren.

_____

_____

_____

_____

Another way of determining how your actions might be affecting him is by asking yourself, "When my partner acts more _____ [fill in the blank with your goal], how does that affect me and, as a result, how do I treat him differently in return?"

So, let's say that your goal is to have your husband be more helpful with the kids. You've been resenting his preoccupation with work. And then let's say that, for some strange reason, he starts pitching in more, being a take-charge dad. Naturally, this will please you. You will be happy. Now, what I'm asking you to do is figure out what's different *about you* when you're a happier person. You must be nicer to him in some way, a more loving partner. How are *you* different when he pleases you?

_____

_____

_____

_____

The reason I'm having you ask yourself this question is that even if your partner's positive behavior wasn't prompted by you, your more positive outlook might be influencing him to keep it up. He may enjoy the "new you" so much that he'll keep doing what works. (He finds your positive actions toward him rewarding. Remember dog-training?) So, if you can't determine what you've done to get him started, figure out what you're doing to keep him going.

Perhaps your partner's positive actions have less to do with *what* you're doing and more to do with some other factors. To figure this out, keep the words "who," "when," and "where" in mind.

Who

Sometimes the presence or lack of presence of another person can be associated with good things happening. For example, some women tell me that their partners are more easygoing after they've spent some time with their buddies. So, buddy time is part of the solution. One couple noticed that they got along much better when her mother, who was living with them, went out of town for a few days. So, think about whether the "people variable" applies to your situation.

When

Have you ever noticed that if you approach your partner with a particular concern on one day, all hell will break loose, but on another, everything works out just fine. This may have something to do with your timing. People are more receptive during certain parts of the day, week, month (you know this one), year, and so on. We deal with the people in our lives somewhat inconsistently, depending on our mood, energy level, physical condition, and stress level, which varies over time. Smart people think about timing when they deal with their partners on issues that matter. Good timing can mean the difference between achieving your ends and waging a war.

For instance, if Jim and I are arguing about something, I know that it's fruitless to try to resolve it at night, before he goes to sleep. From past experience, I've learned the hard way that my efforts to find a resolution when he's tired only make matters worse. Much worse. It's better to give him some space to de-escalate and then go to sleep. In the morning, he's much more reasonable, conciliatory, and even apologetic, upon occasion. So waiting until dawn to find a solution is something I do when we have arguments in the evening. I only wish it hadn't taken me so long to figure this out.

Is timing a factor in your more enjoyable, productive moments with your partner? Is he more attentive on weekends? Is he in a better mood after he goes for a run? Is he more willing to communicate or do things you want him to do after great sex? Should you avoid him entirely when he's preparing for a presentation at work? Does the transitional period he's going through due to his stopping smoking make him less approachable at the moment? So, ask yourself, "Is there something different about the timing of our positive interactions with each other?"

Where

Some couples say they can have productive conversations at restaurants, other people's houses, car rides, and on walks. At home, these talks don't go so well. The point is that environment really can make a difference in how people feel and how they interact with each other. If your more successful times with your partner happen in certain places, create opportunities for you to be in those places more often. Do what works.

At the beginning of this chapter, I told you that solutions to your relationship problems can be discovered by noticing what's different about the problem-free times. But there's another place to look for potential solutions. Sometimes, even in the midst of our most challenging situations, we notice things could have turned out worse. Throughout this book, I've emphasized the importance of noticing small steps forward, and this is no exception. So in addition to your scrutinizing what's different about your problem-free times, you'll want to pay attention to the following clues.

Clue #3: Note what's different when the problematic situation occurs, but for some reason, it doesn't bother you at all.

Janine and Stan argued a lot about the amount of time he devoted to golf. In fact, it seemed that they were arguing all the time lately. Janine was at her wits' end about it and wondered whether she could tolerate being a golf widow any longer. I asked her, "What's different about the times when Stan plays golf but it doesn't bother you?" and she admitted that occasionally his outings were fine with her. "Think about it," I said, "what's different then?" She replied, "I guess when I take better care of myself, spend some time with my friends, get a massage or get out a little, then I don't mind when he plays golf. I get infuriated at how easy it is for him to take off and ignore his responsibilities at home. But if I have a chance to recharge my batteries, I'm more understanding about the time he needs to unwind." Solution accomplished. Here's another example.

Lucy and her husband, Gary, were arguing a great deal because she kept accusing him of drinking too much. When Gary protested, saying he didn't drink very much at all, Lucy admitted he was right, but this didn't stop her from feeling upset when he had an occasional drink. Eventually, Lucy admitted that her fears might be partially due to the fact that her own father was an alcoholic. I asked her, "What's different about the times you're not troubled by Gary's drinking alcohol?" and she replied, "If he has a glass of wine or a beer with dinner once in a while, that's okay. In fact, if he drinks a little, I'm fine with it, as long as he drinks at home."

After some discussion, it became clear that alcohol wasn't the problem. Lucy had trust issues she hadn't dealt with. Her father had many affairs when he was out late at night drinking at bars. She feared Gary would fall into that pattern if he stopped for a few drinks now and then with friends. Once Lucy aired her feelings, Gary said, "I don't have a strong need to go to bars with friends. If that's what bothers you right now, I won't do it. It will be great not to have you jumping on me for having a glass of wine once in a while at home. That's a trade I'll make in a minute." So, again, a solution was born from noticing the difference between times Lucy became upset with Gary's drinking and times when it was acceptable to her.

Think about your own situation. Are there times when you would normally get upset by something that happens, but for some reason you're okay with it? If you determine why you reacted differently, you'll be on to a solution.

Clue #4: Note what's different about the times the problem is less intense, less frequent, or shorter in duration.

We all like it when our lives are problem-free. But blissful times don't last forever. Even in the very best of relationships, "shit happens." In my practice, I teach women to pay attention to problem-free times, but I also teach them to notice when problems are kept at bay or held down to a dull roar. Therefore, it's very common for me to hear, "Michele, I'm really excited by what happened last week. We had an argument . . . but it didn't last more than fifteen minutes. Generally when we argue, he holds a grudge for a day or two, and this time it was over when it was over. I couldn't believe it." Or "We're doing so much better. We had two fights this week. We usually argue about something every day, several times a day. This is great for us."

It's just as important to notice times when the problem is less intense, less frequent, or shorter in duration as it is to notice times the problem doesn't happen. So, in addition to asking yourself, "What's different about the times when we're getting along well?" you can ask, "What's different about the times when the arguments are less intense or less frequent?" Instead of asking yourself, "What's different about the times when he doesn't criticize me?" ask yourself, "What's different about the times he's less critical or his criticism is less hurtful?" Instead of asking yourself, "What's different about the times he arrives on time for a change?" ask yourself, "What's different about the times he arrives more promptly than usual?"

When you figure out your answers to these "less intense, shorter in duration, less frequent" questions, you may not feel that you're home yet. And maybe you're not. You still may have a way to go to feel satisfied with your partner. But trust me when I tell you that if you know why a situation is improved, even slightly, though you may not be home, you're on the home stretch.

Clue #5: Note what's different about the times that something constructive comes from "the problem."

Samantha was angry at her boyfriend all the time. She would even wake up in the middle of the night with her teeth clenched after dreaming about something he had done. She felt that these intense feelings of rage were harming her health, not to mention her relationship. Her boyfriend was losing patience with her.

In addition to asking her the usual exception question—"What's different about the times you feel calmer and more in sync with your boyfriend?"—I asked, "What's different about the times your anger is constructive?" My question really surprised her because she had only been considering the destructive side of her anger, and on that count, there was a lot to consider. However, she found her response to the question eye-opening. Here's what she said.

"Now that I think about it, there are times when my anger is constructive. My usual way of handling anger is to stuff it inside and let it eat away at me. I do that for a period of several weeks, and then he does one more small, irritating thing and I let him have it. Stuffing anger inside and letting him have it are not great ways to deal with anger. But there have been a few times when I handled my resentment differently and felt better about myself and about him.

"During my more constructive moments, I tell him what's on my mind, but I do it in a peaceful manner. I'm very direct and honest, but not hurtful. It surprises him when I handle things constructively because he's used to either hearing nothing and thinking everything's okay, or seeing me act like a screaming meemie. He really listens to me when I talk to him like a person."

The more she thought about my question, the more she realized that there are many times her anger is constructive. She recalled times at work when she funneled her angry feelings into a positive direction. "Those are the times," she said, "when I make an appointment to talk with my supervisor about the things at work that drive me crazy. My supervisor really seems to appreciate my feedback and often restructures the way things are done based on what I've told her."

At the end of our discussion, Samantha learned something new about herself. Although she had always thought that anger was an evil force inside of her needing to be exorcised at any cost, she now knew this wasn't so. She realized that she had a choice as to how to handle her anger, and when she made the right choice, the end result was actually beneficial. Handled correctly, anger actually brought her closer to her boyfriend and elevated her in the eyes of her supervisor. She now knew what she needed to do to turn her unbridled anger into constructive anger, and she planned on doing it more often. Here's another example.

Judy was feeling totally burned out. She worked fifty hours a week as a head-hunter and also was the primary caretaker of her three kids. Her husband and kids hadn't been much help at home. When I met Judy, she told me that her goal was to feel less stress in her life. She recently had had several panic attacks, which were very unnerving to her.

Although I asked the usual exception question—"What's different about the times you feel more relaxed and at ease?"—I also asked, "What's different about the times your anxiety results in something positive or constructive happening?" This question caught her a bit off guard, but she responded by saying, "You know, that's an interesting question. I've been feeling low-grade stress for a long time, but it wasn't until now that I knew something had to give. I realized that I have to make changes in my life and that's why I'm here. I've already joined a health club and made a chart outlining chores for the kids and my husband. If it hadn't been for the panic attack, I'd still be walking around feeling crazed."

Although Judy hadn't made substantial changes in her life until her anxiety escalated to the point she was having panic attacks, she realized that in the future she didn't have to wait until panic set in. I helped her to recognize that if she was feeling stress, it was a signal for her to take action. In the weeks that followed, anytime Judy felt a hint of anxiety, she looked at the places in her life where she was overextended and promptly reprioritized her time. Once Judy realized that something constructive can come from an unpleasant feeling, she saw the feeling of stress as a "friend." It became the red flag signaling the need for her to do something different.

Now think about your own situation. Are there times when the usual problem pops up—but something positive comes from it? Are there times you feel jealous (resentful, annoyed, irritated), and instead of allowing that feeling to divide you, it somehow brings you closer? If so, ask yourself, "What's different about those times? What am I doing differently? What is my partner doing differently?" and so on. And then do those things.

Clue #6: Pay attention to how your conflicts end.

One day I was watching Pastor Robert Schuller on television. He was talking about an important meeting he had attended years ago along with Margaret Thatcher, George Bush, François Mitterrand, and Mikhail Gorbachev. The purpose of the meeting was somewhat unusual: they were going to brainstorm what they believed accounted for the *end* of the Cold War. What a refreshing goal for politicians and religious leaders—to analyze how nations make peace rather than war, how "fights" on a global level end rather than how they begin.

This story struck me because that's precisely what I had been doing with couples for years—helping them identify how their conflicts ended rather than how they began. I learned that analyzing how conflicts begin usually leads to the same dead end: "You started it." Starting points depend on one's perspective.

Conversely, I've found it much more useful to ask couples, "What did each of you do to put an end to that argument?" For one thing, I love watching the look on people's faces when I ask that question. No one has a clue as to why conflict ends. No one even questions it. People seem to think that peace happens unintentionally or accidentally whereas conflict is caused by ill will. It's an interesting perspective, one with which I wholeheartedly disagree.

I believe that when couples begin to argue, they have their routines, their highly predictable ways of acting toward each other. She knows exactly what he's going to say and vice versa. Remember the scripts! Similarly, when people *stop* fighting or when they make up, their actions are equally predictable. Each couple has its unique, highly patterned reconciliation method. We have distinct methods for signaling when it's time to declare a truce or kiss and make up. In other words, there's a method to more than just our madness. Let me give you an example, one of my very own. Most couples I know strongly identify with this story because gender differences play a big role in the way Jim and I respond to each other. Maybe this story will sound familiar to you, too.

When Jim and I argue, I will stop the argument and make peace if one of two things happens: we find a resolution—which doesn't always happen—or Jim says something affectionate like "Look, I love you, let's not do this anymore," or "This isn't worth arguing about," or "Why don't we just drop this and spend some time together." If Jim shows affection, I stop fighting.

Jim is different. When we're in the midst of an argument, like me, he'll stop arguing if we find a resolution, but if that doesn't happen, he wants to be left alone. He isn't looking for affection or connection. He needs time to himself to de-escalate. After he's worked himself up, the last thing he feels is a need to be close to me. So, the upshot of all of this is, if I want Jim to be more connected to me when we're at odds with each other, all I have to do is give him some space for a while. If Jim wants me to leave him alone, all he has to do is say something loving or reassuring. I refer to these solutions as truce triggers.

Now, here comes the interesting part. Perhaps you've noticed that my truce triggers are the exact opposite of Jim's. How in the world have we stayed together for so many years? That's a good question. Before we knew about truce triggers, our arguments frequently looked like this: I would continue talking to him in hopes he'd say the right thing. The more I talked, the more he wanted me to leave, which made me want to pursue the conversation even more, which made him want to withdraw even more. Get the picture?

Sometimes, he'd get so frustrated that he would leave the room. Guess what I did. You got it. I followed him right out the door into the other room. He'd say, "Michele, why do you want to argue?" and I'd say, "I don't want to argue, I just want to find a solution," and he'd say, "Why don't you just leave me alone for a while?" and I'd say, "How will leaving you alone help us find a solution?" Boy, we were going nowhere fast.

Well, one day after I figured this stuff out about truce triggers, I went into the room where Jim was sitting and told him about the different ways each of us ends arguments. Aware of the polarity of our needs, he said, "What are we going to do?" I told him, "I have no idea." And he replied, "I know, the next time we have a fight, we'll flip a coin, heads I hug, tails you leave." That was good for a laugh.

The truth is, we've never done that. But I've noticed that since we've had that discussion about truce triggers, we've handled our arguments differently from the way we used to. Sometimes when we argue and I can tell that he's reaching the point of no return, I muster up all of my personal strength and get myself out of the room. I leave him alone. Although this goes against my nature and is therefore a challenge for me, I notice I can handle it if I keep myself busy. And, oh, do I keep myself busy. I'll do anything to distract myself. I'll even wash the dishes or clean the house.

When I've been strong enough to do this, what I've noticed is that a short time later, Jim will come downstairs. He'll come over to me and say something silly like "You want to be friends?" or "You want to make up?" Sometimes we discuss what happened and sometimes we don't. We might put it off until later or let the subject drop entirely. But what does happen is that we stop fighting. We start loving again. I've also noticed that there are times when our arguments have reached the point of no return—when Jim's eyes glaze over—and he reaches his arms out, stiff as a board, and says, "Come here." And he gives me a hug. You know the kind. It's a cardboard hug. It's plastic. But it's a hug nonetheless. And although I know he really doesn't feel like hugging me, I'm very grateful that he's making an effort to take care of my feelings. So, in return, I think about his needs and I very happily leave the room. But, I must say, my happiness doesn't compare with the ecstasy that he feels in watching me go.

So think about it. Even if you and your partner argue, your arguments don't last forever. They end eventually. Even though you might not know it, I bet there's a pattern to how your fights end. I bet you and your partner act in certain ways when you're ready to make peace or take a respite from the arguing. Are you more likely to make up after you've had some time away from each other? Can you count on your partner to react badly the first time you bring up a heated subject but recognize that once he adjusts to the idea, he's a bit more understanding? Will your partner fight you tooth and nail when he disagrees or feels attacked, but if you watch his behavior closely in the days that follow, can you predict that he'll probably take your feelings into consideration? Will your man rant and rave all day long, but refuse to go to bed without making up with you? Does he expect you to be the one to initiate peace after the war? If so, what are the exceptions to that? When you make up, do you say, "I'm sorry"? Does he? Do you kiss? Do you have sex? Do you just let things go without discussing what happened? Do you call him at work? Does he call you?

Sometimes, when I ask women how their arguments end, they say, "I'm always the one to initiate making up, and that infuriates me." First of all, it is rarely the case that relationships are so one-sided, even though it might feel that way. If you're someone who feels that you do more than your fair share when it comes to making up, you have an option. You can start doing less of it. Remember the seesaw analogy? The more you do of something, the less he'll do. This applies to making up, too. Now I can just hear you saying, "If I don't approach him, he'll never approach me," but my guess is that you haven't tried this strategy long enough to see what happens. You probably hate conflict, so you're quick to rush in and patch things up.

But perhaps you're still saying, "I have tried that and it doesn't work. He'll hold a grudge for days, and unless I give in, nothing changes." In the next chapter, you'll learn additional methods for changing your man, and if getting him to take more responsibility in the reconciliation department is a burning desire of yours, you'll have more tools at your disposal. But there's one more thing I want you to consider.

I bet that there are times you've approached your man to make up and he's been receptive, whereas other times, he's not. My guess is that you've developed a sixth sense about this. If you think about it, when you sense "a green light," that he'll be open to your gestures of reconciliation, it means he's sending signals to you, truce triggers. Granted, they may be subtle signals, but they're signals nonetheless. In essence, your man is reaching out to you in an indirect way. His actions are saying (it's that action-oriented thing again), "Come closer." So maybe the responsibility for making up is more evenly split than you think after all.

You might not have given much thought to your truce triggers. I suggest you do. Once you know your peacemaking signs, you can get your partner to stop arguing and start loving you more quickly. You can decide to have more peace in your house. You can consciously and intentionally find faster resolution to all kinds of relationship problems. So the next time you fight, notice what happens at the end. Stop wondering what causes your problems and start wondering what causes your solutions. Start figuring out what creates peace in your life after you've been at war. You'll find that happiness is not as mysterious as it seems if you can see the pattern leading up to it. And, as always, do what you know will work, even if you don't feel like it. Do it anyway. In the long run, you'll be glad you did.

Clue #7: Pay attention to what's doable.

Often when I ask women what's different about their relationships when there's more romance or more communication or when they fight less, they'll describe a situation that isn't feasible. For example, I might hear, "We got along better before the kids were born" or "We get along just fine when we're on vacation." In other words—since the decision to have kids is a one-way street, and unless you're independently wealthy and retired, perpetual vacations aren't an option—these aren't realistic exceptions. If those are the exceptions you're noting, you're in big trouble. You've hit a dead end—that is, unless you pay attention to what it was about those situations that made it easier to reach your goal. Here's an example.

Julie was one of many women who have told me that she and her husband were closer before the kids were born. (Surprise, surprise.

Did you know research shows that marital satisfaction goes down with the birth of each child?) I asked her, "What were the two of you doing differently before the kids were around?" She replied, "We were more spontaneous back then. We spent more time together. We did fun things like going out for dinner, going away for the weekend, skiing and hiking. And we talked more. Now we hardly see each other at all. He's so busy working, and when I'm not working, I'm making sure the kids are happy."

Okay, it's easier to focus on a relationship when the kids don't compete for your attention. That's true. It's easier to be spontaneous when they're not around. That's also true. But if you take a close look at what Julie and her husband were doing before they had kids, some of that is still doable. For example, there is absolutely no reason in the world that they can't spend time together. Get a baby-sitter. Ask a relative to help out. (I recently warned a couple in my practice that if they didn't apportion time and money to have a date night once a week, they'd be allocating time and money for a divorce attorney.) So even though things change when you have children, it doesn't mean you can't continue to do many of the things that were central to your relationship before kids. Focus on what's still doable and do that. Here's another example.

When I asked Amanda what was different about her marriage when she and her husband got along better, she replied, "We used to drink together, and while it's true that drinking sometimes led to arguments, we also shared lots of good times. It seems as if we had more friends back then, back when we were partying more. We both decided to cut back on our drinking and I'm glad about that, but we don't go to parties or even out on the town anymore. Our lives have become boring."

This one is pretty obvious, isn't it? Going back to drinking more and destroying their health isn't an option. But Amanda might find a solution by asking herself, "What needs were we satisfying by drinking together?" She already provided an important clue: they used to socialize together more. Obviously, that's a missing ingredient for her. She misses having friends. If her old friends were her drinking buddies, then guess what she needs to do? That's right. She needs to make new friends. She needs to go out with her husband more. There are plenty of things to do sober. If they can't think of anything, they need to start a new hobby together.

Back to you, now. If in your search for solutions you identify an exception that is something you no longer want to do, ask yourself, "What need was it satisfying?" and then find another, more acceptable way to fulfill that need.

Clue #8: Focus on the future.

Maybe after reading this entire chapter you still haven't been able to think of any exceptions. So you've been wondering, "What's wrong with me?" or "Boy, my relationship must really be the pits. I can't think of a single exception." Well, there's nothing wrong with you or your partner (that isn't fixable, anyway). Some people just have a hard time finding exceptions. Don't worry about it.

Instead of examining your relationship for past successes, I'm going to help you fast-forward into the future. I'm going to give you some future-oriented questions you can ask yourself any time you feel stuck, questions that will help you discover solutions. The future is a great place to go shopping for ideas. And I'll be your personal shopper. Ask yourself questions along the lines of the following:[1]

> When you go to sleep tonight, if a miracle happens so that when you awake tomorrow the problems you and your partner have been having completely disappear, what will you be doing differently tomorrow?
>
> _____
> _____
> _____

Many times when people answer this question, they talk about how their feelings will change—"I'll be happier" or "I'll feel more secure in the relationship." That's a good start, but you're not quite there yet. You need to identify what you'll be *doing* differently when you feel happier or more secure. Action, baby. That's what I'm after.

Imagine that your children (a friend, your boss, your relatives) are watching you. What will there be about your actions that will tell them that a miracle has happened?

_____

_____

_____

What will these people notice about you that's different? Will your children see you hugging each other? Will they notice you smiling more? Will your boss notice that you're being more productive at work? What will they see?

Who in your life will be the first to notice the miracle has happened?

_____

_____

_____

Once you've envisioned the miracle picture, ask yourself,

What would be one or two small things you could do immediately to begin making the miracle happen?

_____

_____

_____

Are there pieces of the miracle that are already happening? If so, what are they and what do you need to do to keep them going?

_____

_____

_____

Let me give you an example of a woman who was very much helped by asking herself the "miracle question." When I met Amy, she was unable to identify what was bothering her about her marriage, she just knew she was desperately unhappy. And because she wasn't clear about the problem, it was impossible for her to identify "problem-free times." She just drew a blank. So I asked her, "When you go to sleep tonight, if a miracle happens so that when you awake tomorrow, the problems you and your partner are having totally disappear, what will you be doing differently?" After some thought, she replied, "We'll be doing things together and enjoying each other's company. We'll be active, going for walks, going to museums, out to dinner, and to the theater. We'll have friends over for dinner; we haven't done that in a long time. We'll go on a vacation. The last vacation we were on was twenty years ago, before the kids were born. On a day-to-day basis, we'll talk more and touch each other more. Plus, we'll laugh together. We stopped laughing a long time ago." The longer Amy talked about her miracle, the clearer it became that she and her husband, like so many couples, had put their marriage on the back burner for years. No wonder she couldn't recall an example of times things were better. Their happy times occurred too long ago to be easily remembered. However, by projecting in the future and imagining what her marriage would be like if the closeness returned "miraculously," she could begin to flush out the details of what her life would be like without the distance and sadness. Answering the miracle question offered Amy some clues about what she and her husband could do to make things better between them in the present. She realized that she didn't need to wait for a miracle in order for them to spend more time together. Envisioning a positive future allowed Amy to feel more optimistic, which in turn energized her to start breathing life into her marriage.

Welcome back to the present. I hope this chapter has helped you start thinking like a solution detective. Once you start living and breathing solutions, problems don't take their toll the way they used to. In fact, what you once thought of as an obstacle now becomes a creative challenge. It's actually fun to think of new ways to get your needs met. When I come up with a new idea I plan to use with Jim, I often pick up the phone and call one of my friends: "Here's what I'm going to try tonight . . ." That's a far cry from picking up the phone to bitch. It's exhilarating to discover new man-changing strategies!

Perhaps as you're reading this chapter and applying the ideas to your own situation, although you're enthusiastic, you've got some questions. Lots of people do. In fact, here are some of the most commonly asked questions about becoming solution detectives.

Q. Once people identify exceptions and they know what to do, why don't they do it?

A. Emotions derail us. Even if we notice what's working, sometimes it's hard to put it into practice. When we're in the throes of heated debates or unpleasantries with our partners, we tend to get too emotional. We get caught up in the bad feelings. We're not clearheaded. When emotions cloud our vision, we often react without thinking, which is usually not in our best interest. When you're in the thick of things, it takes strength to stop and do something sane. We have to remind ourselves to take a deep breath and focus on solutions.

Another reason people don't do what works is that they think they shouldn't have to. They believe that it is above and beyond the call of duty. Here's an example.

I know a woman whose pet peeve is that her husband ignores her when they go to parties. I asked her what's different about the times he doesn't ignore her, and she said, "If I remind him before we go to take a few minutes during the party to pay attention to me, he's pretty good about doing it and we get along better that way." So I asked, "Why not do that?" and she replied, "I shouldn't have to. He should just know that I want him to be more attentive."

Perhaps this sounds familiar to you. I've heard stories like this a million times before. Women know what they need to do to get better responses from their partners, but they hold back because they want the guys to figure it out themselves, or they think they shouldn't have to do it. True, my dear, in an ideal world, you shouldn't have to. But wake up and smell the roses. You do have to. And when you do, he'll be a better partner. So, maybe you "shouldn't" have to do it, but I say do what works. It's a lot more expedient. It can save years of heartache.

Remember the story I told you about my resentment over Jim's complaining about being Mister Mom? And remember how I resisted thanking him for holding down the fort with the kids in my absence? When I realized how far one small compliment would go in terms of making him more accepting of my out-of-town trips, I started complimenting him regularly. My initial resistance was due to the fact that I didn't think I should have to praise him for being a father. But in the spirit of being goal-oriented, I decided to do it anyway. So the point is, once you figure what works, do it, even if you don't think you should have to. You have to. I said so.

Q. What if focusing on what works isn't enough?

A. Sometimes doing more of what works isn't enough. You have to stop doing what isn't working. You have to devise a plan to approach your partner more creatively when you get stuck. Most women know when they've hit a dead end, but they just aren't sure what to do instead. Well, help is on the way. The next chapter will give you all the tools you need to figure out what to do when what you're doing isn't working.

CHAPTER EIGHT

Do Something Different for a Change

Never go to bed angry. Stay up and fight.
—Phyllis Diller

I've often been amazed at the number and variety of diet books that are available when, in truth, we all know the two things you must do if you want to lose weight. You know what they are—eat less and exercise more. Period. My mind is also boggled by the vast number of relationship books that are on the shelves when, in fact, the process of creating great relationships can actually be distilled down to two similarly simple principles: If what you're doing works, don't fix it, and if what you're doing doesn't work, do something different. Simple though they might be, these are mottoes well worth remembering.

Let's look a bit more closely at this relationship formula, starting with "If what you're doing works, don't fix it." The last chapter offered tools for figuring out which of your relationship tactics are the most effective. You learned that no matter how exasperating things might be from time to time, there are the exceptions—times when your partner responds to you positively. You've identified what's different about those times, and my guess is that you've been doing more of what works. Approximately 75 to 80 percent of the women in my practice are able to make significant changes in their relationships simply by identifying the exceptions and building on these successes. When you think about it, this technique is a pretty powerful tool.

However, sometimes doing more of what works isn't enough.

You also need to stop doing what doesn't work, hence, "If it doesn't work, do something different." In chapter 5 I outlined the pitfalls of doing more of the same, the major one being that doing more of the same makes matters worse. That's why the adage "If at first you don't succeed, try, try again" is really lousy advice. Here's better advice: If at first you don't succeed, do something different. But what? In this chapter, you'll discover six creative strategies that will prevent you from doing more of the same. By the time you're done with this section, you'll have learned new and improved methods for changing your man.

But a couple of words about the structure of the chapter before you jump in. The techniques you're about to read are like recipes in a cookbook. Some will be more appealing to you than others, and that's fine. Try the ones that look delicious and disregard the rest. You are your own best relationship expert. You know best which techniques might work given your situation, your man's usual way of responding, and your own personal preferences.

Although all of these strategies have been field-tested, so to speak, some will work better than others for you. Remember, the most important thing for you to keep in mind is that man-changing, like everything else in life, is a trial-and-error process. Approach all that you do with an open mind and watch the results carefully. If you get the response you're after, you're on to something. If not—well, you know what to do. Do something different.

Another point. You'll notice that all of the techniques in this chapter are action-oriented. They focus on what you should *do* differently to get more of your needs met in your relationship. If you've relied on verbal communication to change your man, you've probably talked until you're blue in the face. These action-oriented techniques will restore natural color to your face because you'll finally be speaking *his* language—Actionese. This is your Berlitz course in Actionese.

And, finally, there's one more thing you need to know. In keeping with the solution-oriented spirit of this book, this chapter is organized around solutions. You'll learn six new techniques that you can use in practically any situation. They're like master keys—keys that can open many doors regardless of the unique shapes of their locks. In the same way that focusing on problem-free times can be a lifesaver in a wide variety of situations, the methods in this chapter are equally versatile.

So, if you feel tempted to scan this section, looking for categories of problems that fit your diagnosis of your man ("The Lazy Husband," "The Immature Man," "The Sneaky Guy"), you can search as hard as you want, girlfriend, but you're not going to find what you're looking for. I want you to stop thinking in terms of problems and start thinking solutions. The antidote to both lazy husbands and sneaky guys might just be the same technique. So read each solution carefully and imagine how it might be adapted to your situation. Ready to do something different? Here goes.

Do Something Different Strategy #1: Do the Unexpected

When I work with women, I first help them figure out what they're doing that can be considered more of the same, their man-changing strategies that are worth forgetting. Then, once they agree to try something new, I give them a homework assignment. Following the technique of therapist Steve de Shazer, I tell them, "The next time you find yourself just about to do the same old thing that you know won't work, stop for a minute and do something different. Do something you've never done before, no matter how weird or crazy it might seem at the time. Just do something different."[1] I have to tell you that I've collected the best stories from women who put an end to doing more of the same. Here's an example.

Lynn was a woman who complained that her husband would keep his feelings bottled up inside for months at a time. Then upon the slightest provocation, he would explode. This troubled her and she frequently asked him "What's wrong?" anytime she sensed he might be upset. Typically, his response to her question was "Nothing's wrong," to which she'd respond, "I can tell something's bothering you. What's wrong?" After several rounds of this, he would finally get angry and yell, "I hate when you ask me what's wrong. Why don't you just leave me alone?" and they'd end up not talking to each other. One night, as they were leaving the house to go to a movie, she remembered my homework assignment and decided to turn over a new leaf.

Lynn sensed her husband was annoyed by something, and she asked, "What's wrong? You seem to be in a bad mood. Did I do anything to annoy you?" And he responded with the usual "Nothing's wrong." This time, since she had promised herself she would do something different, she said, "I'm glad nothing's wrong," and got into the car. Instead of grilling him, she turned on the radio and started to hum as if she were really content. Several minutes later, he asked if she would feel okay with his turning the radio down because he wanted to talk to her. "Sure," she told him.

He turned down the music and shared with her that, although she might not have done it intentionally, she had hurt his feelings. He told her exactly what she had said that made him feel bad. Surprised by his openness, Lynn reassured him that she meant no harm by what she had said, that she was sorry his feelings were hurt, and that she was really happy that he told her. They hugged and had a great time that evening.

I asked her, "How did you stop yourself from interrogating him when he said nothing was wrong?" She replied, "I knew it wasn't going to do me any good. I wasn't sure if keeping quiet would bring better results, but I was determined to try something new. I was really amazed at how quickly he responded differently to me. Actually, it shocked me. But it was great and I plan to be more creative from now on."

Now you might be saying to yourself, "How is it possible that Lynn could change what was probably a long-standing interaction between them simply by making a minor shift in her own behavior?" That's a really good question, and to answer it, I need to backtrack for a moment.

Human beings are creatures of habit. We don't think much about our actions because we do the same things every day. We're very ritualistic. We sleep on the same side of the bed every night. We sit in the same chair at our dining room table and feel out of sorts if another person takes our place. Our mornings don't vary much. We take the same route to work each day. We greet others with the "Hi, how are you? I'm fine, and you?" routine, and have our coffee or tea. We celebrate holidays in the same way and have our preferred methods for doing everything right down to how we eat Oreo cookies. Habits allow us to go through our lives without having to concentrate on what we're doing.

Think about driving a car. Most of the time we're on automatic pilot. We can wonder what we're going to eat for dinner, whether our laundry is ready to be picked up, how late the post office remains open. We can listen to music or grab the car phone with little conscious awareness about the road. But if something unusual happens—like a car darting in front of ours or a driver turning without using a turn signal—our attention becomes focused on the road immediately, and all of our other distractions disappear. Novelty gets our attention. A break in a usual routine forces us to become aware. It shifts us out of automatic pilot.

Being on automatic pilot is not necessarily a bad thing. Habitual responses are economical. We'd get overloaded if we had to think about or be acutely aware of the thousands of actions we take each day. Being on automatic pilot is only a problem when relationship difficulties arise. If you act like a robot when you and your partner are at odds with each other, it could really be disastrous. An angry gesture on the part of one person leads to the next unfortunate response, and the next and the next. (The circular connection, remember?) Then your interactions become linked together sequentially, A→B→C→D→A→B, and so on. When your man does A (criticize), he expects you to do B (get angry), which prompts you to anticipate his doing C (defend himself), which creates in him an expectation that you will do D (get even angrier), which prompts him to do A (criticize), and so on. You know exactly what to expect because you've done it so many times before (skits, skits, and more skits). Your actions are cues that link one antagonistic behavior to another in a powerfully spellbinding way.

Pavlov was a Russian physiologist who observed something very interesting about the ways cues can trigger responses. He did his research with dogs. (Here I go with the dog thing again.) Pavlov placed powdered meat on a dog's tongue—which made it salivate—and simultaneously sounded a tuning fork. He did this repeatedly. Within a short period of time, he was able to get the dog to salivate simply by sounding the tuning fork. He no longer had to place the powder on the dog's tongue. The dog associated the sound of the fork with the taste of the meat and therefore salivated with each bong.

This happens in the world of humans, too. Certain cues in our surroundings trigger us to react in specific ways even without our awareness. Think about the cigarette smoker who lights up without knowing it after meals, after great sex, during tense moments, or in smoky bars. Great food, sex, stress, and fellow smokers elicit the knee-jerk smoking response. When we're in the midst of relationship problems, our buttons get pushed by many different things. I explained how your partner's actions can be one such trigger, but that's only a start. Triggers are all around us. From chapter 7, you'll remember that if you always fight in the same place, at the same time, and in the same manner, you start programming yourself to launch into one of your usual fights whenever you're in one of those familiar settings or situations. In other words, the setting or the situation becomes the meat, and you start salivating, even if you're not hungry.

For example, if you always argue on Christmas Eve when you're decorating the Christmas tree, the next time Christmas Eve comes rolling around, you'll probably be expecting an argument, you'll broadcast your expectations to your partner, and, lo and behold, you'll find yourselves arguing. Too many lights or too few? Tinsel this year or is it too messy? Or if you've argued every time the two of you go to a particular restaurant, it's fairly certain you'll argue the next time you're there. Christmas Eve and that restaurant trigger you and your partner to respond in the same old way to each other.

The beauty in all of this is that any change in the routine can get you out of your hypnotic trance. Novelty is a wake-up call (remember what happens on the road?). If instead of doing B after your partner does A, you do C or even Z, your partner won't be able to do his same old thing in response. You'll be forcing him to shift gears. Any change—a change in your actions, the setting, the timing of your dispute—has the potential of yielding better results between the two of you because the novelty forces both of you to think, to become more conscious of how you treat each other. And that's a good thing. Novelty goes a very long way. Let me give you an example.

The letter you're about to read was written to me by a man who decided to do something different when he and his wife argued. Although all of the solutions in this book are woman-driven, I include this because it is truly wonderful. Sometimes men have good ideas, too.

Last week Sue and I discussed how we could make our conflicts more productive. I suggested we use one of your techniques, Do Something Different. I told her that the next time we started to fight, we would have to take our clothes off. If we followed this rule, we could not argue in malls, during family outings, or any other place outside, since our winters are brutally cold. Our three children have left home, making this idea a doable one. Nonetheless, she was still somewhat hesitant to agree. We had tried many other problem-solving techniques before, with little success.

A few days later we started to argue, and I decided to stick to our plan. If we were younger and in better shape, then peeling off our clothes might have changed our focus. However, despite our old, decrepit bodies, something wonderful happened. As I was arguing with her, I started to take off my clothes and throw them emphatically on the floor, one piece at a time, punctuating the points I was making. Sue was shocked. She said, "I can't believe you're really doing this." I continued to argue, taking off my socks, pants, shirt, and underpants. Sue began to laugh. She laughed so hysterically that tears ran down her face. I was laughing, too, but I continued making my points. Believe it or not, we soon found ourselves agreeing with each other.

Since then, we have laughed and laughed about that interaction. Sue said that she will never be able to remain serious in an argument again because she will always think about how silly the two of us must have looked that day. When I think about it, I can't

> even remember what we were arguing about. I just
> know it was the best fight we ever had.

Okay. Don't panic. You don't need to strip if you don't want to. But you have to admit, it's a pretty funny idea. Humor prevented them from doing what they usually do during their solemn, serious altercations. Here's another example of doing the unexpected.

Sally was furious at her partner, John, because he started the morning off by offending her with a rude comment. Typically when this happened, she called him on his car phone when he was on his way to work and really let him have it. Naturally, this displeased him no end, but that's exactly what Sally wanted. She hoped he'd be as bruised as she was. Other than this phone call, they usually had no contact during the day, so when they reunited in the evening, they were still mad at each other and often went to bed in silence. Sally disliked this but felt she had no alternative— until I got my hands on her, that is.

I asked her what she wanted to have happen when her partner was rude, and she said, "I want him to recognize how mean he is and apologize." I asked if barraging him with insults was moving her toward her goal, and she admitted that it wasn't. "Do the unexpected the next time it happens," I suggested, "and come back and tell me what you did and how it worked." Although I don't think she had a plan in mind, she set off to do the unexpected.

She returned a couple of weeks later and said, "Well, the inevitable happened. He got up on the wrong side of bed and started complaining about one thing after another. I was really pissed at him and felt tempted to let him have it, but I remembered what you said. So I kept my feelings to myself until I could figure out what I was going to do. He left for work, and I'm sure he expected a call from me. So that's exactly what I didn't do. But I decided that wasn't enough. I thought of a really crazy idea.

"I waited until he arrived at work and then I sent him flowers and enclosed a note card that read, 'I love you.' He immediately called and asked, 'What's this about?' and I said, 'After you left this morning, I got to thinking about how much stress you've been under recently at work. I know things must be tough for you or you wouldn't have been so unhappy when you woke up. I realized that you are probably pushed to the limit and that's why you had so short a fuse with me. So, I thought I'd send you flowers to brighten your day.'" Then she added, "Michele, he was dumbfounded. There was dead silence on the phone. He thanked me profusely and then the impossible happened—he apologized. I was blown away. I couldn't believe it."

Isn't this fun? I love it. Shock your man into being more loving. Get him off dead center. Be unpredictable. Avoid stale, stuffy, run-of-the-mill strategies. Dare to be different. Ask yourself, "Have I had any wild ideas about how I would like to handle a particular situation but was too conservative to actually do it?" If the answer is yes, cast your inhibitions to the wind and give it a shot. If your answer is no, let me give you a hand.

In the last chapter, I suggested that when you look for solutions, you think about the words "what," "who," "when," and "where." If you're at a loss as to what you should change about your approach to your partner, you might find it helpful to continue to keep those words in mind.

What: Change what you do.
Who: Vary who's in charge of certain issues.
       Vary who's present during conflictual times.
When: Approach him anytime other than the usual time.
Where: Try a new location to sort things out.

Here are some short examples of the Do the Unexpected method in each of these categories.

Changing the What

I've already given you several examples of changing what you do or how you handle your dilemma. Lynn stopped asking her partner, "What's wrong?" and took his response at face value. A man and his wife agreed to strip naked to have their usual argument. Another woman sent flowers instead of insults to her husband after a tiff. If you're still having trouble figuring out what you could do differently, go back to chapter 5. Recall what you do that's more of the same. Stop doing that and do *anything* else instead. Anything other than what isn't working has a better chance of getting you the results you're after.

Too often we stop ourselves from trying something new because we aren't completely sure it's the "correct" thing to do. Once you truly understand that novelty is the correct thing to do, it gives you a great deal of latitude in terms of what you can try. Years ago, I heard a story that illustrated this point exceedingly well.

Gregory Bateson, a renowned anthropologist and one of Margaret Mead's many husbands, was asked to come to a zoo to observe the otters, who were extremely listless. As you might know, otters are very playful animals, and their stillness concerned the zookeepers. After observing the otters for several days, Bateson attached a piece of paper to a string and dangled it in the area where the otters were lying.

Within a short period of time, one of the otters spotted the paper and got up to investigate. It began batting the paper around. Shortly thereafter, another otter got up to get into the action. It wasn't long before the rest of the otters were actively involved in playing with the paper. Moments later, Bateson quickly removed the paper. The otters continued playing with each other. Days later, they were still back to their frisky selves. (I remember hearing this story for the first time and thinking, "I wonder what it said on the paper?")

Bateson's conclusion about this prompt turnaround in the otters' activity level was that if nothing new was introduced into the environment, nothing new would happen. If something new were introduced, the odds of change were greatly improved. Who would ever have thought that a dangling piece of paper would have restored the otters' vim and vigor? I bet no veterinary medical books prescribe this sort of treatment for otter lethargy.

The moral of the story is that there are many, many paths to a solution. Don't hesitate to try something new because you're not completely sure of its efficacy or because you're waiting until you've found the Correct Way to handle your man. The correct thing to do is the thing that works, and you won't know if it works unless you try it. So try it. Do anything that is out of the ordinary. Ask yourself, "What would I have to do that would make my partner sit up and take notice?" Do that. Give it a shot. Stop doing more of the same, do the otter thing.

Changing the Who

If you and your partner always argue about who initiates sex, how bills are paid, how the dishes are done, the way your fifth grader should solve his math problems, curfew issues, or how vacation time should be spent, vary who's in charge of these matters. If you've been in control, let him do it for a while. If he's been in charge, suggest a changing of the guard. I'll give you an example that revolves around child-rearing, but as you read this example, know that this technique applies to almost any other topic about which you and your partner disagree.

Lots of couples argue about how to handle the kids. Every parenting book says that you should present a united front when dealing with the kids and, in an ideal world, this is probably true. However, my world is anything but ideal and sometimes this isn't possible. I imagine the same thing is probably true for you, too. So if you and your partner argue continually about kid issues, take turns being in charge. You deal with the kids one week (or one month) and then alternate. Or make a list of all the issues you're dealing with at the moment and agree to divvy them up. You handle some and he handles the others. Or flip a coin next time you find yourselves doing the same old thing. Instead of arguing about who's right and who's wrong, have chance dictate how things will be handled.

Now I know that you might feel horrified at the thought of allowing chance to decide important issues. You may be even more horrified at the thought of your partner making those decisions. But the truth is, what's really horrifying is that the kids see you fighting all the time. Furthermore, when you're debating who's right and who's wrong, you are undermining each other's efforts to find a solution. You dilute what he wants to do. He dilutes what you want to do. And your kids fall through the cracks. So if you're not in agreement about things, take turns, divide up areas of jurisdiction, or flip coins. It will be better than what you've been doing.

Changing the who made a huge difference in Pat and Jack's relationship. Pat frequently complained that Jack wanted to have sex at the most inconvenient or undesirable times, when the kids needed her attention, very late at night or very early in the morning when she was tired, five minutes before they had to walk out their door, and other equally inopportune moments. At first, Jack tried experimenting by initiating sex at other times during the day, but according to him, no time was a good time. He became totally frustrated and angry. His anger permeated their relationship.

When he talked to Pat about his feelings, she felt he was exaggerating, which made him feel worse. Eventually, a cold war ensued and there was little communication between them. That's the point at which I met them. Within a short period of time, I made a suggestion. I asked them if they would be comfortable trying an experiment. I suggested that for the next several weeks, Pat be in charge of initiating sex. That way, every time would be the right time. They agreed. I saw them three weeks later.

Jack said he was unconvinced that the experiment was working the first week because Pat wanted no sex at all. However, Jack resisted complaining or putting her down. The following week was better. Pat initiated sex twice, and they both commented how much they enjoyed it. Jack eagerly told me that the third week was great, not because of the frequency of their lovemaking but because of Pat's renewed passion when they made love. Jack felt as if the Pat he had met long ago had suddenly returned. He was thrilled.

I questioned Pat about her feelings, and she said, "I used to feel so much pressure. If we had sex when I didn't want to, I wasn't relaxed and therefore didn't enjoy it. If I turned Jack down, I felt bad because I knew it was hurting his feelings. I walked around feeling crummy all the time. When you suggested that I take over for a while, the pressure lifted and I could pay more attention to my own feelings of sexuality which, up until then, had been the last thing on my mind. With the pressure off, I remembered that I used to love sex and now we're having fun again."

So "changing the who" can be an effective way to change the dynamics in a relationship. Try it, you'll like it.

Changing the When

A woman told me that she dreaded weekends because every Friday night she and her husband argued about money. The bad feelings from this argument spilled over to the weekend so that their time together was quite unpleasant. After learning about "changing the when," she decided to avoid discussing finances on Friday and try a different time.

Friday evening came rolling around, and she and her husband met at home. As usual, he broached the subject of money. She responded, "Hon, let's not ruin our evening tonight. Let's talk about it some other time." After several unsuccessful attempts to get her to discuss their point of disagreement, they ended up having a very pleasant time together. In fact, the remainder of the weekend was a time of renewal for them. By Sunday evening, they liked each other again. And that's when she decided to raise the money issue. Surprisingly, they resolved what had been a chronic problem on the spot. The good feelings engendered from their positive interactions over the weekend enabled them to be more conciliatory with each other, and they thought of a completely creative solution.

So follow the lead of the woman who no longer has money problems. If you notice an uncanny coincidence—problems seem to pop up the same time of day, week, month, or year—make an effort to deal with them at some other time and watch the results.

One other "timing" suggestion here. If your arguments seem to have a life of their own, that is, they seem to come out of the blue and ruin a perfectly good time together, it's often helpful to schedule time-limited conflict resolution sessions. You might try scheduling these discussions once or twice a week and limiting all debates to those prearranged times. Many couples find the structure of the scheduled conflict resolution times extremely helpful. Whereas a hurtful deed is the usual trigger for most discussions (aka arguments), this is not necessarily the case if discussion times are prearranged. People often have more productive conversations when they're not angry.

Changing the Where

In the last chapter, I suggested that certain environments might be more conducive to getting along or successful problem-solving than others. If you've noticed that your disagreements tend to occur in a particular location, be experimental. Try working things out someplace else.

Joan and her husband had an ongoing battle about who does what around the house. Joan felt that her husband had little regard for all the work she did. At her wits' end, she wanted him to pitch in more. Their arguments never went anywhere. They'd scream at each other, and he would go back to watching television.

One day Joan decided to invite her husband out for dinner at one of their favorite restaurants. The ambiance was lovely and the food was great. In the middle of the meal, she approached the heated subject of housework. Whether it was due to the pleasant environment, being in a public place, or just doing something out of the ordinary, Joan and her husband were able to come to some agreements. She vowed that from then on, whenever they found themselves going round and round about something, she would extend an invitation to her husband to go out for dinner.

Another place "changing the where" comes in handy is in lovemaking. Sometimes women complain to me about having a low sex drive. After we eliminate hormonal causes, feelings of resentment that quash sexual interest, or ignorance about various sexual issues, lots of couples use the "changing the where" method to spice up their lackluster love life. Need I say more? Use your imagination.

So, the key to triggering change in your partner is novelty. With this in mind, sometimes simply making a small change in the usual way you do things may not be novel enough. You may have to do something radically different to get your partner's attention. This next technique, Do a 180°, is radically different. Trust me.

Do Something Different Strategy #2: Do a 180°

Back in the seventies, I remember reading a book called *Provocative Therapy*, by a psychotherapist named Frank Farrelly, Ph.D. He noticed that when he tried to bolster the self-esteem of his insecure clients by reminding them of their personal strengths, they would debate him. They would tell him that he was misguided and offer evidence of their frailties. The more reassuring he was, the more they belittled themselves. This dynamic interested him immensely. He wondered if he was inadvertently making things worse for his clients by being so supportive. And so he decided to do an experiment. He decided to Do a 180°.

From that point on, whenever depressed or insecure clients talked about their reasons for feeling unhappy, he agreed with them and provoked them by exaggerating their claims—a Don Rickles of psychotherapy. I've heard audiotapes of this man's work, and at first you can't believe how insensitive he seems. But if you listen carefully, what you begin to notice is that his clients got angry at him and started standing up for themselves, defending their strengths and quickly dismissing Farrelly's put-downs.

By the end of these sessions, Farrelly's clients became absolutely determined to prove their doctor wrong about his negative assessments of them. They returned to subsequent sessions with grins on their faces, having improved their lives immensely. Strange behavior? In truth, not so strange.

Take little kids, for example. If you're a parent, I bet you anything that, at one time or another when your child was small, you told him or her, "Don't you dare eat those peas," when you really wanted the peas eaten, or "Don't you dare clean up your toys," when that's exactly what you wanted. Because you banked on the fact that children don't like to be told what to do, you fully expected your little one to defy you and eat the peas and straighten up his room. In other words, you expected your child to resist you by doing the opposite of what you were requesting.

Well, guess what. Most adults are like that, too. We all have a little stubborn kid inside us screaming to get out. Especially men. As I said in chapter 3, most men really like to call the shots, to be in control. So if your man fits this description, he won't respond well to being asked to do something he doesn't want to do. He simply wants to do things his way, on his timetable. Instead of getting frustrated and going crazy, get smart. Use your knowledge about this dynamic to get him to change.

Years ago, I figured out that Jim has an extremely strong need to be self-determining. It may be one of his most compelling needs. If he feels pushed into a corner about anything, he'll do just the opposite, even if means doing something he really doesn't want to do. I think he's incredibly stubborn that way. Occasionally, he would approach me with an idea for something he wanted to do and if I said, "I don't want you to do that" or "That doesn't sound so great to me," I could always count on his doing it. I fought him about this for a long time before I figured out a much simpler solution. Anytime he broached a subject that made me wary, I would either keep quiet or encourage him to do it. Inevitably, his intense desire to do the undesirable would dwindle in the face of my encouragement. It worked every time. The unforbidden-fruit technique.

Now trust me when I tell you that keeping quiet or encouraging Jim to do something I really didn't want him to do wasn't easy. It required a tremendous leap of faith. It's like rappelling off a mountain for the first time and being told the rope is going to catch you. Maybe so, but you can't help feeling somewhat skeptical. But after I did a 180° a few times, I realized that, as uncertain as I might have been about its effect, the real risk was in putting my foot down with Jim. I finally got smart.

So here's my advice to you. If you notice that the harder you try to get your man to change, the more stubborn he becomes about his position, you may have to do a 180°. Doing a 180° means just that: doing the complete opposite of what you usually do when you approach him. Let me give you some more examples.

One of my favorites concerns a woman whose husband began staying out late after work with his buddies. She complained that these after-work escapades were lasting longer and longer into the evening, which really bothered her. She couldn't understand why he didn't share her feeling that it was important to spend time with the family. In the past, he used to return home at about eight o'clock on the occasional evenings he went out, but now he was going out three nights a week and staying out until ten or ten-thirty. She was infuriated.

I asked her what she had been doing about the situation, and she said, "On most days, I called him at work and asked him about his plans for the evening. He'd always say the same thing, 'I'm not sure.'" She'd always respond in the same way: "Well, figure it out," and he'd end up announcing that he was going to be late that night. Then she'd promptly hang up on him.

In an effort to do something different, she had tried not saying anything to him about his late nights out, but it didn't seem to make much of a difference. They were fighting a bit less, but he was still coming and going as he pleased. That's when I suggested that she do a complete 180°. I told her, "Tomorrow when you call him, I want you to give him a big surprise. Tell him that you've finally realized how important it is for him to let off some steam after work with his friends. Tell him that you had lost sight of how much stress he's been under and that you have been somewhat insensitive. Suggest that he take all the time he needs to be with his friends that evening and not to worry about you. Say good-bye—no questions asked."

She was quite surprised by my suggestion. I also told her, "Later in the week, call him again and tell him not to rush home. Tell him everything's handled and that you've made plans of your own. Don't elaborate, just tell him to have a good time." You want to know the end of this story?

She returned to my office saying, "The first time I told him to stay out and have a great time, he was completely quiet on the phone. He did go out that night but came home at 9:00 P.M., which surprised me because he'd been coming home later. He went out the next night but again returned home earlier than usual. I also called him two days later as you suggested and told him not to rush home. I mentioned that I had plans with some friends. He asked for details, but I gave him none."

When she got home that evening, she found her husband waiting for her. He had taken the baby-sitter home and spent the evening with the kids. She was shocked. Over the next few weeks, she kept encouraging him to stay out and going out herself. She noticed that he was going out less and less and that their times together were more enjoyable. She also learned something about herself in the process. She realized how much she enjoyed getting together with her own friends, and she decided to do that more regularly. Here's another example.

Shelley had been asking her partner to hang wallpaper for several months. He would agree to do it, but when the time came for him to get started, something always diverted his attention. Shelley nagged and nagged, begged and criticized. You get the picture. Then one day she decided to do a 180°.

Over dinner, she apologized for putting so much pressure on him concerning the wallpapering, especially since he had so many things on his mind. Plus she admitted that she was probably overestimating his ability to hang wallpaper. Although he had done it a few times before, it was long ago. She intimated that he might be a bit rusty and therefore not the best person to do the job. So she told him not to worry about it, that she would find someone else who was really skilled. She ended by thanking him for being willing to do the job anyway and said no more.

Mysteriously, the next evening after work, her husband announced that he wouldn't be sitting down to eat dinner because he was going to start hanging the wallpaper. Shelley resisted his offer, reminding him that he might not know how to do it right, but he walked off in a huff and worked until the wee hours of the morn, getting a majority of the job done. And a beautiful job it was, she added. Now what's that about not eating peas?

If your partner is incredibly stubborn, it might be time for you to do a 180°. Here's what you need to do:

1. Identify the problem behavior you're trying to change.
2. Assess how you've been approaching him up until now. What have you been doing to try to make things better? What's your most usual approach?
3. Do a 180°. Shifting gears will be hard because you've undoubtedly been doing what you've been doing because it makes sense to you. It's fair to assume that doing the opposite will seem strange or bizarre, at least initially. But once you begin to see positive results, the only thing that will seem strange is why you didn't do a 180° sooner.
4. Watch what happens. Remember that no matter what technique you try, you have to watch your partner's reaction. This is the most important lesson you can learn in this book—keep your eyes glued to your partner's reactions to you. If what you're doing works . . . Well, I've said it enough, I won't say it again.

Lots of people tell me they're afraid to do a 180° because they think they'll make things worse. If you're one of those people, I completely understand. Logic tells you that doing a 180° is crazy. But by now you should understand that logic isn't always the best rule of thumb when choosing man-changing strategies. Crazy situations call for crazy interventions. Period. So stop worrying. I want to reassure you that the only way you can truly make things worse is by continually doing what you know won't work.

Secondly, if doing a 180° has yielded positive results, you might feel tempted to begin to approach your partner in a more straightforward manner. Don't give in to that temptation. If you do, he'll backslide. For instance, if he's taken over doing his laundry because you told him not to help you, that you didn't want his assistance, then you need to continue to give him regular gentle reminders not to help. If you start asking for help, he'll go back to being lazy again. Don't fool yourself into thinking that your partner's changes are due to the fact that he understands your feelings better. He may, but don't count on it. His more desirable behavior may simply be the result of his resisting your "don't help" message. So don't quit saying, "Don't help," or you'll be going it alone.

Perhaps you don't have a "who does the laundry" problem. Maybe your partner needs to shape up in some other way. Suffice it to say that regardless of the nature of your partner's particular problem areas, if doing a 180° gets him to change, then that's what you need to keep doing.

Finally, some women say that doing a 180° sounds manipulative, like game-playing. But I say that continually doing what doesn't work is no less gamelike than doing a 180°. Whether you admit it or not, when you nag, complain, or express your feelings, you're hoping to influence your partner in some very specific way. In a sense, that's manipulative, too. But nagging, complaining, and expressing feelings can be ineffective, which means he'll resist you. When he resists you, you're angry at him and vice versa. These harsh feelings are bad for relationships.

If doing a 180° can short-circuit bad feelings, in my mind, doing otherwise is absurd. So, if you think your partner's a control freak, the key to more loving interactions is now in your hand. Go ahead and use it.

Do Something Different Strategy #3: Act As If...

Problems often arise in relationships because people think they can predict the future. "I just know how my husband will respond when I tell him I'm going out," or "Steve will undoubtedly fly off the handle when my parents come for dinner," or "I can tell that we're going to have an argument tonight because he's so quiet." The problem with predicting dire outcomes in the future is that, whether we know it or not, we begin acting in certain ways that broadcast our expectations to our partners. And these subtle signals often bring about the very results we fear. The self-fulfilling prophecy is alive and well in households across America. Even mine.

A few years ago, I was returning from a four-day conference and my husband, Jim, was picking me up at the airport. Just before landing, I turned to my friend and said, "I just know he's mad at me and he's going to be unpleasant because he got really tired of playing Mr. Mom while I was gone." I felt the knot in my stomach tighten as I anticipated a less than friendly greeting. I promised myself not to talk much about the conference because if Jim knew how much fun I had had, it would only exacerbate the situation. My plan was to get off the plane, give him a tentative hug, and wait to see what kind of mood he was in.

My wise friend listened intently and then asked me, "If you thought Jim was going to be happy to see you and that he wasn't resentful at all, how would your greeting be different?" "That's easy," I told him. "I'd race off the plane, throw my arms around him, and start bubbling over about the events at the conference."

Now think about it for a minute. If, in expecting coolness from Jim, I met him with a reserved and aloof greeting, what might he be thinking? Envision things from his perspective: I'm away for four days, and when I return, I say very little and appear to be aloof and tentative. If our greetings after time apart are typically warm and expressive, don't you think he might be confused by my behavior and uncertain about how to respond? Wouldn't *my* behavior at the airport (and not necessarily my absence) trigger more tentativeness in him? And then, when he appeared to be cautious, unaware of the impact I was having on him, I would have incorrectly concluded, "See, I'm right. He is mad at me. I just knew it." The self-fulfilling prophecy in action.

So thanks to my friend, I reminded myself to get off the plane that night expecting a positive outcome. I imagined Jim dying to see me, missing me a lot, and I greeted him exuberantly. I'm glad that I did because the evening ended happily. Much more happily than I originally expected. Although I'll never know for sure how Jim would have responded if my friend hadn't coached me before we deplaned, I can't help but think our encounter would have gone sour given my plan to enter guardedly. My friend's comment made me wonder how often negative interactions with Jim were actually unintentionally triggered by me. Expecting positive outcomes may not be everything, but it's a lot more than you think. But don't just take my word for it. Here's another example.

Paula sought my help because she feared her marriage was falling apart. She and her husband, Jason, were separated. Jason moved out when he could no longer stand Paula's unsubstantiated accusations that he was having an affair. Although, initially, he tried to reassure her of his fidelity, eventually her insecurities took their toll. He started spending more time at work and less time with her. He avoided her completely when they were home together and eventually moved out. She saw his withdrawal as further proof that he was having an affair.

I asked Paula how she would treat Jason differently if she knew for a fact that he had not been unfaithful. "I would be like the old Paula: self-confident, outgoing, attentive, and vivacious. I'd stop asking him for reassurances all the time. I'm sick of talking about this situation." As soon as she said this, she realized how much she had changed recently and admitted she probably wasn't much fun to be with anymore. I knew that she and Jason had a "date" arranged for the following week, and I asked her to stop talking about her feelings and start "acting as if." "When you see him next week," I told her, "remember the old Paula. Do all the things you used to do when you were feeling confident about his love. Then watch what happens."

Two weeks later, she returned to my office and told me that she had made a decision to get herself in a good state of mind before Jason arrived at her house. She worked out, showered, dressed in a new outfit, and turned on their favorite CD in the background. She was determined to exude her old self-confidence. Instead of grilling Jason when he walked through the door, she greeted him affectionately and enthusiastically and shared with him the details of her week. Great conversation, compliments about her appearance, and an enjoyable dinner followed. Jason ended the evening by initiating lovemaking, something he hadn't done in months. Paula was on cloud nine.

Because Paula could see how her fear of rejection and her incessant need for reassurance had actually increased the likelihood that Jason would leave the relationship, she promised herself she would continue to "act as if" and restrain from voicing her insecurities even when she felt less than confident. Over time, their relationship improved dramatically and her fears gradually vanished. Jason returned home, and they've never been closer.

If this technique makes sense and you want to apply it to your own situation, here's what you have to do:

1. Ask yourself, "Am I anticipating that my partner will disappoint me in some way?"
2. Ask yourself, "How would I act differently if I were expecting him to be cooperative or more responsive?"
3. Once you identify exactly how your approach would differ if you felt more confidence about a positive outcome, "act as if."

In chapter 7, you learned about the importance of focusing on the problem-free times and doing what works. You might be wondering how "act as if" is different because you do what works with this technique, too. When you focus on the exceptions, you search your memory for current or past times that have gone well. And then you repeat what worked. When you use this technique or "act as if," you project into the future and imagine how your behavior would change if you were to expect positive outcomes. And then, of course, you "act as if."

Here's one more example for the road. Greta and her friends decided that they wanted to go on a week's vacation, just the girls. In the past, Greta's husband wasn't too supportive of the separate vacation idea. She felt certain that he would balk when she approached him with this request because a week was longer than she had ever been away. She told me that she could just imagine his response: "No way. I don't go away with my friends. Why is it so important to you to do that?" As she related the story, I could see the tension building in her body. I asked how she usually responded when he gave her a hard time, and she said, "I get very angry at him and point out all the fun things he does with his friends on a regular basis. He may not leave town, but he does as he pleases. I go into those talks with my dukes up, there's no doubt about it. Our conversations generally end badly."

I asked her how she would approach her husband differently if she expected him to go along with her plan. She said, "I'd have a good attitude and I'd approach him lovingly, taking his feelings into consideration. I'd be willing to work out an arrangement that he'd feel comfortable with." I told her, "Go home and when you bring up the subject of your out-of-town trip, act as if he'll be supportive, even if you're not so certain he will be." Act as if.

When she returned, she told me, "When he got home that night, instead of saying, 'I know you're going to give me a hard time about this, but I'm going . . . ,' I started the conversation more positively. I told him about my friends' plan to go on a vacation and asked him how he would feel about my joining them. He was somewhat hesitant, but he didn't say, 'No way.' I told him that the plans were very flexible at that point and if a certain time of year was better than another time, I would certainly honor that. I also filled him in with the details of what we'd be doing on vacation. Usually, I feel it's none of his business. He seemed really happy that I was considering his feelings and he said, 'I guess that's okay. Just don't make it the week of June fifth because I have an important meeting that week.' I said, 'Fine. No problem. Thanks for being understanding. I'll keep you posted as we make plans.' I gave him a kiss and left the room."

Greta was quite surprised at how understanding her husband had been. She began to reflect on how often she anticipated dead ends when she approached her husband with things. She decided that, from then on, before she asked him for anything, she would do a "self-check" to make sure she was envisioning a supportive response from him and adjusting her approach accordingly.

Do Something Different Strategy #4: Easier Done Than Said

Throughout this book, I have emphasized the importance of taking action if you want to influence your man. This particular technique, Easier Done Than Said, requires that you stop talking entirely. You pretend that you ran out of words and you have to get your message across through the actions you take. One of my favorite examples of this involves a feisty woman in her seventies.

Her pet peeve was that her husband would come to their dining room table without a shirt on. This greatly offended her. She tried talking to him about it, nagging, pleading, threatening, but nothing worked. Every meal was a shirtless meal.

One Sunday morning, after preparing an elaborate breakfast, this man joined her at the table in his usual attire. She excused herself, went to the bathroom, returned naked from the waist up, and seated herself beside him. Upon seeing her, he turned white as a ghost, got up, put his shirt on, and never returned to the table again without being fully dressed. (If this story sounds familiar to you, I'm not surprised. I find this woman's story to be so inspirational, I tell it all the time!) Here's another example.

A woman in my practice complained that she and her husband had very little time together, and she really resented that he slept late on weekends. She felt that his sleeping-in prevented them from doing anything enjoyable on Saturday or Sunday. For months, she tried reasoning with him about this, but nothing she ever said made a difference. I take that back. It did make a difference—it made things worse. He always got angry at her for not being more compassionate about all the pressure he was under during the week.

So one morning she decided to try the Easier Done Than Said method. She woke up early on Saturday, and instead of nagging her husband to get up, she took her dog on a very long walk. Unexpectedly, she ran into a friend, and they spent the rest of the afternoon together. By the time she got home, her husband was more than awake. In fact, he interrogated her at length. She promptly told him that she had no intention of sitting around waiting for him any longer. Guess what happened. Sunday morning he arose bright and early, asking if she wanted to go on a picnic. Hmmm. In fact, she told me that her husband became much more interested in being active during the weekend from that day on.

I know another woman who asked her partner repeatedly to pick up his massive collection of Coke cans from the den, but somehow he seemed deaf. He never complied with her wishes. One day, out of frustration, she emptied out every can, gathered them up, and placed them under the covers on his side of the bed. That night when he went to bed he was exhausted. He peeled back the covers, and without paying attention, he sat down on the pile of Coke cans. The woman confessed that her husband wasn't thrilled about the situation, but, oddly enough, he became more diligent about recycling the cans after that.

One more example. Jenny had been asking her partner to fix a leaky faucet for what seemed like a million years. She heard every drip at night when they went to sleep, and it drove her crazy. Her partner was a handyman who fixed everyone else's house but his own. She understood that he was tired of repairing things around the house, but she was beginning to feel exasperated.

Finally, one evening, in full view of him, she took out the complete do-it-yourself manual for fixing anything at home, found his plumbing tools, and starting fixing the leak herself. No more than two minutes passed when he came over to see what she was doing. Naturally, he had lots of advice for her. Within a few minutes, he took over completely. That's when Jenny had a flash of insight. She realized that this was a pattern: anytime she tried her hand at fixing something, he stepped in, took over, and finished the project. Not a bad thing to keep in mind, eh?

Men are so action-oriented that sometimes they don't believe you really mean business until you get your feet moving. That's why too many men don't listen to women's requests for change until these women file for divorce. Divorce is an action. Don't let things get to that point. If you've said everything you can possibly say to try to get your man to change, stop talking. Pretend you are playing the game of charades—no words allowed. Do mime. Get creative. Have fun. Just stop talking. Here's what you have to do:

1. Identify what you've been saying over and over.
2. Think of some action you could take that would get the message across without using words.
3. DO IT. DO IT NOW.

Do Something Different Strategy #5: Do Nothing

Remember, relationships are like seesaws. The more one person does of something, the less the other person has to do. If one person initiates sex all the time, the other person won't. If one person takes out the garbage every week, the other person won't. If one person is pessimistic, the other becomes optimistic. If one person is frugal, the other spends money as if it grows on trees. If women want their partners to change, a simple solution can be discovered by remembering the seesaw syndrome. If she wants her partner to do more of something, she has to do less of it.

One of the perpetual disagreements my husband, Jim, and I have had in our twenty-four years together is how we handle our daughter, Danielle. Although she is quite strong-willed (she comes by this honestly), I think Jim is too harsh with her and he thinks I am too lenient. For years, I've tried to influence him to be a kinder and gentler father. I must admit that my regular lectures about effective parenting skills have fallen on deaf ears. We've had more arguments than I care to count about this difference in our parenting styles.

Despite my best intentions, I've noticed that our situation always goes from bad to worse if I intervene in Danielle's behalf when Jim is angry at her. He becomes incensed at me and even angrier at Danielle. So while I think I'm helping the situation, in reality, I'm only making matters worse. I'm fully aware of this, but knowing it and doing something about it are two very different things.

One day, I decided to try something new. I travel quite a bit to do seminars, and one evening, upon my arrival in my hotel room, I received a call from Danielle, who was crying her eyes out. Her dad was "being mean" to her. He was yelling and being unpleasant. Being so far from home, I felt totally helpless and was just about to do my usual thing. I told Danielle to get her dad on the phone. I was determined to confront him about his actions.

It took a minute for Jim to pick up the phone, just enough time for me to reconsider my plan. So when he said "hello" in a gruff voice, I replied, "I just wanted to say good night to you." Since he expected a confrontation, there was a moment of silence, and then he said, "Good night." I must say that not stepping in and "saving the day" required every ounce of personal strength I could muster.

The next day, I called home from the airport just before my flight to check on Danielle. I assumed she had just gotten home from school since it was around 3:00 P.M. But much to my surprise, Jim answered the phone. Since he generally arrives home later, I asked why he was home and he said, "I left work early to pick Danielle up from school so I could apologize to her. I bought her a dozen roses [Danielle loves flowers], and I took her out for a bite to eat." I was speechless, an unusual state of affairs. Jim broke the silence by saying, "You feel better?" I responded, "Yeah," and he quickly added, "Me, too." I was incredibly touched by his sincerity and his efforts to make amends with Danielle. Not exactly the brute I made him out to be, huh?

The moral of that story? I'm convinced that that ending never would have occurred had I intervened in my usual manner. Jim's predictable response to my attacking him is to defend himself. This allows him to focus on his anger at me and not have to reflect on his actions with Danielle. By my not interfering, it gave Jim the opportunity to contemplate what had happened and work things out on his own. And what a splendid job he did without me! When I fix less, he fixes more—the seesaw theory in motion.

So think about a problem you've been dealing with for a long time. Recognize that one of the strategies you may not yet have tried is doing nothing. After days, months, or years of trying to remedy a situation, your doing nothing will be quite noticeable. And, remember, the main idea in this chapter is the importance of novelty. If you take a sabbatical from fixing things, it will probably be very new. Your partner is likely to wonder what's going on. He might even do something productive to solve the problem. So give it a try.

Doing nothing is fairly self-explanatory, but let me point you in the right direction.

1. Identify the times you feel compelled to "fix" things.

If you aren't sure about your "more of the same," just recall the times your partner tells you that you're always jumping in or interfering.

2. The next time that situation occurs, do nothing.

3. Watch the results.

If you are a compulsive fixer like me, when you back off, you might worry that you're not doing anything when a problem occurs. But that's needless worry because doing nothing isn't nothing, it's something. It's really something.

Do Something Different Strategy #6: The Medium Is the Message

Good teachers know that students have different learning styles. Some students learn information visually. These students do well with visual aids such as charts or movies. Other students are auditory learners. Lectures or music might be good ways to reach these students. Still other students are kinesthetic learners. This means that they learn through touch and movement. Such students would have an easy time learning math concepts by being able to hold objects in their hands. Role-plays that involve moving their bodies through space would also be an effective means of teaching them. Skilled teachers match the teaching method with the preferred learning style of the student. Unskilled teachers often blame students who aren't progressing instead of questioning whether there's a better way to reach them. The same might be true for your man.

When you are trying to get a message through to him, there really are countless ways you could do it. Some work better than others. For example, I know a woman who had been begging her husband for months to be more forthcoming about his out-of-town trips or his late nights at work so that she could make her own plans. Simple enough request, right? Well, despite what seemed like several thousand reminders, he never did what she asked. This enraged her and they fought constantly. One day, she left a calendar and a Magic Marker on the kitchen counter along with a note urging him to mark his schedule for the following week. When she came downstairs, she discovered her calendar marked with his plans for the next three months. The visual approach worked like a charm.

I know another woman whose partner is very stubborn when they have face-to-face conversations, but if she talks with him over the phone, things usually go remarkably well. Go figure. Now this woman felt that something was wrong with their relationship because they had such a hard time working things out face-to-face. Although I could understand her desire to have more productive talks in person, I felt it was important that she be a bit more pragmatic. As long as there is a way to cooperate, don't knock it. Many couples should be so lucky.

Terri was a woman whose husband drank heavily. She hated this about him and had considered leaving the marriage. Because they had three children, she was determined to try everything before she left. When I met her, she felt fairly certain she had said everything she could say to her husband, and she was at a loss as to what to do next. I asked her, "Have you ever written him a heartfelt letter about some issue in your relationship?" and she replied, "Yes, I have. Years ago I felt he was spending too much time at work, and after many months of arguing, I wrote him a letter expressing my thoughts. We never really talked about the letter, but I noticed that he started spending more time with the family." I told her that if she had good luck with writing a letter once before, it might work again, so why not give it whirl? She agreed.

Several weeks later, she told me that the letter worked. Her husband wasn't completely sober yet, but he admitted he had a problem and was trying to figure out whom to contact to get help. For the first time in their marriage, he promised he would change. She recognized that the road to sobriety was going to be a bumpy one, but she was ecstatic that they were on the road.

So if the method you've been using to get through to your man hasn't been working, get creative. Leave a message on his car phone. Write him Post-it notes. Send him E-mail. Find the perfect Hallmark card. Take out a classified ad. Or do what one woman I know did to profess her love to her insecure boyfriend. She rented a billboard and confessed her love for the whole world to see. He got the point.

Do yourself a favor and give yourself permission to expand your horizons. Good communication involves more than just face-to-face, eyeball-to-eyeball, verbal tête-à-têtes. If some of your best and most productive communications occur in unconventional ways, don't judge it. Just do it. Nike has the right idea.

Okay. Now that you've learned Actionese, you might be thinking, "I know it makes sense for me to be more action-oriented with my man, but there are times when I want him to talk to me and I want those talks to be more productive. How do I get him to listen? How do I get him to turn off the television and hear what I have to say to him?" Although I've made it clear that talking might not be the best way to reach your man, I know that talking is very important. It's one of my favorite things to do. So if you promise you'll be more action-oriented, I'll give you a few tips on how to talk so your man will listen. Stay tuned. But before I give you the tips on talking, I have one more action-oriented method you should strongly consider if your partner has refused to budge no matter what you've done so far.

The Medium Is the Massage: The Siren Solution

I assume that you and I know each other well enough for me to be completely honest with you. Since the guys have left the room, I'm going to tell it like it is, and I'm going to make it short, sweet, and to the point. If you want your man to be nice to you, to do the things that make you happy, stack the deck in your favor—keep him happy sexually.

When women ignore their partner's sexual needs, men feel incredibly hurt, rejected, and angry, and as a result, they shut down. They do little around the house. They're insensitive. Days pass with their saying little more than "Pass the salt." This infuriates women. Show me an infuriated woman, and I'll show you a woman who cringes at the thought of kissing, touching, and loving, which of course makes her man even more of a curmudgeon, which in turn makes sex an even more remote possibility, and so on.

So, once again, we're back to that old familiar Catch-22, aren't we? Women need to feel satisfied emotionally in order to satisfy their partners sexually. Men need to feel satisfied sexually in order to satisfy their partners emotionally. When relationships are rocky, women wait for men to be more loving, more communicative, to spend more time together before they pay attention to their sexual relationships. Men wait for women to be more sexy, flirtatious, and receptive to their sexual advances before they put energy into their relationships. As you might imagine, this can be a very, very long and lonely wait.

Are you someone whose mate hasn't responded to anything you've tried so far? Is your sex life virtually nil? There may be a direct relationship here. Whether it's obvious to you or not, you need to acknowledge and internalize that without a satisfying sexual relationship, your man is going to be edgy and combative. He's not going to be motivated to please you. So you have a choice. You can keep your distance from him physically and perpetuate the unhappiness between you, or you can make a decision to stop the ongoing cycle of blame and counterblame and start caring about his needs. This doesn't mean that you have to have sex every time he gets the urge, but it does mean that you should pay more attention to your sex life.

You might be surprised by this suggestion. After all, it's not exactly politically correct advice. But in case you haven't noticed, I abandoned the idea of being politically correct long ago. I'm more practical now. I'm helping you keep your eyes on the cheese, remember? And practically speaking, if having a better sex life yields a more loving man, it's a wonder women don't do everything they can to keep their love lights burning.

Do you remember the good old days when sex was more of a priority to you? Do you recall having butterflies in your stomach when he walked into the room? What was it like when he touched you or brushed against you back then? How were you different during your more passionate times? Were you more adventurous?

Did you take the time to dress differently to get his attention? What did you do to make him feel like a stud?

When you start showing your love for your man by placing more importance on your sexual relationship—even if you're out of practice—you'll trigger a solution cycle; he'll be happier and more loving in return. He'll spend more time with the kids. He'll fix the leaky faucet and put up those shelves you've been asking for. He'll stay up late at night talking even though he really doesn't feel like it. Then you'll like him more and feel more attracted to him, which will inspire him to be even nicer, and so on. You get the picture.

So the next time you notice that you're just not getting through to your man, ask yourself, "When was the last time we had sex?" and if you have a hard time answering the question, or if your last sexual encounter was more than a few days ago, it's time for you to get cookin'. Even if you're not convinced that being more sexual will make a difference, why not try it anyway? You have nothing to lose and everything to gain.

Some women feel that if sex isn't as important to them as it is to their mates, why should they have to be more sexual? But I say that that's the wrong way to look at this. In good relationships, people are willing to take care of each other's needs. The problem in so many relationships is that people tend to give to others that which *they'd* like to receive. But that's not real giving. Real giving entails giving your partner what he wants and needs, whether you understand it or agree with it or not. Contrary to conventional pop psychology that warns people of the risks of putting others ahead of yourself, I say that's garbage. Ask anyone in a long-term, happy marriage about the secret to his or her success. You'll undoubtedly hear something about the importance of placing your partner's needs in front of your own from time to time. You can't have real loving without real giving. Putting your sex life higher on your list of priorities is what real giving is all about.

Many women turn down their mate's sexual advances because they're not in a sexual mood. They may be preoccupied, busy, tense, or just plain disinterested. But it's important for you to keep in mind that just because you aren't in the mood at the outset doesn't mean you won't get in the mood after a while. Hundreds and hundreds of women have told me, "Once I get going, I get into it." Since you can jump-start your desire, it doesn't hurt to get started and see what happens. You may be pleasantly surprised.

But sometimes, no matter what your man says or does, your interest in having sex is nonexistent. When this happens, you have a few options in addition to declining. You can give your man a rain check. He'll like that. Or you can make him happy without expecting anything in return. If you do, he'll be putty in your hands.

Some women are hesitant to be more sexual with their men because it feels manipulative to have sex simply as a ploy to get them to be more responsive. And if that's the *only* reason they push themselves to be more affectionate, I'd have to agree with them. It is manipulative. However, women who decide to become more sexual notice that the benefits of doing so go far beyond simply getting their men to change. They feel happier and more connected to their partners. They rediscover the pleasures of sex and the bond that comes from being in sync sexually.

Having said that, you should never do something that conflicts with your values or makes you feel uncomfortable. If, for any reason, you're uneasy about the idea of becoming more sexual with your partner, don't do it. You know yourself best. Do what works for you.

However, revitalizing your sexual relationship is a wonderful thing to do. Nothing but good can come from it. He'll be happier, he'll be nicer, you'll be happier, and—who knows?—it may bring out the siren in you. Remember what Annie Hall said about sex? She said, "It's the most fun I've ever had without laughing."

Now on to talking.

CHAPTER NINE

Smart Talk: How to Talk So Men Will Listen

C an we talk? Are we friends yet? I hope your answer to these questions is "Yes," because I'm about to tell you things only a good friend would say. I'm going to tell you what drives men nuts about the way we communicate. I've heard it all, and since men are out of the room, I'm going to spill the beans. Though I don't necessarily agree with this male perspective, I think you should be privy to the information. Like it or not, if we want to have meaningful discussions with our partners—particularly about touchy subjects—we have to take their perspectives into account. If we don't, they'll tune us out. Then we'll be back to where we started. Nowhere. We need to find ways to talk so men will listen.

The tips you're about to read pertain to conflict-ridden conversations. I don't think you need assistance making superficial talk or with discussions that are void of emotional content. Those are no-brainers. Emotion-packed conversations are where we get in trouble. They bring out the worst in everyone. In keeping with the "It takes one to tango" spirit expressed throughout this book, when you change your steps in the dance of conflict between you and your guy, he'll respond more sanely and your heated talks will become more productive. So consider this a primer in conflict-busting. Here's the scoop.

Twelve Tips for Talking

Talking Tip #1: Let him say when.

You already know that men aren't crazy about talking things out. That's why it feels as if you're infringing upon your man when you say you want to talk. Consequently, it is extremely helpful to try to catch your man when he's most amenable to conversing. Earlier in the book, I talked about the importance of choosing your timing wisely when you approach your man with something important. I can't stress this point enough. If your man is otherwise preoccupied or is unprepared emotionally to deal with your issues, it won't be a productive conversation. He'll become defensive, nasty, or shut down.

When you announce that you want to talk about something, you should ask him whether now is a good time for him. If he says, "No," respect that and ask him, "When would be a better time?" Many relationship experts suggest that a twenty-four-hour time frame should be sufficient. Then honor your man's request and wait it out patiently. If he asks what you are going to talk about, briefly describe the subject, but don't go into too much detail. If he's not ready to talk, it behooves you not to get him going. Some women notice that by giving their partners the power to decide *when* these confrontations will occur, their men are more willing participants in the conversation.

Talking Tip #2: Be brief and to the point.

Men are not particularly patient with long-winded explanations about things. In fact, when it comes to verbal communication, they're not very patient at all. Please don't forget this. You have a very narrow window of opportunity to be heard. Like kids, they have an extremely short attention span. So you have to make the most of the time you have.

One thing to avoid at all costs is doing something guys refer to as rambling. I've come to figure out that when guys say "rambling" they generally mean one of two things: that we're jumping from topic to topic or we're talking about feelings. Let's take jumping from topic to topic first. Women often briefly discuss one point and quickly move on to another. This "stream of consciousness" style of relating is very comfortable to us. We think out loud. When we talk with our women friends, speaking in half sentences is the rule. Our friends follow along without blinking an eye. They fill in the blanks effortlessly. We expect this sort of understanding with our friends and we're rarely disappointed.

But here comes the problem. We talk to our men as if they are our women friends—but they're not. Guys can't fill in the blanks. If we switch topics midstream, halfway through the second topic, they don't hear a word we're saying because they're trying to figure out what topic one has to do with topic two. They get lost easily, and when they do, boy, do they get angry. "You're so illogical!" they inform us. "Why can't you ever stay on one subject at a time?" Sometimes they say worse things. Then we think they're being obstinate because we can't, for the life of us, understand why they can't understand . . . but they can't.

If your man has criticized you for jumping from topic to topic, here's what you need to do. Prior to your discussion, plan one or two points you want to make. It might help for you to write down your points in short sentences. You might even rehearse your lines before you approach him. When you start talking, make sure he understands point one before you move on to point two. Then, prior to switching topics, it's helpful to say, "I'm changing topics now. I'm on to something different." This will make the transition a lot smoother for him.

Okay. That's the jumping-around thing. What about the business of talking about feelings? Why do guys get off track when we talk about feelings? In chapter 3, I explained what makes guys tick. Perhaps you recall my saying that men are goal-oriented. When men are unhappy about something, they try to identify the problem and then quickly want to figure out what to do about it. They're not interested in "wallowing around" in discussions about feelings. To them, that's a waste of time. Get the issues out on the table and start fixing them. To us, talking about feelings is anything but a waste of time.

I've worked with many couples who have gotten stuck because of this difference between men and women. She identifies a problem and starts talking about her feelings. He can handle listening to her discuss the nature of the problem, but when she expounds on her feelings about it, she loses him. And because she senses he's lost, she keeps explaining her feelings rather than identifying potential solutions. This makes him crazy. Here's an example.

I was working with a woman who wanted her husband to commit to making one meal a week. He said that he didn't mind cooking, but he didn't want to commit to any particular night. She offered her rationale for wanting him to do so, and within a few minutes, he agreed. However, she wasn't really listening because she was busy justifying her request. Since cooking had always been her responsibility, she felt somewhat guilty asking him to take over. As a result, she explained, "I've been doing it all for so many years. I want time to myself. I know you're busy, but I can't understand why it's so hard for you to commit to cooking a meal one day a week," and on and on. . . .

After five minutes of her monologue, he started getting defensive, justifying why he never cooked, a bad turn of events. So I intervened. I asked her to rate on a 1-to-10 scale, with 10 being extremely agreeable, and 1 being not agreeable at all, how agreeable her husband was at that moment to cooking one night a week. After some thought, she said, "Five."

I turned to him and asked, "How would you rate yourself?" He replied, "Ten." I asked them what they thought accounted for the difference in their perceptions, and he said, "I agreed to do what she was asking several minutes ago, but she wouldn't stop talking. It's frustrating. We do this a lot at home. When she keeps going, I finally make some snide comment and end up hurting her feelings. I don't mean to hurt her feelings, but at least I get her to stop." He admitted this wasn't a good practice.

I offered two suggestions to them. I told her that, prior to their discussion, she should make certain that she's very clear as to her request. She should narrow her speech down to several sentences for starters. Then she should continually check out whether her husband is getting it. If she's not sure, she should ask, "Am I making sense to you?" or "What do you think about what I'm saying?" Then STOP when there's a meeting of minds.

I told *him* that the next time they got into a conversation, once he understands what she's asking or saying, he should tell her so, more emphatically. He should say, "Okay, I get your point. You want . . ." If this didn't work, I suggested that he get a visual aid, like a red flag, and wave it when she hits a home run. They laughed and thought it was a good idea. In the weeks that followed, they noticed a vast improvement in their communication.

The point to remember is that if your man keeps telling you that you're losing him or you're repeating yourself, it may mean that all he wants is the facts, just the facts, ma'am. If you want something from him, make an effort to be more succinct. Describe the issue, tell him what you want, and talk less about your feelings. It might help.

Talking Tip #3: Notify him if you want to discuss feelings.

Sometimes, you want to share your feelings with your man. After all, why be in a relationship if you can't talk about your feelings, right? Then why is it that every time you talk about negative feelings, even if it has nothing to do with him, it ends up in a fight? I can tell you why this happens and what you can do about it.

Earlier in this book, I told you that guys have an incredible need to fix things that are broken. When you talk about feeling sad or unhappy, he thinks you're broken and that he needs to do something about it. So when you start talking about being concerned about your job, the kids, your weight, other family members, he thinks he needs to give you a solution. He believes that's what you want from him. He starts telling you what to do, and you get furious. You think he's not listening. You think he's not caring. You believe he just wants the conversation to be over. Because if he did care, you tell yourself, he would give you empathy, not advice. You get angry at him. And he gets even angrier, because from his perspective, he's helping and you're not appreciating him. So you end up mad at each other. Sound familiar?

Well, the good news is that you can talk about feelings, even negative ones, but you have to give him directions first. Prior to discussing your emotions, tell him, "I just want to talk to you about something I'm feeling. It doesn't have anything to do with us and you don't need to fix it. I just want to share my feelings with you. So just listen." Most guys will go along with the program if they know the rules. And once they know that "just listening" is really doing something, they feel they've been helpful. This will satisfy their urge to fix things, after all.

Talking Tip #4: Start softly.

Sometimes the negative feelings you're experiencing have something to do with your partner. And, believe it or not, you can talk to him about these feelings, too, if you get off to a good start. Psychologist John Gottman, Ph.D., has done some very interesting research on couples' communication patterns. One of the characteristics of conversations that go well is something he refers to as "a soft start." Some say that the outcome of a chess game can be dictated by the first move. Gottman would probably say that this metaphor also applies to conversations between loved ones.

A soft start simply means that you approach your partner gently. You don't want him to feel attacked, even if you're angry about something. For example, if your man was insensitive at a party and said some things that embarrassed you, although you might feel like clobbering him verbally, it's not in your best interests to do so. You should start your conversation by saying something like "You probably really didn't mean to hurt my feelings, but something you said last night didn't sit right with me." Or "Maybe I'm off base here, but I found something you said last night kind of confusing. Could you help me out with this?" If you've been going round and round about housework, instead of saying, "I want to talk to you about something. I'm so sick and tired of doing everything around here," you might try softening the blow a bit. Try "You know, I really love you and I can't stand all this fighting we've been doing about the housework. Let's find some solution we can both live with."

Even if your conversation gets more heated as time progresses, research shows that if you start softly, you'll end up in a better place. So get yourself into a good frame of mind before you tackle hard issues. Don't approach your man until you can genuinely begin your conversation with something he won't mind hearing. If he feels attacked from the start, he'll spend the rest of the time defending himself, and that's not what you want. A soft start will lower his defenses and make it more likely that he'll listen to you and take in what you have to say.

Talking Tip #5: Say what you want.

In chapter 4, you learned about two important aspects of goals-setting. Think about what you want versus what you're unhappy about and be concrete. These principles apply to conversations with your man as well. If you talk about those things that make you unhappy—"You always ignore me"—you're bound to have more trouble than if you discuss what you want him to do instead—"I really would like to spend a half hour each evening talking together." If you talk in negative terms, as far as he's concerned, you're nagging. He hates that and he'll tune you out or resist. Positive statements, ones that say what you want, are not viewed as nagging. They're requests for change, and to him that's a whole lot better than complaints.

In addition to stating what you want in positive terms, it pays to be concrete. Instead of saying, "I want you to be a better lover," which may be Greek to your man, say, "When we make love, I'd like you to start by kissing me, make eye contact with me, and spend more time touching parts of my body other than my genitals," and so on. Men are much more responsive when things are spelled out in black and white. So before you approach your partner with anything important, do a self-check. Make sure what you're about to say is positively worded, specific, and action-oriented.

Talking Tip #6: Say what you mean.

Men need for women to be positive, specific, and have our words accurately reflect what we mean. That's because they're so damn literal. That's why when you're saying, "We don't spend time together anymore," instead of understanding that you're missing him and you'd like to be together, he'll dissect your sentence to bits.

"What do you mean that we don't spend time together *anymore?* You mean we *never* spend time together? You mean we *never* see each other anymore? What exactly do you mean?" Isn't it frustrating when that happens? It sure is. But that's the way their minds work. They're just literal beings.

Jim, our daughter Danielle, and I were out to dinner the other evening. The waiter came over to our table. Jim asked him, "Do you ever eat here?" After an inordinately long time, he said, "Yes." I didn't quite understand what was so tough about Jim's question, but what happened next made his long silence more understandable.

The waiter asked if he could take our order, and we told him that we were ready. Before making a final decision, Jim asked, "How do you like the veal?" and again, after a few moments, the waiter replied, "Well done. I've served it medium-rare a few times, but it's too juicy for my taste." I had to stop myself from chuckling. Obviously, Jim wanted to know whether or not the waiter liked the veal, not how thoroughly he liked it cooked. But the waiter didn't have a clue because he was so literal. In fact, I realized why the waiter hesitated when Jim asked, "Do you ever eat here?" He must have thought that Jim was asking whether he ate at that particular table! Oh, well, what can you expect? He was a guy.

If you don't want your discussions sidetracked, be careful to say what you mean. Don't exaggerate to illustrate your point, or your point will get lost. Be simple and direct and remember that he is going to take you literally.

Talking Tip #7: Heed his effort to make amends.

John Gottman also noticed that in healthy relationships, one person often reverses the flow of negative communication by attempting to say something conciliatory. Then the other person acknowledges it and becomes more conciliatory in return. For instance, after fighting for a while, one person might say, "Well, I suppose there's something to what you're saying" or "I think we both do that [admitting culpability]." Hearing the attempt to diffuse anger, the other person might make a U-turn and be more positive in kind. In unhealthy relationships, if one person says, "I admit it, you're right about that," the other person might be so angry that he or she will be oblivious to the comment and just keep going. In other words, repair attempts go unnoticed.

A word to the wise. If you and your partner are in the midst of a heated conversation and he says something even mildly positive, acknowledge it. Any effort on his part to get things back on track is effort worth reinforcing. You want to catch him in the act of getting it right—being conciliatory—and underlining it, remember? Don't allow the heat of the moment to deter you from doing what will be more helpful to you in the long run. The next time you have a fight, listen very carefully to what your partner is saying. Look for the small signs that he's trying to make up with you.

Talking Tip #8: Acknowledge his position and feelings.

The premier communication principle is this: Seek to understand before you seek to be understood. When people feel understood, they're much more cooperative and conciliatory. When couples argue, most of the time it's a debate about who's right and who's wrong. Neither person is really listening. We're too intent on making our points. Little effort is put into trying to make sense of the other person's point of view. That's when conversations get very destructive.

One of the most common things to occur when we don't acknowledge our partners' perspectives is that they won't acknowledge ours. We all keep repeating ourselves over and over in hopes we'll finally get through. Good luck. When I do seminars, I tell people, "If for some perverted reason you wanted your partner to keep repeating himself over and over, I have the fail-proof formula. Don't acknowledge what he's saying. Just keep repeating your point over and over."

If you're someone who can't believe how stubbornly your man clings to his way of looking at things, I'm going to tell you something that works like magic during heated confrontations. If you want your partner to cooperate with you, to understand your point of view, to appreciate how you might be feeling about something, there are two things you need to do.

The first: *Really* listen to what he's saying. Now you might be wondering what I mean by that. I'm not just saying that you hear the words that are being spoken, I'm saying that you truly try to understand your partner's point of view. Put yourself into his shoes. You don't have to agree with his opinion, but you should make a concerted effort to understand why he might be feeling that way.

The second step: Tell your partner that you understand what he's saying. Check out whether he thinks you grasp his point. Agitated people often become calm, conciliatory, and cooperative when they feel understood. But there's another reason that acknowledging your partner's point of view often leads to more positive outcomes.

Throughout this book, I've discussed the all-too-common problem-solving strategy—doing more of the same. When we keep stating our position over and over, that's exactly what we're doing—more of the same. But when we acknowledge our partners' points of view, not only are we demonstrating that we understand them, we're also stopping a bad habit. We're doing something different.

Some time ago, my husband and I were out to dinner and we were having a really pleasant time when I decided to discuss the purchasing of a new car. Although I felt certain that I had finally decided what kind of car I wanted, I thought it would be a good idea to discuss my decision with him. I had tentatively decided on a sedan that was a bit more upscale than my usual style. When I shared my choice with him, he immediately suggested I get a more practical car, like a Jeep.

Oddly enough, although I'm not particularly picky about the kind of car I drive, the more he favored practicality, the more I leaned toward overindulgence. As our conversation got more heated, I realized we were ruining a perfectly lovely evening together, and I also realized that, down deep, I don't care all that much about cars, I just like reliable transportation.

So, at the peak of our dialogue I turned to him and said, "You know, I can see your point. Given my lifestyle and my driving needs, a practical car makes more sense," and kept right on eating my dinner. After six seconds of silence, he looked at me and, referring to the car that I had originally picked out for myself, said, "Okay. Did you pick out the color you want? I'll go get it for you."

Once he said that, something mysterious happened. I didn't care at all what kind of car I bought. All I knew was that it felt great that he was considering my feelings. And I know why he did so—he felt good that I had considered his.

If you've ever felt your partner is stubborn and that arguments have gotten blown up way out of proportion, it may be because you and your partner have ignored this one little rule: Conflict resolution begins the moment people feel understood. Listening is an act of loving, and when you give love, you'll get love in return.

Talking Tip #9: Ignore the zingers.

Unless they're attorneys, men complain that their women are so much more adept at arguing than they are. Many men feel women run circles around them verbally. To even out the score, guys often throw zingers. Zingers are sarcastic comments that don't feel very good, to say the least. If you want your conversation to go downhill at lightning speed, throw a zinger right back at him.

But I say, you be the big one. Know that the main reason he's hurling a hurtful comment at you is that he feels threatened in some way. He's trying to protect himself, and although being mean isn't a healthy or fair way to protect oneself, for that moment it's his way. But regardless of what he does or says, you have a choice. You can stoop to his level or you can take the high road. To take the high road, you can do a number of things, the most obvious of which is to just ignore him and keep going. If you're new to this ignoring thing, he'll be surprised that he didn't push your button, and he might even challenge you again. Throwing zingers is only one of many ways he tries to derail you. He has other methods for pushing your buttons. By now, you should know what they are. (Remember your skits?) That's when it takes a great deal of self-control to deflect his comments. But it can be done. Once he sees he's not getting you to react, he'll eventually stop testing you. Regardless of his method of choice, always remember that ignoring him will work in your favor.

When you ignore his zingers, you'll feel good about yourself. You'll feel as if your life is in your control. This is all really good stuff, but there's also icing on the cake. You should notice that by detouring around his zingers, your arguments won't get destructive. In fact, they might even be productive. It may not happen overnight, but if you're patient, eventually he should come around.

Now maybe you're thinking, "Michele, that sounds like a good idea, but how in the world do I stop myself from blasting him if he's nasty to me?" First of all, you have to feel convinced that it's your choice. I already told you that you're in charge of what you say, no matter what he says to you and no matter how his zingers make you feel. Even if you're furious, you still have to decide what you do about it. Feelings don't force us to act certain ways. *We* decide how we're going to act and react.

Second, you probably know exactly when he's about to spout something ridiculous or hurtful. My guess is that you even know what he's going to say. Being able to predict this stuff doesn't lessen the sting when it happens, but it does prepare you for its occurrence. And since you know it's coming, you can take a deep breath, count to three (or one hundred, if you have to), and calmly continue with what you were saying before he interrupted. Just keep telling yourself, "Don't react. It's not worth it." If you really set your mind to it, you can do it. I know you can. Remember, you're changing your steps in the dance of conflict to get better results!

Talking Tip #10: Take a time-out.

Have you and your partner ever been in a heated conversation and in the midst of things, your man checks out? His eyes glaze over. He stops talking. He looks away. He utters, "You're right, you're always right. I'm always wrong." All meaningful conversation comes to an abrupt halt. Or in the middle of an emotionally charged discussion, does he walk out of the room or leave the house? There's a name for what your man is doing. Researchers John Gottman and Robert Levenson call it "stonewalling." Lots of men do it. And when I tell you why, you'll probably be surprised.

The researchers asked the couples to discuss a major area of disagreement in their marriage. Throughout their conversations, these couples were videotaped and monitored for physiological arousal. Heart rate, blood velocity, skin conductance, and gross motor movements were tracked. The data suggested that during conflict, men become significantly more aroused physiologically than women. This allows women to tolerate longer, escalating rounds of conflict. Men need to lower their arousal because if they don't, they might feel overwhelmed and lose control. Stonewalling protects both partners from this sort of escalation. Furthermore, it takes men longer than women to recover from being worked up physiologically.

Even though you now know there are physiological reasons for your man's tuning you out, you may not feel any better about him when he does it. But you should know that he's not doing it to make you angry, he's trying to soothe himself. He needs the downtime. Since many men really do need time to de-escalate, it's often helpful to build in a time-out period when you have heated discussion.

If you see your partner stonewalling, you can suggest that you stop talking about things for a while. You may decide to separate or just do something entirely different. You can have a predetermined time-out period, or you can make it more open-ended. If it's open-ended, wait a while and then ask your partner if he's ready to talk. Honor his feedback, and if he's not quite ready, set another appointment to finish your conversation. Or, if you'd like, decide that you've gone as far as you will go on that particular subject and drop it.

You may think that instituting a time-out period during heated debates is too artificial for you. That's okay. The most important thing for you to remember is that if your man walks out of the room or tells you to leave him alone for a while, there's a good reason for it. He's not just being difficult. He needs to settle down. Your conversation will not be a good one if you keep going when he's highly agitated. So whatever you do, don't pursue him no matter how angry you are. A time-out period can give both of you a chance to clear your heads and approach each other in a more level-headed manner. Give it a shot.

Talking Tip #11: To cry or not to cry, that is the question.

A short but sweet tip. Some women tell me that when they're arguing and they become emotional and cry, their partners tune them out, get angry, or leave the room. Other women say that their tears make their men soften. So I have a suggestion: Once again, keep your eyes on the cheese. If your becoming emotional—crying, being sad, looking despondent—triggers your man to be more sensitive to you, then let it all hang out. If your emotional side makes him become less cooperative and angry, get a grip. Let your feelings out with a good friend instead. I'm not saying you should manufacture feelings or pretend you don't have feelings when you do, but I'm suggesting that you keep your end goal in mind no matter what you're feeling.

Talking Tip #12: Unless he's deaf, he heard you.

It took me lots of years to figure this one out, and I want to spare you the exasperation. Long ago, when Jim and I argued about something, I would keep at it until he either agreed or acknowledged what I was saying. More often than not, I didn't get what I was looking for. I had chronic frustration. But as I got older and wiser, I noticed something interesting. Even though Jim didn't agree with me (in fact, he usually vehemently disagreed with me), in the days that followed, his behavior changed. He started doing what I asked of him.

That's when I realized that my microscope was too narrowly focused. I was looking for understanding and cooperation within the time frame of our conversation only. If he didn't verbally commit to pleasing me, I felt I hadn't gotten through to him and I was angry. Since I now know that, even if he tells me I'm crazy and that there's no way in hell he's going to do something, I don't jump to any conclusions. I know from years of experience that when he's had a chance to cool down, he might just change that stubborn little mind of his. He often does.

If your man is fanatical about self-determination like Jim, it's much more likely that he'll come around *after* you've stopped trying to convince him. Then if he complies, he's doing it because he wants to, not because you told him to. He's saving face. So don't think if you haven't reached an agreement during your talk with him that he isn't listening or hasn't heard. Unless he's deaf, he hears you. Stop pressing your point (and don't feel bad about it); step back for a few days and watch for signs that he's mellowing. Be patient. Guys are slow learners. It takes time for good ideas to catch on.

So now you're armed with lots of tools for influencing the man in your life to be a better partner. And when he's less than wonderful and you need to talk with him about it, you can make your life easier by taking the talking tips to heart. I'm assuming you've already started putting many of these techniques to work. If you haven't, SHAME ON YOU. You need to get off your butt and do something. Don't read another page until you get your feet moving. Otherwise, all this is meaningless. Action turns these techniques into magic. But you and you alone are the magician.

Perhaps you've seen some changes in your man and you're happy about that, but you're wondering, "How long is this going to last?" or "What do I need to do to keep these positive changes going?" In reality, maintaining positive changes is not all that difficult. But you have to know how. And that, my dear, is what the next chapter is all about—keeping it up!

CHAPTER TEN

....

Keeping It Up

I'm sitting at my desk right now, thinking about you. I'm imagining that, because of your actions, your relationship is a happier place to be. If not, you probably wouldn't have gotten this far into the book. If I'm in error about that—if things have remained somewhat stagnant—skip this chapter and immediately go on to the next one, entitled "The Immovable Man." After you fine-tune your strategy and start getting better results, come back to this chapter. See ya later.

If you're still reading, it means that whatever you've been doing has been working. Even though I don't know you personally, I want you to know how great it makes me feel that you've changed your relationship single-handedly! You should feel proud of yourself. You've stopped blaming your man and you've taken control of your life. That's fantastic! And I know that whatever you've been doing hasn't been easy. I know because, even though I teach seminars and write books about being solution-oriented, I still find it challenging when push comes to shove.

So give yourself a pat on the back. You deserve it. In fact, why not reward yourself in some way? Go out with friends, have a tiramisù, buy yourself a new sweater, get a massage. Pamper yourself, woman. You've obviously made a decision to stop fighting and start putting positive energy into your relationship, and that's a decision that will make your life richer every day. So, congratulations!

Now's the time for you to step back for a moment and take an inventory of what's gotten better since you made your partner your project *du jour*, how these changes have impacted on your life, and which of your actions prompted these improvements. You also need to know which aspects of your relationship still need your attention. In other words, it's time to assess the progress you've made and to start plotting the course ahead of you. To do so, it will be helpful to answer the questions below.

If you're like me, you might be tempted to skip this Q&A section entirely. Don't. These exercises, based on the work of Steve de Shazer, will really help you identify the ways you've already strengthened your relationship and they'll enable you to see how much work you have still cut out for yourself.[1] So take out your pen and get going. And one more thing, as you answer the questions, always keep in mind that you have to be specific. Concrete, observable, action-oriented responses only, please.

Start by thinking back to a time when things were really rough between you and your man. Ask yourself,

> 1. "On a 1-to-10 scale, with 10 being great and 1 being the pits, where on the scale would I have rated my relationship back then?"

_____

Due to the progress in your relationship, ask yourself,

> 2. "On that same scale, how would I rate things now?"

_____

When you answer question number 2, you may be thinking, "Every day is different. Some days are better than others." I know that. Just average things out. Rate a typical week, now that things are better. Also, even if there's only a small difference between your responses to questions 1 and 2, appreciate the fact that there is improvement. Any improvement, no matter how small, is a sign that you're moving in the right direction. Be patient.

As you reflect on the difference between your responses to questions 1 and 2, ask yourself,

3. "What has my partner been doing differently that allows me to feel better about our relationship?"

_____

_____

_____

_____

_____

Take your time answering this question. List as many changes as you can think of. You might need more space than I've allotted. If so, use additional paper.

Think about your relationship over the past few weeks. What differences have you noticed in his behavior? Is he less combative? Is he gentler? Does he help more with the kids? Is he trying to be more communicative? Make sure your response describes his changes in action-oriented terms. For example, if your man is more communicative, you might write, "He's talking more in the morning" or "He's letting me know if he's going to work late." Be specific.

4. "What have I been doing differently that may have triggered a better response in him?"

_____

_____

_____

_____

This is one of the most important questions for you to answer. You need to know what it is about your actions that has prompted change in your partner. Over the past few days or weeks, I'm certain you've been noticing what you've been doing that works with your man, but now I want you to make note of it for a couple of reasons.

The first is that once you know what works, you know what you need to do to keep the changes going. I'm going to tell you a lot more about that in a little while, but for now, know that the key to continued improvement is doing more of what works. Second, since there undoubtedly will be times in your life when you get sidetracked, having a list of solutions to which you can always refer can really make a big difference. I often encourage women to keep a solution journal—a diary in which they record daily everything they do that works—for that very reason. You might consider doing the same thing.

When you respond to the question "What have I been doing differently that may have triggered a better response in him?" make sure you isolate which of *your actions* deserve credit. Granted, there are factors beyond our own actions that influence our partners. However, if you assume that all of his changes are due to mental telepathy or to things beyond your control, you might as well hang it up. I'm telling you that you affect him. I'm convinced that if your partner has changed since you've been reading this book, it's not a coincidence, my dear. Your behavior is a big part of the reason he's different. So, whatever you do, don't attribute the improvements you see to balmy weather, a good hair day, or mind reading. Focus on your own actions.

5. "How have these changes in both of us impacted on our relationship? What have we been doing differently as a couple?"

_____

_____

_____

_____

Now's your chance to really investigate how all the changes, big and small, have spilled over into other areas of your life, making your relationship, family life, work, and free time more enjoyable.

For example, one woman told me that once she was able to enlist her husband's help around the house, her resentment vanished. She felt more loving toward him and was more affectionate. Their sex life improved, and she noticed that he was making more of an effort to communicate regularly with her. This pleased her no end. Their getting along better allowed her to feel more confident at work, and she noticed she was achieving more of her career goals.

In addition to the increased communication and improved sex life, she became aware that they were spending more time together, doing many of the things they used to do in the past, such as biking and hiking and playing tennis. These activities further solidified the positive feelings between them.

In this example, you can see how putting an end to the chore war had far-reaching effects on their relationship. My goal in asking you the previous question is to help you see similar positive patterns in your relationship.

Now that you have a clearer idea of what's better and how you got it that way, it will be useful for you to know what you need to do to keep these improvements going. Well, it's pretty obvious, isn't it? You've got to keep doing what works.

Doing More of What Works

Remember my mantra "If it works, don't fix it"? Good. Because that's exactly what you need to do. If things have been better between you and your man, you've made them that way and you have to keep going. You can't get complacent or go back to "the old you" or rest on your laurels, because if you do, your partner will regress, too. He'll go back to "the old him."

Let me say this loudly and clearly. The reason—and the only reason—your man has changed for the better is that you've changed for the smarter. You've been more productive in how you approach him. Your actions have helped to make him look good. Stop taking those actions and he'll stop looking so good. I promise you. It's not a coincidence that he's been coming around. You've been taking the lead. You have to keep leading.

Everyone knows that you can't expect to lose weight simply by dieting hard for a few days or even a few weeks. If you want to lose weight, you have to make good eating habits a way of life. Similarly, you wouldn't be foolish enough to expect your car to drive forever on one tank of gas or without regular maintenance checks. If you want reliable transportation, you have to pay attention to your car while it's in working condition. The best way to maintain the loving feelings between you and your man is to make a promise to yourself that you'll continue to be diligent about doing what works when things are working. Preventing problems is a lot easier than fixing them when they occur.

Nervous Is Natural

Many women tell me that they're really apprehensive about the good things lasting. They worry that their partners will revert to bad habits or that they, themselves, will have a hard time remaining solution-oriented. This is entirely natural.

If you're fearful that your partner's changes are only temporary, there's a good reason for it. When your relationship was rocky, you built a wall around yourself. That wall protected you. It prevented you from feeling too much hurt when your partner disappointed you. However, I told you earlier in this book that having a wall around you has its price. Although the wall kept out the pain, it was also impervious to feelings of love and joy. So it kept you at arm's length from truly being close to your partner.

As your relationship improved, the wall began to crumble. Feelings of love have been creeping in again. Although these wonderful feelings are long-awaited, you can't help but notice a gnawing sense of vulnerability. "What if he backslides?" "What if he starts criticizing again?" "What happens if all the progress we've been making goes right out the window?" "How will I survive the disappointment?" A sense of cautiousness permeates your life.

Just as the wall has both benefits and disadvantages, so, too, does caution. From a positive standpoint, a healthy dose of caution prevents you from taking the improvements for granted. It forces you to keep a close eye on how things are going and makes you more diligent about not allowing minor setbacks to spread insidiously.

On the other hand, caution can turn you into a pessimist. You may constantly be waiting for the other shoe to drop. You may start to expect your man to go back to his old ways, and when you do, you'll start acting differently toward him. Your skepticism may actually precipitate the negative self-fulfilling prophecy I've warned you about so many times in this book.

If you're someone who believes it's better to expect the worst than to be disappointed, that's fine, if you're only anticipating rain on the day of a family hike or a loss when playing blackjack. But it's really not a great philosophy when you're involved in the man-changing business. It's too big a gamble. Norman Cousins said,

"We fear the worst, we expect the worst, we invite the worst." So be cautious, but keep it in check. Know that your cautiousness is a means of self-protection, not necessarily an accurate view of reality. Be cautious about your cautiousness.

Maybe you're less worried about your man reverting to his old ways than you are about yourself. Perhaps you wonder if you can keep up what you've been doing right. If so, let me allay your fears. Your self-doubt will pass with time. Now, when you stop yourself from doing more of the same, it feels as if it requires super-human strength and concentration. That's because being solution-oriented and avoiding knee-jerk responses are new to you. It's still hard to do sometimes. No wonder you question how long you can stay focused.

But let me remind you that learning any new skill—like learning how to ride a bike—requires intense concentration at first. With practice, you don't have to concentrate at all. Your ability to keep your equilibrium becomes a given.

Thankfully, the process of being solution-oriented unfolds in much the same way. Eventually, doing what works becomes a habit. And when being solution-oriented starts to feel more natural to you, your confidence grows. You start feeling more assured that you will do *your* part in keeping the changes going. When *you* feel more convinced that *you'll* stay on track, you'll be less concerned about your man because you'll know that no matter what he does, you'll be able to point your relationship in the right direction. When that happens, you'll begin to relax and enjoy the fruits of your labor. So, take a deep breath, harvesttime is right around the corner.

Expect Bumps in the Road

Maybe you couldn't identify with the women I described who worry about staying on track. You may be someone who assumes that once things improve, life will be smooth sailing from that day forward. Let me shatter that fantasy right now. No matter how great things become between you and your partner, you're bound to hit speed bumps along the road at some point or another. It's the nature of the beast. Try as you may, there's nothing you can do to completely eliminate conflict from your lives. It just won't happen. Your man is bound to have a bad day now and then, and so are you.

Getting off track, in and of itself, is not a problem. Getting bent out of shape about it, however, is a *big* problem. If you get upset about the bad times, it will prevent you from doing what you need to do to get things back on track. You'll be so busy either blaming yourself or your man that you will forget to be your old solution-oriented self. Feeling bad about minor setbacks clogs your thinking.

Instead of allowing bad feelings to misguide you, you need to say to yourself, "Oh, well, things didn't go as well as I had hoped today. Tomorrow's another day" or "Boy, I really handled that situation badly, but I'm sure I'll have another crack at it later in the evening." You need to forgive yourself and move on. You have to give yourself permission to screw up once in a while. If you don't, you run the risk of getting so despondent about every mistake you make, you may feel like giving up for a while. You may allow your mistakes to set you in a tailspin. Don't do that to yourself!

No matter how hard you work at this thing, you, your partner, and your relationship will never be perfect. If you ever find a way to achieve perfection, honey, please write me because I want you to be my mentor. But even though you'll never achieve perfection, you can make a decision that will truly change your life forever. Promise yourself that from now on, whenever there's a setback of any sort, you'll approach it with a spirit of curiosity and experimentation. Try to determine, as quickly as you can, what you can do to set things back on course. Get up and get back on that horse.

I once worked with a guy who was an incredibly skilled golfer. When I asked him the secret of his success, he said, "I learned how to leave my disappointment about playing badly at the hole where I got it. I look at each hole as a new start." If you play any sport at all, you can probably appreciate what an accomplishment it is to leave bad feelings behind and concentrate on each play. No wonder he was so good.

Now you have to do the same thing. If you get off track in the morning, don't say, "What's the use?" and blow the rest of the day. If you have a bad day, don't allow your frustration to make you lackadaisical in the evening or in the days that follow. If you and your partner are edgy all week, look at the weekend as being an opportunity to start anew. Every moment offers a new chance to start with a clean slate. Don't ever forget that.

Look, I've never been more convinced about anything than what I'm about to tell you. What separates the winners from the losers in life isn't whether or not they get sidetracked, it's what they do about it once they do get sidetracked. When winners get off track from their goals—whether it's great relationships, weight loss, or career success—they get back on track without skipping a beat. Even if you've failed to keep the good things going in your relationship in the past, it can be different now. You can be a winner this time. Expect the bumps in the road but remember that you have great suspension.

Successful Man-Changers Are Good Planners

One way to negotiate the road bumps is to be able to predict when they might occur. If you're driving and you see a road sign, "Bump Ahead," you have a chance to maneuver around it or, at the very least, slow down. You can develop a plan. The same is true in relationships. If you spend some time identifying when and where the potential bumps might occur, you'll be prepared to deal with them when they're upon you.

Perhaps you're wondering why I'm asking you to predict potential bumps in the road, because earlier in this chapter I said that you shouldn't expect failure. There's a difference between expecting failure and expecting challenges. Expecting challenges is a good thing because life is full of them. Your car will break down occasionally, your husband will be grouchy once in a while, your boss will overload you with work, your kids will spill ketchup on your new carpeting, someone you know will become ill. Those things will happen. You can count on it. But you have a choice as to how you will handle those situations. If you focus on solutions when you hit the speed bumps, you'll stay on track. On the other hand, if you expect failure, you're predicting that you and/or your partner will resort to dysfunctional methods to handle life's inevitable ups and downs, and that, my friend, is not a good thing. And you already know why.

The bottom line is that as long as you anticipate what's ahead and arm yourself with a plan, you're actually preventing problems. So keep your eye on the road and look for the warning signs.

Below are a few more questions by Steve de Shazer designed to help you predict the challenges you might encounter. Ask yourself,

> 1. "What, if anything, might pop up in the next week or two that would present a challenge to either me or my partner, making it difficult for us to stick with the positive changes?"

_____
_____
_____
_____

Perhaps you and your partner experienced positive changes in the past, but something happened that made it really hard to stay focused. It's fair to assume that if something tested your resolve to stay on track in the past, it will probably be just as challenging if it occurs in the future. For example, in response to this question, one woman said, "I'm expecting my mother-in-law to stay with us for several weeks starting next week, and things always seem to go downhill when that happens." Another responded, "My husband is just about to quit smoking, and I know he gets really tense at night. It will be hard to stay on track in the next few days." A third woman told me, "I have a very important presentation to give at work in two weeks, and as that time draws near, I'm positive that I'll be preoccupied and nervous. That will make it more challenging for me to continue doing what works."

Think about your own life. Can you think of any particular stressor that might take place in the next few weeks that will test your resolve to stay on track? Do you have to make an important decision together about an emotional subject? Are you anticipating PMS? Is an out-of-town trip going to throw you off center? Really give this question some concentrated thought. Then ask yourself,

2. "How will I handle that situation differently this time?"

_____

_____

_____

_____

The next time you're confronted with a trying situation, think about how you will handle it differently. What would you have to do for your man to notice you're doing something different in re-sponse to an old trigger? As you answer this question, be creative and don't forget your sense of humor.

Okay. Now you've identified the positive changes in your relation-ship and how you've gotten them to happen. You've even identified potential challenges in the weeks ahead and how you might deal with those challenges. That means you have a pretty good idea about what you need to do to keep it up, that is, keep those changes going.

But what if you're not where you want to be yet? What if, after taking a closer look at how far you've come, you realize that you still have a way to go to reach your goal. Now would be a really good time to review your answers to the questions in chapter 4, the goal-setting chapter. I'm going to help you determine what you need to do next to get to your destination. Go back to questions 1 and 2 of this chapter. That's where I asked you to rate, on a 1-to-10 scale, where things were when you started and where they are right now. Compare those answers with your responses to the following questions.

Given your progress and knowing that relationships are never perfect, ask yourself,

3. "Where on the scale would I need to be to feel satis-fied?"

_____

Where on that scale would you have to be to wake up in the morning and say to yourself, "We still have occasional ups and downs, but I am really happy. If things were to stay this way, I could certainly live with that."

Assuming you're not quite where you need to be yet, ask yourself,

> 4. "What are one or two things that I could do or that could happen in my relationship to raise my score a half step higher on that scale?"

_____

_____

_____

_____

There are two things I want to point out about this question. The first is this: I've talked many times about the importance of breaking your goals into small, achievable steps. That's why I'm interested in knowing what would have to happen for you to rate your relationship "a half step higher on that scale." I realize that, even when you achieve that minigoal, you still might not have accomplished your end goal. That's fine. With each sign of progress, you keep asking yourself question 9 over and over until you get where you want to be. Let me give you an example.

Imagine for a moment that you were at a "3" when you started on your man-changing journey, and because of your efforts, you're now at a "7." And, let's say that in order for you to feel satisfied, you want to be at a "9." Fair enough. So, the first step is to ask yourself, "What are one or two things that could happen that would bring me up from a '7' to a '7½' or an '8'?" And once you do those things and achieve your minigoal, you should ask yourself the very same question again, "What are one or two things that could happen that would bring me up from an '8' to an '8½' or a '9'?" Take one step at a time.

Second, in response to this question, some women identify what *they* would need to do in order to feel there's improvement in the relationship. For instance, one woman said, "Things are going well, but I will feel better about us when I can say no to him and not get a knot in my stomach. Instead, I will feel confident that saying no is okay." Another responded, "For things to improve even more, I would need to be able to feel more secure about his love when he goes out of town. I'll know I'm doing better when I don't sit by the phone when he's gone."

Other women identify what *their partners* would need to do for there to be further improvement. For example, one woman said, "Our relationship will move to the next level when he says, 'I love you,' again. I need to hear the words." Another woman said, "I'll feel better when we start making love again." Still another response: "Our relationship will go from '7' to an '8' when my husband starts to keep the promises he made to me about helping with the kids."

If, in the previous question, you were able to identify what you need to do to move to the next level in your relationship, then make a commitment to yourself to start doing those things. You'll feel great about yourself when you do. If, on the other hand, instead of identifying a task for you, you identified something your man has to do, then ask yourself,

> 5. "What would *I* have to do to make *his* doing that more likely?"
>
> _____
> _____
>
> _____

Throughout this book, I have made it clear that you can prompt positive behavior in your partner through your own actions. If you want him to be more thoughtful, what do you have to do to inspire him to be that way? If you want him to say, "I love you," under what conditions is he more likely to do that? If you yearn to make love with your man, what do you have to do to get him in the mood? If you push the right buttons, you increase the odds that he'll do exactly what you want him to do.

Change Is Like a Zigzag Rather Than a Straight Line

So now you know what to do to get it up and keep it up. Good for you. I want you to know that most people who can get it up can keep it up. You should find that encouraging. I know I do. I have faith in you. There's absolutely no reason that you can't maintain these changes in your relationship. You can make being solution-oriented a permanent way of life. But there's one more thing I want to tell you about the process of change before you move on to the next chapter.

Change is like a zigzag rather than a straight line. You already know that no matter how swell things are going, there are going to be off days once in a while. But that's not what I'm talking about here when I say that change is like a zigzag. Authors James Prochaska, John Norcross, and Carlo Diclemente describe this zigzag process in their book *Changing for Good*.

They suggest that there are six stages people go through as they make real changes in their lives: precontemplation, contemplation, preparation, action, maintenance, and termination. When people are in the precontemplation stage, they can't see the problem. They're in denial. In the contemplation stage, people acknowledge the problem and start thinking about doing something to change. People who are in the preparation stage still feel some ambivalence about changing but start making definite plans to take action. In the action stage, people finally do what they've been planning to do. In the maintenance stage, people try to solidify gains and prevent relapse. In the termination stage, people feel no apprehension about going back to old ways.

These authors suggest that even after making significant changes in their lives and maintaining those changes over time, it is not uncommon for people to stop doing what works for a while and return to previous stages before taking positive action again. For example, they say that most people who eventually give up smoking undergo three or four serious attempts before they actually achieve their goal.

I tell you this not to discourage you or make you feel bad—I would never want to do that. I tell you this because I want you to know that real change, the kind that sticks, is three steps forward and two steps back. And sometimes five or six steps backward. The important thing to remember is that even if you take a significant step backward, going back to square one the second or third time is *very different* from being there the first time.

No two setbacks are alike. Time one is not time two. After a taste of success, you're not the same person you were before. You've gained new knowledge and skills. You have more confidence. You've had glimpses of what it feels like to get the love you want from your partner. You will get back on track because the machinery to be solution-oriented is well greased.

Let me give you an example from my own life. As you know, Jim and I have been together for many, many years. And although we argue from time to time, our relationship is so much better now than it was long ago. Back then, our arguments were incredibly hurtful, and the fallout from those fights would linger for days, sometimes weeks. Now we don't do that anymore. If we fight, we fight, but generally within twenty-four hours, it's over. And there's usually an apology to boot.

Lord knows, we didn't get here overnight. In fact, there were many times, after long peaceful periods, that I thought we were "cured." I thought we were done with our ugly fights. But I was wrong. We went back there many times before we stopped completely. But the peaceful times got longer and the ugly times got shorter. And our determination to stay clear of the unhappiness became more resolute. And now I can honestly say that those unhappy days are gone for good. I truly think we've forgotten how to get there.

So, if you find yourself going back to square one or square two just when you thought you had a particular problem completely licked, know that you're zigging at the moment and that in no time at all you'll do what it takes to start zagging again.

The next chapter, "The Immovable Man," is for women whose partners have managed to do whatever they can to resist change. Obviously, that's not you. However, you might want to read the chapter anyway, because on those days when you're zigging, you'll need all the help you can get.

CHAPTER ELEVEN

The Immovable Man

Is your partner an immovable man? After all you've been doing to effect change in your relationship, is he still resistant, unbending, and inflexible? Does he still tune you out or veg out in front of the television, or refuse to assume more responsibility in your home or with your children? Has he made it clear to you that, no matter how you approach him, nothing will change him? Well, I'm going to help you figure out why you haven't gotten the results you've been hoping for and, even more important, what you can do about it.

Without knowing you and your partner personally, it's hard to decipher the precise reason your man has resisted your efforts to change him. However, after years of working with change-resistant men and the women who love them, I can tell you that there are some definite patterns. As you read these common scenarios, think about which one(s) might apply to your situation. Some of the ideas will sound familiar to you because they are reviews of basic concepts discussed throughout the book. I just want you to double-check if you've forgotten something.

Immovable Isn't Immovable

Sometimes, your man may not be as resistant as he seems. If you're desperate for major changes in your relationship, it's easy to make the mistake of overlooking small improvements. This is completely understandable because the teeny steps forward may not feel like much. But as I told you in chapter 6, if you want your man to make a hefty change in his life, you have to shape his behavior, one step at a time. If his efforts are overlooked, he won't know when he's on track. And if he doesn't know when he's on track, he ain't gonna get to the end of the line. Let me give you an example.

Deb wanted her husband, Joe, to have more faith in her ability to manage money. Because she was a stay-at-home mom, Deb had no income of her own and resented having to ask Joe for money every time she needed it. Joe paid all the bills and had complete control of the family income. They argued a great deal about how money should be spent and who had the authority to make those decisions. She urged him to allow her to pay the bills and manage the family money for a while. She also wanted to have her own account so that she didn't have to ask Joe for money.

In the weeks that followed, Joe did not undergo a major transformation in regard to his need to control money. He continued to pay bills and debated Deb about how their money should be spent. However, there was one concession. Deb set up her own account and received a monthly allowance, thereby preventing her from having to ask Joe for money. While she thought this arrangement was somewhat more tenable, she was still unhappy about Joe's controlling attitude about money. Therefore, although he went along with one of her suggestions, she said nothing about it to him. He was upset that she didn't recognize his efforts to please her, and their arguments about money escalated.

Truth be told, if I were in Deb's shoes, I wouldn't be happy, either. No one likes to feel controlled. Joe wasn't demonstrating his respect for her as an equal partner. Having said that, though, he did go along with one of her suggestions, and for that he should be acknowledged. I know it's hard to give someone credit for making small changes when what's needed is a major overhaul. But that's precisely what you need to do. Deb needs to make it clear to Joe that he's taken a step in the right direction and that she appreciates it. That's the most efficient way to get him to make further, more fundamental, changes in his controlling outlook.

Now let's go back to your situation. Think back over the last few days or weeks and see if you've missed anything worthy of your attention. Since you've been applying the ideas in this book, has your man changed anything about himself, anything at all? Be honest. If he did, did you cheer him on?

Most important, if the relationship pattern between you and your partner has been long-standing—he disappoints you and you nag about it—it will be just as challenging for you to break away from your negative mind-set as it is for him to change. You need to switch gears and positively reinforce his baby steps forward, even if, in your mind, he doesn't deserve it. I realize that it's challenging to reinforce the small improvements, particularly when you feel your partner should know better in the first place or that his efforts are a drop in the bucket. But this book is about rising above your feelings and doing what works. That's what I always want you to keep in mind. So, if after thinking about it you realize that your man has made some minor changes, it's never too late to let him know he's getting warmer—even if he doesn't gratefully accept your acknowledgment.

Impatience Isn't a Virtue

Women often get so excited by the upbeat tone of my enthusiasm that they expect to see instant results. However, change sometimes takes a bit more time. Certain men are more set in their ways than others.

Many women make the mistake of trying a particular strategy for a day or two, and if they see no positive results, they quit. They might move on to something else, or they might just say to themselves, "This isn't going to work," and go back to their old ways. Impatience gets the better of them. Does that sound familiar?

Look, I know I've been telling you that if it doesn't work, do something different, but you first need to make certain that you've given whatever you're doing enough time to do its job. So now you're probably wondering, "How much time is enough time?" Although the answer varies from situation to situation, I'm going to try to give you some general guidelines.

When you experiment with a new technique, you might not get an immediate response from your partner. It may take a few days for him to come around. In fact, you might have to use that same technique several times in a row to see if it's going to work. Advertisers have figured out that most buyers need to see a commercial 2.2 times to pick up the phone or pull out their wallets. Maybe the same philosophy applies to man-changing. The point is, don't abandon ship prematurely.

As a general rule of thumb, try a technique for a period of two weeks and then evaluate the results. Mark your calendar for a two-week period and then let 'er rip. If you're still uncertain as to the value of something you're doing, try it a little longer. But if you don't get good results very quickly after that, it's time for you to switch gears and try something else.

Think over the last few weeks. Did you dabble with a variety of strategies, never giving any particular strategy a fair shake? Regardless of how eager you are to have change in your life, you still have to be methodical about the whole thing. If you're not, you'll never know what works with your man and what doesn't. So, take a deep breath, go back to technique chapters 7, 8, and 9, and start experimenting slowly and systematically. It's the only way to go. One last point here. If, after you try something new, things appear to get worse, by all means STOP DOING IT. You don't need two weeks to convince yourself that making things worse is a bad thing. However, there is one exception worth mentioning.

Sometimes, when you set out to change your man, he might respond negatively. He may challenge you, become unpleasant, or even avoid you. You might think that your efforts to change him are really making matters worse, and from a temporary perspective, they are. However, some women report that after an initial balking stage, their men settle down and become more cooperative. This is another reason for sticking with your approach a little longer just to see if your man's unpleasant responses are simply temporary growing pains. As a rule, the more controlling your man is, the more likely he is to initially bristle at your efforts toward change.

Different Isn't Different Enough

Some women get stuck because, when what they're doing isn't working, they try something different, but it isn't different enough.

Dot is a good example of this. She had a pet peeve: her husband consistently left his shoes all over the house. If you were to ask Dot, she would tell you that she's tried everything to get him to be less forgetful about his shoes and to take her feelings into consideration. Nothing worked. I asked Dot, "What have you tried?" and she replied, "I asked him politely to remember to put his shoes in the closet where they belong. I've reminded him to move his shoes when they were in my way. I've pleaded with him to be more considerate of my feelings. I've left notes for him around the house. I've even sent him a fax at work telling him how frustrated I've been about the whole thing. Nothing has even made a dent."

Although I thought that Dot was very resourceful and creative, I couldn't help but notice that all of her strategies had one thing in common—words. I gave her a lot of credit for trying the written word when talking and begging and nagging didn't work, but I couldn't help but be curious as to how her husband would respond if she abandoned words entirely. So I suggested that she give it a shot.

Every night when he came home from work, Dot strategically placed two or three pairs of shoes in the entryhall. This way, he had to notice that they were there. In fact, if he didn't notice, he would trip on them. Dot wasn't totally averse to this outcome. In a matter of three days and one near fall, Dot's husband got the message. His shoes magically found their way to his closet.

Becoming more action-oriented isn't the only way to be "different enough." Remember the technique Do a 180°? That's when you do the complete opposite of what you've been doing if you haven't gotten the results you're after. That's about as different as you can get. If you've been stuck for a while and you're wondering whether your new approach is different enough, you might consider doing a 180°. Review the last chapter to refresh your memory if you're not quite sure what you need to do. Let me give you an example.

Cathy is a single woman who very much wants to be married. She is involved with a man who is reluctant to make a commitment. Over the past few months, Cathy pressured him to step up to the plate. The more she pressured, the more her boyfriend backed away from her. Out of desperation, she decided to do something different. She promised herself that for the next two months, she would say absolutely nothing about marriage to her man. At the end of this two-month period, Cathy noticed that they fought less but absolutely nothing changed in regard to the status of their relationship. She was devastated and ready to throw in the towel.

After thinking about her situation a bit more thoroughly, Cathy realized that her restraining herself from complaining about their relationship might not have been different enough. It was entirely possible that her boyfriend might have thought she was taking a breather, and it was just a matter of time before she started in on him again. When she realized that, she decided to do a 180°. They went out for dinner one evening, and she told him that after thinking about it long and hard, she decided that it was time for her to date other men. She said that she realized he wasn't interested in making a commitment, and she thanked him for being honest with her. "At first," she said, "I couldn't understand why you wouldn't want to share your life only with me, but the more I got to thinking about it, the more I realized that making a lifelong commitment is a really big deal and you'd better be damn sure of what you're doing. I figured out that I'm as unsure as you, and so I encourage you to go slowly and take your time because I need to do the same thing."

Much to her surprise, her man didn't like the idea that she wasn't certain of her feelings for him. He liked even less that she was considering playing the field. But it didn't take long for him to start pursuing her like crazy—wanting to spend more time together, planning special dates, sending her cards, and calling her more often. Cathy sensed he was about to pop the question. But the strangest thing happened.

The more he pursued her, the more she doubted whether he was the right man for her after all. Once she started dating other men again, she remembered that she had other options. When I stopped seeing Cathy, she was still uncertain as to what she was going to do about her relationship, but she learned an incredibly valuable lesson nonetheless. In her opinion, doing a 180° is a technique every woman should know. She's right.

Your Heart Wasn't in It

Sometimes, when women put the techniques to work, their efforts are halfhearted. There are a couple of reasons for this. The first is that some women have a hard time believing that their new approach can work. The old tapes continue to play in their heads: "I know he'll never change" or "I can't imagine how anything I do will make a difference." If these are the thoughts you're still thinking, it's hard to put your heart into what you're doing. You have one foot in solution land and another in the land of doubt. Believe me, your man will be very good at reading your uncertainty. He might think you don't really mean what you're saying or that your actions are a fluke. He will discount anything you say or do—which may explain why he isn't coming around.

In addition, if you've never tried these methods before, it will be hard for you to have confidence in them. If, over the past few weeks, you've had nagging doubts about the effectiveness of your approach, reread the technique in chapter 8, Act As If. . . . Imagine how you would approach your man differently if you had a great deal of confidence that what you're doing will work. Then do that and notice the results.

Another reason women don't put their hearts into their man-changing strategies is that they're not 100 percent comfortable with them. If you're new to these techniques, you're probably going to have some level of discomfort with them. That's only natural. But that's not what I'm talking about here. Some women are downright uncomfortable with certain techniques because they're unconventional.

For example, if you decide to do a 180°, it might require encouraging your husband, who's staying out later than you would like with his buddies, to stay out even later. That's counterintuitive, and some women are uneasy about it. That's fine. I told you that you'll find some techniques more appealing than others. Let me say it one more time—if a particular technique doesn't feel right to you, don't do it. If you do, you'll probably come across as insincere. If that happens, whatever you're doing won't work. Your man will see right through you and react in his usual way. So don't waste your energy. Unless you can really get behind a method I've outlined, it's not going to be effective.

Does any of this ring true for you? Have you been trying a particular technique but feeling that it's not completely right for you? If you're unsure, quit doing it. There are many more techniques from which you can choose. Find one that feels comfortable to you and do that instead. When you feel in sync with your actions, you'll exude confidence about your ability to change your man, and that will work wonders.

It Doesn't Work If You Don't Do It

Sometimes women tell me, "Things improved for a while, but then the techniques stopped working." When I heard this complaint as a rookie therapist, I scrambled to help my clients think of new things to try. But eventually I got wiser. I finally figured out that it wasn't that the techniques hadn't been working, it was that my clients had stopped *using* the techniques. After they noticed some improvement, they slacked off and so did the progress.

Back to you for a moment. Although you're feeling frustrated that you're not making progress right now, was there a time a few days or weeks ago when you had even a small taste of progress? If so, that's great news, because it tells you that you were on the right track. Now I don't know why you stopped doing what you were doing, but it really doesn't matter, does it? The only thing that matters is that you start doing it again.

Here's a classic situation I encountered when I worked with adolescents and their families. There was an out-of-control teenager with parents who had a hard time setting limits. Once the parents decided to exert more control at home, the teenager complied. Then, as he started being more cooperative, the parents relaxed their rules and the teenager started taking advantage of them again. Although I could see why the parents might have felt "nothing is working" when their son started acting out again, it was even easier for me to see what they needed to do about it. So take a lesson from these parents. If you saw any positive change in your man at all, go back to your more effective approach and stick with it this time.

When Fixing Things Becomes a Problem

When it comes to your relationship, is your motto "Never stop trying"? Are you someone who keeps working on your relationship issues no matter how uninvested your man seems to be? Are you up on all the latest relationship enhancement courses, tapes, books, and therapy? Do you cut out articles from magazines with tips on how couples can get along better and give them to your man? Has fixing your relationship become your full-time job?

Well, first I want to tell you that I admire your dedication. I think the world needs more people with your spirit and persistence. Having said that, I also want to remind you of a seesaw and the Do Nothing technique, one last time. Remember, the more you do of something, the less your partner will do. Well, here's the bad news. If you and your man have fallen into the roles of The Fixer and The Dodger, you're in big trouble. He's come to expect you to be the one who takes all the responsibility for making things right in your relationship. And if you do, you're creating space in the universe for him to do nothing. You become a fix-it addict and he checks out. In extreme cases, regardless of *what* you do to fix things, your simply taking the initiative to repair your relationship becomes "more of the same." If that's the case, there is only one sane thing for you to do and that's *stop fixing things*, at least for a while. To get him to be a more responsible partner, you have to back off for the time being. Let him take the lead.

Now I know that this is easier said than done because you've been in the habit of taking care of your relationship. But research tells us that the easiest way to break a bad habit is to substitute the undesirable behavior with a desirable one. That's why when smokers quit smoking, they often do something else with their mouths—chew gum or drink pop, for example. So the best way for you to stop fixing your relationship is to stop thinking about it. And the best way to stop thinking about your man is to think about other things. Get a life. Get involved. Go do something you've never done before that will really require your full attention. Change the focus in your life for a while.

I know what you're thinking: "This won't make a difference be-

cause he won't even notice. He'll just be glad that I'm off his back."
You may be right. But, then, on the other hand, you may be wrong.
My guess is that you've never backed off long enough to know. You
may have experimented for a few days, but when you saw no results, you started harping on him again. I'm telling you that if
you're a fix-it addict, your man won't notice that you've backed off
until you're truly invested in something else. You can't fake it.
Once you apply the same level of commitment to something else in
your life, your man will finally figure out that the roles have
changed in your relationship and that if something needs fixing,
he's going to have to do it. And that's where you want him to be.

So, be honest with yourself. Are you *always* the one to suggest relationship repair at the expense of your own needs? If so, perhaps
in your more reflective moments, you've had some crazy ideas
about things you'd like to do in your life that you've put off for one
reason or another. If the things on your wish list are not illegal, im-
moral, or too expensive, go for it. Stop trying to change your man
for a while. You can always go back to your fix-it job later if you
want to. You don't have to worry about anyone else filling your position in your absence. That won't happen. It doesn't pay well
enough.

One last thought about fix-it addicts. Being a fix-it addict is
never a great thing, but there is an extreme situation in which being a fix-it addict can have absolutely disastrous results. If your
partner has told you that he is no longer interested in your relationship and appears to have half a foot out the door, the worst
thing you can do is keep pursuing him, even if it feels natural to
you. I can guarantee that if your relationship is really shaky and you
keep pursuing your reticent man, you might as well say good-bye
to him. It will be over.

No matter how desperate you feel, you have to stop trying to
convince him to stay. You have to stop reminding him how great
your relationship once was. You have to quit telling him that the
children will suffer if you divorce. You must abstain from begging
him to give things one last try. The more you long for your relationship, the less your man will. The more you try to piece it back
together, the less your man will. If you're pushy, the only thing

he'll be thinking about is how to get away from you. He won't think back wistfully about the good times you shared. He'll be thinking of ways to dodge you.

So, you have to stop the chase. But that's not all. In addition to stopping the chase, you have to try the Last Resort technique. The Last Resort technique requires that you do the biggest 180° you've ever done in your life. Extreme situations call for extreme interventions. Here's what you have to do.

Ask yourself, "Given my desperate behavior during the last few weeks or months, what would I have to do to get my man's attention? What would really be out of character for me right now?" When I ask women this question, they say things like "Every time he comes to pick up his mail, I try to lure him in the house and I start crying about our situation. I'm always so depressed. I guess if I seemed happier, like the old me, that would make him wonder what's going on. Also, if I weren't waiting around for him to come over or call, he would be very surprised. It would amaze him if my answering machine picked up, because he believes that he's the center of my universe and, other than him, I have no life." Other women say, "If I told him that, after thinking about it, this separation is really turning out to be a good thing for me, that would blow his mind," or "If I started dating again, I know that would shock him."

Perhaps some of these examples click with you. Maybe not. In any case, think about your situation. Identify what you would have to do to get your man's attention. Give him the impression that you've decided to move on in your life (even if you haven't). And then watch the results. If it works, you have to keep it up until your man is firmly back in your life. If you start being too enthusiastic about his change of heart, he'll develop buyer's remorse, that is, he'll second-guess himself. So keep acting "cool" for a while.

I truly hope that the change you want your man to make doesn't have anything to do with his commitment to you because it's very painful when someone questions his love for you. But if your man is halfway out the door, give the Last Resort technique a try. It might just get him to change his mind. It doesn't always work, but if your guy hasn't left yet, it's definitely worth a shot.

Immovable Is Really Immovable

Let's face it, there are some men who are pros at defying every man-changing strategy in the world. You may be married to or in a relationship with one of them. He may be the guy who holds steadfast no matter how creatively you try to modify his behavior. Perhaps you've asked yourself, "Why isn't he responding to what I'm doing?" or "Why is he so stubborn?" There are lots of reasons some men don't change, and because I'm not big on explanations for why people stay stuck, I'll leave the hypothesizing to you. But there is one exception we need to address before talking about what to do with the immovable man.

Some men defy change because they're involved with serious, deeply entrenched problems such as a propensity toward violence or severe substance abuse. If you are involved with a man who has been physically violent, you must seek professional help immediately. Physical abuse should never be tolerated. If your partner does not recognize the problem and isn't willing to get help, you must remove yourself—and your children, if you have them—from the threat of violence. Do not go another day without getting some assistance with this problem. There can be no fundamental changes in your relationship until your man takes full responsibility for changing himself, his attitude, and his actions.

In regard to substance abuse, I once heard a specialist in that field, Duncan Stanton, discuss what he tells women who are married to chronic substance abusers, women who have tried everything to get their husbands to stop abusing drugs, to no avail. He tells them that they basically have three choices. They can continue what they're doing and be miserable for the rest of their lives, they can leave their marriages, or they can develop a Zen-like detachment from their partner's drinking or drug problem. Since the meaning of first two is fairly obvious, let me explain the third option a bit more.

Women who live with substance abusers often make their partners' problem their problem. They nag incessantly, they cover for their partners when they act irresponsibly, they hide alcohol in an attempt to limit their partner's drinking, and so on. In short, getting the abuser to stop using becomes an addiction in itself. It's easy to understand how this happens because when one person abuses substances, it truly affects the whole family. Nothing is more painful. But allowing one's life to be totally consumed by someone else's failure to act responsibly is a waste of life. It doesn't work. As with the physically violent man, unless the substance abuser is ready to acknowledge the problem and take responsibility for becoming sober or drug-free, there's not much you can do to get him to stop. So if you're committed to staying in the relationship, then detaching yourself from your partner's problem is certainly a good option. But what does this mean?

It means that you will no longer take responsibility for his behavior. You will not try to rescue him. You will allow him to suffer the natural consequences that drunkenness brings. In essence, you allow alcoholism to be *his* problem and go on with your life. Some women need support to detach and often go to programs such as Al-Anon. Others do it on their own. Either way, women who are able to detach themselves emotionally from their partners' problems say that it is truly freeing. They feel much better about themselves and their lives in general.

But what if your man isn't a substance abuser or physically abusive, but he stubbornly resists change nonetheless? What can you do about it? For starters, if you haven't done it already, it's a good idea to talk to other people in your life about what you're going through. Sometimes two heads are better than one. Someone—a relative, friend, or your clergy—might have some additional ideas about what you can do. If you're a private person, I know it can be hard to open up with others, but you should do it anyway. People who love you, especially people in loving relationships, can be great problem-solving resources. But beware of the person who does nothing more than take your side and condemn your man. As I told you earlier, this support might feel good for a short while, but it will only fuel your negative feelings and it won't provide you with solutions. So stay clear of that kind of advice.

Another option is that you can take a relationship skill-building course. In recent years, countless relationship seminars have been popping up all over the country. Some of these courses are affiliated with churches and synagogues, others are not. Many people get a lot out of these seminars and feel closer to their partners.

Some require the participation of both partners (which, in my opinion, is impractical), others do not. Local community colleges and mental health centers often sponsor these courses.

Another option is that you can enter therapy. A therapist may be able to help you brainstorm alternative ways of handling tough situations. Even if your man won't go, and he probably won't, you should go yourself. The therapist might be able to help you figure out what you're missing. But I have to tell you that I'm biased. If you opt to seek professional help, I suggest you go to a therapist who is goal-oriented and focuses on solutions rather than problems. There are many therapists all over the world who practice Solution-Oriented Brief Therapy. And I think that's a good place to start.

But what if you feel you've tried everything—followed the advice in this book, talked to others, taken courses, sought professional advice—and you've made no headway at all. Then what do you do? Well, I like my colleague Duncan Stanton's advice—you can keep doing what you're doing and be miserable or you can leave—*or* you can simply change your perspective so that you don't feel miserable anymore. I think this advice applies to any problematic relationship. Let's look at each option.

Keep Doing What Isn't Working and Be Miserable

Anyone in her right mind would say, "What, are you nuts? That's not a choice." But in reality, it is. You've probably made this choice many times in your life. I know I have. I just wasn't aware that it was a choice. It felt more like a reflex. But now you know that everything you do, every response you make, is a choice. I think that doing what isn't working and being miserable isn't such a great choice. But you decide for yourself.

Leave

If you're not married and you don't have children and you're incredibly miserable, leaving is an option. However, the decision to end a relationship should never be taken lightly. Since most endings are unilateral, they are very painful. You should make sure you leave no stone unturned before you go.

If you are married and have children, I think that you should avoid divorce if at all possible. If you're uncertain as to why I'm so adamant about this, please read my book *Divorce Busting*. If you're in a second or third marriage and you're reading this book, it tells me that you've learned one very important fact about relationships. All marriages have their challenges. Though 50 percent of first marriages end in divorce, the statistics are even higher for second marriages and subsequent marriages. My goal is to help women change their men so they won't have to keep changing partners.

But if your man won't change, it still doesn't mean that you have to leave or resign yourself to a life of misery. There's another option. Change *your* perspective. A new outlook on your man's resistance may be just what the doctor ordered. Here are two methods for getting a new perspective on your relationship.

Focus on the Good Parts

Your man may be unmotivated around the house, but he might be a fantastic provider. He may spend too much time with his friends, but he might be a super father. He might be really hard on you sometimes, but other times he's incredibly sensitive and loving. He might be controlling about money, but also be a wonderful lover. You get the point? Guys are package deals. There are some things you love about them and some things you hate. This is true of every man walking the face of the earth. (And, by the way, the same could be said of women.) You can trade in one man for another, thinking you're upgrading, but, in my opinion, you're just getting a whole new set of problems. In every relationship, there is good *and* there is bad. And I do mean *every* relationship.

While it makes sense to try to change what you don't like about your man, it also makes sense to stop obsessing about what won't change. Throughout this book, I've emphasized the very important point that what you focus on expands. If all you think about is your man's intractable bad habits, that will become your life. That's a crummy life, if you ask me. Instead, why not focus on his good qualities? Why not think about what he has to offer as a partner and cherish that instead? Why not appreciate his strengths?

I also want to point out that deciding to emphasize his strengths rather than his weaknesses doesn't mean that you will *like* the parts of him you find irritating. It doesn't mean you condone behavior you find annoying. It just means that you're not going to make an issue of it anymore because you've decided to accept the package deal. I truly believe that everyone in solid, long-term relationships faces this decision sometime in their lives. Why not make it now? Acceptance can turn an okay relationship into a truly great relationship.

When you let go of trying to change something about your man, it can be truly liberating. Feeling that you can control everything in life is an illusion, an illusion that can cripple you. When you drop the rope in the relationship tug-of-war, your life often takes wonderful twists and turns because you're no longer allowing his behavior to control how you feel and what you do. Freedom at last!

If the idea of focusing on the good and letting go of the bad sounds appealing but challenging, review chapter 7. That's where I talk about the importance of focusing on the strengths in your relationship. Rereading that chapter will motivate and inspire you to appreciate the man in your life even if he's not perfect.

See the Good in the Bad Parts

There's a story I heard about a poor old farmer. He was totally dependent on his horse for his family's livelihood. One day, due to a hole in his fence, the horse escaped. Knowing how much the farmer needed his horse, the people in the village came to his house to express their condolences: "This is terrible. This is awful. We're so sorry for your family." But the farmer replied, "You don't know this is terrible, you don't know this is awful. We'll see."

Several weeks later, the farmer was working the land by hand when he heard a familiar neighing. It was his horse. But to his amazement, his horse was not alone. It had led many other wild horses down from the mountain into the farmer's pasture. Learning of the news, the villagers visited the farmer and rejoiced. "We're so happy for you. This is wonderful. This is fantastic," but the farmer replied, "You don't know that this is wonderful. You don't know this is fantastic. We'll see," and the villagers left.

Several months later, the farmer's son, who was a talented and skilled warrior, was trampled by the horses and had to have one of his legs amputated. Again, the villagers arrived to share their concern. "We're so sorry. This is terrible. This is such bad news." The old farmer responded, "You don't know this is terrible, you don't know this is bad news. We'll just have to wait and see." And, again, the villagers returned home.

Weeks passed and war broke out. All able-bodied young men were drafted into the army to fight the enemy. The farmer's son remained at home. Most of those who went to war were killed.

This story serves as a reminder that, depending upon our attitudes, life's difficulties can be viewed as disasters or opportunities. Adversity often opens doors. In bad, there is good. When I apply this notion to my own relationship, it really makes sense to me. There are many things about Jim I've been able to influence. And, despite my obvious genius, there are many other things about him that have been impervious to my man-changing efforts. And although when I'm mad at him I don't always feel this way, in my more objective moments I reflect on how I've grown as a person having had to deal with his "shortcomings." Let me give you an example.

Jim is very opinionated about the things he likes and doesn't like to do. He's not big on compromising. He hates shopping, tearjerker movies, and a heavy social calendar, and he insists on going to the same vacation spot all the time even though I have other ideas, just to give you a few examples. Years ago, this infuriated me and I spent a great deal of energy trying to get him to do what I wanted for a change. Sometimes, I even succeeded. He would go along begrudgingly and put a damper on the whole experience. Eventually, I started doing things by myself.

At first, I was really uncomfortable doing things alone or with friends that I "should have been doing with him," but I soon realized that I was having more fun without him. I enjoyed my time alone or time with friends. I got over the discomfort of being alone. In fact, I was getting to be an old pro at it.

I discovered that I liked the feeling of independence. I liked missing him when I was gone. I liked his missing me. Nowadays, I travel all the time to do seminars, and I'm convinced that I wouldn't have the comfort level that I do if he had been by my side wherever I went throughout our relationship. His "selfishness" had some positive side effects in my life.

Perhaps you're thinking, "Boy, that sounds like a rationalization." But for me it's not. It's real. Although I know that his motives are purely self-centered, I honestly believe I have grown as an individual because of Jim's fiercely independent view of things. Now, if you ask whether I would have chosen Jim to be that way from the start, certainly my answer would be "No." But given the hand I've been dealt, I've decided to make lemonade out of lemons. And I'm a happier person for it.

If you are having trouble seeing the good in the bad, it might be easier for you to start by thinking about it the other way around—looking at the bad in the good. Remember back to the beginning of your relationship. Do you recall what it was about your man that you found so attractive? I'll bet you anything that it is precisely the wonderful quality in him that is driving you nuts right now. The very thing you once loved about him is the thing you're so desperate to change. The point is, nothing in life is inherently good or bad; it all depends on how you look at it.

I really believe that we have choices in life. We can be miserable or we can try to decipher the lesson life is teaching us in all that we encounter. Seeing the good in the bad is really an option worth considering. Think about your relationship for a moment. Reflect on the parts of your man that have been particularly challenging for you. Now I want you to stretch a bit and ask yourself, "In what ways has this quality in him made me a stronger person?" "How has he inadvertently helped me grow as an individual?"

People's resilience in trying situations always amazes me. If you think about the times you've had to reach inside of yourself to cope with some of your mate's idiosyncrasies, you'll know exactly what I mean. Life doesn't always go the way you predict or want it to, but whatever has happened in your life has made you the wonderful person you are right now. So when nothing seems to be going your way, look for the good in the "bad." It will make you feel so much better.

Boy, we've come a really long way together. You now have skills to transform your man. You even know what to do if he puts up resistance. But there still is one thing you might not know, and that's what the next chapter is about. It's a surprise.

....

CHAPTER TWELVE

The Surprise Ending

Our time together is drawing to an end. I'm going to miss our "girls only" confidential conversations. Speaking of confidential, when I first started writing this book, I asked Jim to read a couple of chapters to get his feedback. But the more I wrote, the more I realized that asking him to read my tried-and-true strategies for changing him was actually insane. Why in the world would I want to give away my secrets? Pretty dense, huh? So I stopped asking him for feedback, and I don't think he even noticed. Or if he did, he hasn't said anything about it. Maybe he's not interested in reading my book because he thinks he knows everything about me, that I'm completely predictable. Well, let's just keep it that way, then. But back to you.

Think back to how you were feeling when you picked up this book. Were you frustrated, disillusioned, or confused? Were you ready to throw in the towel? Were you hoping against hope that one day things would be better between you and your man? If so, I hope this book has been helpful to you. I hope you now have a better idea of what you can do when you're feeling stuck. I hope you're not hopeless about changing your man anymore.

But I do want to ask you a question. By any chance, have you noticed that despite the fact that this is supposed to be a book about changing your man, it's really much more than that? While I discussed your need to change as being pivotal in changing your man, I never told the whole truth—this is a book about changing yourself. It's a book that teaches women to become smarter, more strategic, and more systematic in their lives. It's a book directed at grabbing women's attention and saying, "Change yourself and your life will change." By rights, this book should have been entitled *A Woman's Guide to Changing Herself—Without Her Even Knowing It*. Trouble is, no one would have read it. And that would have defeated my purpose. But you're the person I'm banking on when it comes to relationship change, not your man. It's *you* I believe in. But why?

As a woman, you really know what's important in life. You understand that good relationships are the only things that really matter. You know in your heart that no dying person has ever regretted having spent too little time at the office. You figured that out a long time ago.

Dr. Elisabeth Kübler-Ross is a physician whose pioneering work in the field of death and dying taught us a tremendous amount about this previously taboo subject. She interviewed thousands of people who had near-death experiences and found uncanny similarities in their stories. One aspect of these experiences is particularly relevant here. Kübler-Ross says that people who have had these near-death experiences report having been taught a lesson about life's *real* purpose, the reason we're even on this planet. They say people have two fundamental missions in life: to love and to serve others.

Now, if you were to write a job description for women, I think that would be it, don't you? That means we get it. We understand on a deep level what's important in life. We make sacrifices to make other people happy. We love to love. We know life's lesson way before our final hour. . . . We're pretty smart after all, aren't we?

So that's why I'm depending on you to spread love throughout your life. All you need to do is make a promise to yourself to stay focused on solutions, forgive yourself for slipping occasionally, and get back on track when you do. If you follow those three simple steps, you'll grow closer to your partner than you've been in years. I promise. Plus, something else wonderful will happen, too.

Once you truly embrace the empowering philosophy of this book, you'll feel more in charge of your life, a perspective that will benefit you far beyond your improved relationship with your man. You'll like yourself more. You'll feel energized and vitalized. And this feeling of renewal will spill over into every area of your life.

You'll notice improvements in your relationships with your children, other family members, friends, and coworkers. You'll be more invested in the projects you undertake. You'll find the resolve you've been waiting for to do good things for yourself—sticking to your diet, stopping smoking, exercising regularly, and saying "No," and really meaning it. You'll feel more vibrant and alive. More than anything, you'll be a happier person.

And that's when the fun begins, because the people in your life will notice something different about you. They'll be wondering, "Is it something in her walk or the way she carries herself?" or "Is it that twinkle in her eye?" They might not be able to put their finger on what's changed about you, but they'll be dead certain of one thing—you're a different person now. And because you're more at peace with your relationship and with yourself, people around you are going to respond differently to you. Your whole life is about to change. You're in for a treat.

And who knows? I bet you're going to spread this solution-oriented stuff all around you. You're going to want to share what you've learned with the people you love. You'll want to let the cat out of the bag that life doesn't have to be so complicated, that getting out of ruts can be child's play. Since you know the way, you'll want to lead others to solution land. And I can hardly blame you. This stuff is really exciting.

So forgive me for using the old bait-and-switch strategy on you—first tantalizing you into thinking there's a magical pill you can slip in your partner's orange juice to make him the man of your dreams, and then spending the rest of the time telling *you* to change—but it shows you how determined I am to get your attention. Pretty nervy, huh?

The truth is, I did this because I know how quickly and completely your life will be transformed when you take responsibility for change. Below is a quote from a tombstone of an Anglican bishop in the crypts of Westminster Abbey:

> When I was young and free and my imagination had
> no limits, I dreamed of changing the world. As I
> grew older and wiser, I discovered the world would
> not change, so I shortened my sights somewhat and

decided to change only my country. But it, too, seemed immovable.

As I grew into my twilight years, in one last desperate attempt, I settled for changing only my family, those closest to me, but alas, they would have none of it.

And now as I lie on my deathbed, I suddenly realize: *If I had only changed myself first,* then by example I would have changed my family. From their inspiration and encouragement, I would then have been able to better my country and, who knows, I may have even changed the world.

Anonymous[1]

So, my dear friend, our coffee klatch is just about over. Know that I'll be thinking about you and cheering you on from the sidelines. I have complete faith in your ability to get out there and create the kind of relationship you really want with your man. In fact, I'd love to hear your success stories. Would you take the time to write and fill me in? That would make me one very happy woman. Until then, happy man-changing!

For information about my seminars and audiotape/videotape products, you can reach me at:

The Divorce Busting Center
P. O. Box 197
Woodstock, IL 60098
Fax: 815–337–8014
E-mail: Divbuster@aol.com

Acknowledgments

Throughout this book, I have emphasized the idea that no man or woman is an island. I certainly have noticed the profound effect that many wonderful people have had on my life and, in particular, on the writing of this book. I am deeply appreciative of all they have given me.

To my children, for bringing such intense joy to my life and reminding me of what's really important. To Danielle, whose humor, support, love, and hugs mean more to me than you'll ever know. Thank you for sharing your last year at home with a computer. To Zachary, who faithfully pulled himself away from his obsession with sports long enough to ask, "How's the book coming, Mom?" I love you for that.

To my mother, who taught me about love and inspired me to help others create more love in their lives.

To my father, whose ambition, drive, and passion for his work have obviously rubbed off on me.

To Virginia Peeples, my dear assistant and close friend, without whom none of this would have been possible. Thank you for your meticulous help with the preparation of the manuscript, your being a guinea pig for all my ideas, your ever-positive biased opinions about me, and your above-and-beyond-the-call-of-duty assistance in every aspect of my work. I also want to thank Joe Peeples for graciously sharing his wife with me when she and I burn the midnight oil, which is most of the time.

To my supportive family, Leah and Byll Davis and the Davis clan, Lila Weiner, my brothers, Ken and Chuck, my lifelong friends Noble Golden, Arnold Woodruff, and Therese Quoss for cheering me on and forgiving me when I haven't called.

To Mindy Adams, my Mary Poppins, who, for so many years, has simplified my life so I can focus my efforts in other directions. Thank you for being part of our family.

To my wonderful and talented editor, Laura Yorke, who believed in me from the very start, which was a very long time ago. Your enthusiasm for my work is, as always, greatly appreciated, as are your insightful editorial comments. Lara Asher, Laura's assistant, has been tremendously helpful to me. Also, I'm very thankful to Bob Asahina at Golden Books for generously offering his advice about my career.

To Suzanne Gluck, my literary agent, who had big plans for this book. I appreciate your vision. Thanks, also, for your wonderful sound bites. I'm always ready with my pen when we talk.

To Steve de Shazer, a teacher and mentor; our time together has greatly inspired me.

To all the wonderful women in my practice, thank you for allowing me to be part of your life. I've learned so much from you as we put our heads together to shape up your men. Thanks for having faith in me. And to all the wonderful men in their lives, thank you for being men. Without you, this book wouldn't have been possible.

APPENDIX

Join the Women's Solution Network! Start Your Own Man-Changing Group

G irlfriend,

One night, after working on this book, I had a dream. I envisioned women from all backgrounds coming together and, instead of complaining or analyzing things to death (as we're too often prone to do), they would meet in small groups to brainstorm effective strategies for making their relationships better than ever. Using the amazingly simple, commonsense principles in this guide, they would unearth long-awaited answers to the universal questions: How do I get my man to help more around the house? What can I do to get my man to understand that I need more communication? How do I get my man to be less controlling? What can I do to make my man understand that I need to feel closeness in order to desire him sexually? And so on. Now, my dream has come true. That's why I'm ecstatic that you want to be part of this exciting new solution network.

This section contains all the information you need to get your group started: guidelines for recruiting members, instructions and suggested topics for discussion, and worksheets for practical application. So, enjoy the book, enjoy each other, and go, girlfriends!

Think solutions!

Michele Weiner-Davis

How to Start Your Own Man–Changing Group

There are many different ways to recruit group members. If you are already involved in a book group or reading club, you might ask members to focus on "man changing" for a few weeks. Bookstores are a good place to start, too. They can provide information about how to start a group, they can host a group, or they might be able to locate an ongoing group for you to join. So be sure to give them a call. In addition to approaching the big chain stores, keep in mind that many smaller independent book stores are extremely supportive of groups meeting on their premises.

Besides bookstores, consider contacting local chapters of women's organizations, YMCAs, park districts, libraries, community centers, cafés, churches, and synagogues. A small display or classified ad in your local paper might also work. It could read, "Join a free, four-week women's group aimed at finding positive solutions to relationship challenges, based on Michele Weiner-Davis' book *Getting Through to the Man You Love*." Include your telephone number for more information. Or hang a poster containing information about your group in visible spots throughout your community. Posting a message on the Internet might be a good way to start a group. Tell a friend, bring a friend, and tell members to bring friends, too. To prevent a delay in beginning your group, contact your bookstore immediately to order enough books for group members.

Group members will need lead time to clear their calendars and to read Chapters 1–3 before the first meeting, so start planning a few weeks in advance of the date you'd actually like to begin. When interested members contact you, find out which times and days of the week will work best for them and try to accommodate as many people as possible, or you can arrange your meeting time in advance. Where you meet is a matter of personal preference. Some groups meet in members' homes, alternating to share the load, while others meet in public libraries, bookstores, churches, and synagogues. Some even meet during their lunch hour at work. Your meeting place should be quiet and free from distraction. Stay-at-home moms often meet during school hours, while working women generally meet in the evenings. Although it varies from group to group and the topic being discussed, most discussions last for approximately two hours. But feel free to continue a discussion that is really going strong.

General Guidelines

The following guidelines are meant to be just that. Feel free to modify them to meet the needs of your group members. However, all members should agree on the mission of the group: to provide a safe place to discuss the challenges facing women in their relationships, and more important, a golden opportunity to brainstorm concrete, down-to-earth suggestions for creating the kinds of relationships women really want. Group members should understand that all conversations are confidential.

Most groups meet a minimum of four times. Though this varies from group to group, ideally meetings should be spaced one or two weeks apart. Groups of ten or less seem to work best. The purpose of your meeting is not group therapy; therefore, any woman experiencing severe relationship problems should not consider it a substitute for professional therapy. If it becomes apparent that a particular member's issues are beyond the scope of the group, she should seek professional advice.

Each group should have a facilitator to lead the discussions. If you are organized and motivated enough to start the group, you undoubtedly possess the skills to be a great facilitator. However, should you decline, the group can select a single facilitator or opt to have co-facilitators: two women leading the group together.

In addition to reading the guidelines and agenda out loud at the beginning of each meeting, the facilitator's job is to raise the topics on the agenda, keep the conversation productive (focused on solutions rather than blame), integrate the worksheets at appropriate points in the discussion, make certain no single member monopolizes the conversation, and ensure that everyone who wants to talk has an opportunity to do so. Furthermore, remember that the women attending your group are not seeking unsolicited advice about the goals they've chosen for their relationship, just feedback about methods for accomplishing these goals. If group members begin to offer advice—"Why don't you leave him?" or "Why do you put up with that?"—the facilitator should get people back on track. Finally, the facilitator reminds members about their "homework assignment" at the end of each meeting.

Some women may feel more comfortable listening and learning vicariously rather than sharing personally, and other members should respect that. You don't have to talk about the intimate details of your sex life or other personal issues to benefit from the discussion. You can choose more impersonal goals, such as getting your man to clean up after himself or convincing him to help more with the kids. If members learn how to achieve less threatening goals, they will also be able to tackle more personal goals on their own if they wish. Conversely, do not discourage women who are comfortable discussing personal issues. Variety will make your group interesting and challenging.

The Three Most Important Rules

Ultimately, the group will be successful if the members keep in mind at all times the three most important rules for discussion. The first rule is that man-bashing is prohibited because it's not productive. This isn't to say that a member can't complain about her partner's actions. Many women need to tell their stories before they are ready to make an active change. However, complaints should be kept brief, and the discussion that follows should focus on what women can do to improve their situations. If any member falls into the "I'm just a victim" or "See what I have to put up with" mindset, other members must remind her to get back on the solution-oriented track.

Because it is so important to restrain yourselves from blaming the men in your lives, create a "male-bashing buster" device to bring to all meetings. You can use something as simple as an index card folded in half with the words "male-bashing buster" written on both sides. Any item that serves as a visible reminder to stay on track will do. Place the item within reach of all members, so that if one person spends too much time whining or complaining without striving to find potential solutions, anyone can hold up the card and suggest a new direction in the conversation. Although the facilitator must take responsibility for keeping a solution-oriented focus, group members should share in this responsibility because it's good practice; the more often we can identify dead-end thinking in others, the better we'll get at noticing it in ourselves.

The second rule for discussion is that any positive attempt to change—any small step forward—should be celebrated and congratulated. You are there to encourage and empower each other to risk trying new and improved methods for making your relationships more loving. So bring on the fanfare whenever possible. Remember, small changes count.

Finally, since all women are a wealth of information about solutions, ask members to share what works for them. However, be careful to respect individual differences and preferences. Most of all, adopt the motto "Do what works," cast your inhibitions to the wind, and have fun!

Before the First Meeting

- The facilitator should make nametags for each group member.
- Members should read chapters 1–3.

First Meeting

Introductions

Hand out nametags. Members should break into groups of two (or three if there is an odd number). Person A should then introduce herself and say why she decided to join the group. She can share how long she and her partner have been together, whether they have children, whether she works outside the home, or any other information. After two minutes or so, the women should switch roles. Person B introduces herself to Person A. When everyone has had a chance to talk, members should turn their focus to the group again. Then, each woman should introduce the woman with whom she was paired to the rest of the group.

Discuss chapters 1–3. Read through instructions for each chapter first, then go back to the first question. When someone is done speaking, the facilitator should ask, "Does anyone else have something to say?" In fact, it's a good idea to ask "Anyone else?" frequently throughout your meeting. Even if there is momentary silence, be patient and wait a few seconds. It may give more reserved members an opportunity to speak.

Chapter 1: Can We Talk?

This chapter discusses the pitfalls of blaming your man for problems. What do you think about this? Have you caught yourself falling into that trap? How do you feel about the fact that this book is written specifically for women? What does the story about rats teach you about yourself?

This chapter introduces the idea that women rely too heavily on words to try to change their action-oriented men. What do you think about that? Do you know women who could be classified as "Walkaway Wives?" What do you think about this phenomenon?

Chapter 2: Changing Your Leopard's Spots

This chapter introduces the idea that one person can actually change another, one of the most important concepts in the book. What do you think of this idea? To what do you attribute your man's resistance to change?

The ripple effect is powerful in relationships. Change is like a chain reaction. Can you think of some examples in your own family or relationship that demonstrate that the ripple effect truly happens?

Even though interactions in relationships are circular—A→B and then B→A—why does it always seem that our partners "start" the problems in our lives? And why don't they agree with our assessments? Consider this scenario. Does she complain because he works late, or does he work late because she complains? Think of a conflict that you believe was "started" by your partner. As difficult as this might be, try to imagine what you might have done that could have inadvertently triggered his behavior. If you have trouble answering this because it's hard to see the forest for the trees, ask your group for help.

Are you one of those women who asks, "Why do I have to be the one to change?" or "Isn't it manipulative to try to change your partner?" If so, how do you feel after reading this chapter?

Chapter 3: Testosterone Simplified

This is your one and only chance to commiserate, so go for it. Which of the five beefs resonates most with you? What others would you include on your list?

Talk about how you've struggled to get your man to be more like you—more verbally communicative, more of a team player, more interested in helping around the house, more laid back, and so on. After reading this chapter, what are your thoughts about these struggles?

What did you learn about your man (and men in general) in this chapter? Did it push you to think about your man a little differently?

Leave time at the end of the meeting to write one to three goals on the "Goal-Setting" Worksheet. List what you hope to change about your man. Written responses don't need to be lengthy to be beneficial. (The worksheets start on page 251.)

Homework Assignment

- Read chapter 4. Review the goals you set at the end of the first meeting and complete the "Goal-Setting" Worksheet to make your goals solution-oriented.
- Read chapter 5. Complete the questions in chapter 5.
- Read chapter 6. Complete the "Basic Training" Worksheet.
- Read chapter 7. Complete the "Solution Detective" Worksheet and the questions in the chapter.
- Read chapter 8. Complete the "Do Something Different" Worksheet.

Don't forget to bring your books and completed worksheets to the next meeting.

Second Meeting

This meeting is truly a hands-on session. You will discuss five chapters: the real nuts and bolts of the man-changing material. So roll up your sleeves and get ready to work. This meeting might last somewhat longer than the others. Begin by checking the results on the "Goal-Setting" Worksheet.

Chapter 4: So Many Changes, So Little Time

Discuss whether the goals you set at the end of the last meeting met the criteria outlined in chapter 4. Share what you learned about goal setting as you made your goals more solution-oriented.

Of the three criteria for solution-oriented goals—say what you want, not what you don't want; be action-oriented; and start small—which one presented the most challenge for you? How did you overcome it?

Unlike men, who are usually natural goal setters, taking time to set goals does not come easily to women. We spend a lot of our lives just hoping things will eventually fall into place. Talk about how you felt setting your relationship goals.

Chapter 5: Don't Even Go There, Girlfriend

Understanding what it means to do "more of the same" is extremely important if you want to get a better response from your man. Can you identify your man's "more of the same" behavior? What about your own? Discuss your responses to the questions in chapter 5. What has doing this exercise taught you about yourself?

Chapter 6: Basic Training: Sit, Stay, Come

What do you think about the comparison between changing your man and training a dog? Discuss your responses to the "Basic Training" Worksheet.

Chapter 7: Becoming a Solution Detective

Have you been guilty of all-or-nothing thinking? When you're at odds with your man, do you accuse him of always acting a certain way or never doing what you want him to do? What do you think about the idea of focusing on problem-free times to discover solutions? Discuss your responses to the "Solution Detective" Worksheet and the questions in chapter 7.

Chapter 8: Do Something Different for a Change

This chapter describes many different techniques for breaking bad relationship habits—Do the Unexpected, Do a 180°, Act As If, Easier Done Than Said, Do Nothing, The Medium Is the Message, and The Medium Is the Massage. Discuss how you reacted as you read each technique.

Doing something different counteracts doing more of the same. Discuss your responses to the "Do Something Different" Worksheet. Does anyone need help thinking of something new to try? Offer suggestions.

Homework Assignment

- Between now and the next meeting, commit to holding yourself back from doing more of the same at least one time. In its place, try doing something—anything—different. Let your imagination run wild.
- Read chapters 9–12.
- Answer the questions in chapter 10.

Third Meeting

In this session you'll examine what you're trying and how it has been working. Discuss positive results first. This sets a solution-oriented tone to the meeting. Begin by asking, "What are you doing differently, and what's been better?" In specific, action-oriented terms, describe what you're changing about your own behavior. For example, if someone says, "I'm giving him space for a change," help her to be more specific by asking, "What exactly have you been doing?" Then she might respond, "When he's in a bad mood, I leave the room and keep busy. I do the dishes or pick up the phone to call my friend." The more clearly you can assess which actions are productive, the better you'll be at resolving future problems.

In addition to describing what you have been doing differently, discuss how your man has responded differently. Again, concrete and specific answers are key. Remember, cheer all positive changes, big and small. After sharing success stories, ask if anyone tried something new with little or no success. Remember, if a strategy works at all, it's worth keeping in mind as a solution to build upon. Anyone feel stuck? Try brainstorming other, more productive solutions. Be open to many different ideas without vetoing or evaluating. Then discuss chapters 9–12.

Chapter 9: Smart Talk: How to Talk So Men Will Listen

This chapter offers methods for keeping your man's attention when you're talking. Review the tips. Which do you find most illuminating or helpful? Which will be most challenging for you to do? What can you do to resist the temptation to handle conflict in unproductive ways?

Chapter 10: Keeping It Up

This chapter encourages you to take an inventory of your man-changing progress to see how far you've come and assess the work that still needs to be done. It is very important to monitor your progress on a regular basis. So why not do it now? Discuss your answers to the questions in this chapter.

A word of caution: Worrying about setbacks is natural. Consider what you can do to feel more confident that the changes you made will stick. Is it more time under your belt, or some other kind of "proof"? Getting off track from time to time is inevitable. Discuss how you will remind yourself to get back on track quickly and without blame. Does anyone still feel stuck? Brainstorm creative solutions.

Chapter 11: The Immovable Man

Here's a checklist of questions to ask people who might still be feeling stuck:

1. Are you overlooking small but important changes? Is anything different at all?
2. If you noticed only minor changes in your man, did you stop trying because you hoped for major changes?
3. Are you giving each technique enough time to work?
4. Is the new method you're trying different enough from your usual method?
5. Is your heart really into what you're doing?

This chapter also discusses the idea that you may be a fix-it addict. What do you think about that idea in general and how it might apply to you?

Acceptance is important in any relationship. Even if there are things you want to change about your man, he undoubtedly has many good points. Think about and share what's great about your man. How have his less-than-desirable traits made you a stronger person in the long run?

Chapter 12: The Surprise Ending

This chapter reminds you of the basic premise of the book: You are at the core of relationship change. How do you feel about this responsibility/opportunity now that you've completed the book? What are the benefits of looking at your life through this lens? How does this compare to how you used to think about your relationship and your life?

Homework Assignment

- Notice signs that things are staying on track and note what you do to keep them that way. If you've been stuck, commit to doing something different again.
- Complete the "What Works" Worksheet.

Fourth Meeting

Start the meeting by discussing what's been working in each woman's life since the last meeting. As usual, celebrate improvements. Then allow time for members who might be stuck to brainstorm other solutions. Discuss the "What Works" Worksheet.

Wrap up by sharing something you appreciate about having been in the group. Your comments can be directed toward the group in general or to individual group members.

• • •

As the author of the book, I can't tell you how excited I am that you have participated in this group. I would love to know how your man, relationship, and life have changed. Because a woman's work is never done, you may decide to continue meeting. Or you may be enthusiastic enough to want to start another group. You're an expert now, so why not?

In any case, know that I'm thinking about you and would love to hear from you. I would be thrilled if you would take a few minutes to fill out the feedback form on page 255 and drop it in the mail.

The "Goal-Setting" Worksheet

Exercise 1: Ask Yourself

What are the three things I'd most like to change or improve in my relationship?

Stop! Read chapter 4 before proceeding to exercise 2!

Exercise 2: Make Your Goals More Solution-Oriented

1. Make Your Goals Action-Oriented

Your goal will be vague unless you describe exactly what you and your partner will be doing when your goal is achieved. For example:

Vague Goal	Action-Oriented Goal
I want my husband to communicate better.	1. He'll turn off the TV when we talk.
	2. He'll make eye contact with me when we talk.
	3. He'll offer comments after I share something with him.

Go back to the goals you set in Exercise 1. Now, make these goals action-oriented. What will you and your man be doing that will let you know you have reached each of your goals?

2. State Your Goals Positively

When you set a goal, make sure you express it positively. Think about what you want to happen instead of what you want to avoid. For example:

Negative Goal	Positive Goal
I want you to stop being so critical of me.	I like it when you compliment me. I'd like you to do it more often.

Review your relationship goals. Are they stated positively? If not, write your goals in positive terms.

3. Start Small

If you want to accomplish major goals, you must break them down into small, achievable steps. Take a look at your relationship goals once again. Ask yourself, "What will be the very first sign that I am making progress toward my major goal?"

The "Basic Training" Worksheet

1. If you asked your man whether you emphasize the things he does right or the things he does wrong, what would he say?
2. Since rewards need to be rewarding, what works with your man?
3. Do you compliment your man on small improvements or hold out until he gets it completely right?
4. Would he say that you hold grudges for long periods of time? Is this a good thing?
5. Expecting prompt compliance is one of the basic dog-training rules. What do you do if your man ignores what you say the first or second time?

The "Solution Detective" Worksheet

With your relationship goals in mind, answer the following questions:

1. What's different about the times when we're getting along better, we're communicating well, or our sex life is great (or whatever your goal is)?
2. What am I doing differently at those times? Think about as many actions as you can. Are you being kinder, more forgiving, more playful, more relaxed?
3. What is my man doing differently when we get along?
4. What are we doing differently as a couple when we get along better? How is our life different at that time? What activities do we do together when we like each other?
5. If you are having a difficult time recalling recent examples of problem-free times, look to your past successes. Ask yourself: What was different about our relationship years ago, when we were doing better? What was different about our lives when we first met?
6. If you can't think of any exceptions, ask yourself: What is different about the times when our problem is less frequent, less intense, or shorter in duration?
7. What's different about the times when the problem occurs, but something constructive comes from it?
8. Sometimes the problematic situation occurs, but you don't seem to get upset by it. If so, ask yourself: What's different about the times when the problem occurs, but it doesn't bother me?
9. When you're experiencing a problem, instead of figuring out who started it, it's helpful to figure out how you got the problem to cease being a problem. Ask yourself: How do our conflicts come to an end? What are our "truce triggers"?

The "Do Something Different" Worksheet

This worksheet will help you identify several creative approaches for improving your relationship. Instead of "doing more of the same" when you are faced with a challenge, you'll have some ideas about what to do differently. Review the specific techniques in chapter 8. Then review your answers to the questions in chapter 5 regarding your "more of the same" behavior. Which of the techniques might work in your situation?

Ask yourself: What could I do that would be totally different from the usual way I handle things?

Sometimes a minor change in your behavior isn't enough to get the results you want. That's when you need to make a complete U-turn. Review your "more of the same" behavior.

Ask yourself: What approach would be the exact opposite of how I typically have been handling things? What would be a 180°?

The "What Works" Worksheet

Step 1: Identify the changes. Ask yourself: What is happening that I want to continue to happen? How have changes in our relationship affected the rest of my life?

Step 2: Identify what you have been doing to help create the positive changes that have occurred. Ask yourself: What strategies have I tried recently that have led to good things happening between us?

Step 3: Keep using your most effective strategies. Do what works!

Step 4: Make being solution-oriented a way of life. Stop complaining and start thinking, living, and breathing solutions in all areas of your life. Help the people in your life to "think solutions," too!

Feedback Form

I've been talking to you for a while now; here's your turn to talk back to me. I promise to read your feedback personally. So brag a little. Share your success stories with me. Tell me how you have used *Getting Through to the Man You Love* to improve your love relationship.

Describe what you liked most about the book._____
_____

What about your relationship has changed most since you've read this book?_____
_____

In what ways has participating in this group been helpful to you?
_____
_____

Would you change the group structure in any way? If so, how?
_____
_____

Would you recommend being part of a group such as this to a friend?_____
_____

Additional Comments:_____
_____
_____

Your Name:_____
Address:_____
E-mail address:_____

Please send this form to me at the address on page 235.

Notes

....

Chapter 2. Changing Your Leopard's Spots
1. Kay Butler, "The Anatomy of Resilience," *Family Therapy Networker*, p. 25.
2. Anthony Robbins, *Unlimited Power*, p. 77.

Chapter 3. Testosterone Simplified
1. John Gray, *Men Are from Mars, Women Are from Venus*, pp. 146–47.
2. John Gray, *Men Are from Mars, Women Are from Venus*, pp. 16–18.
3. Theresa L. Crenshaw, M.D., *Alchemy of Love and Lust*, pp. 5, 143.

Chapter 6. Basic Training: Sit, Stay, Come
1. Gina Spadafori, *Dogs for Dummies*, p. 131.
2. Ted Baer, *Communicating with Your Dog: A Humane Approach to Dog Training*, p. 11.
3. Gina Spadafori, *Dogs for Dummies*, p. 199.
4. Ted Baer, *Communicating with Your Dog: A Humane Approach to Dog Training*, p. 22.

Chapter 7. Becoming a Solution Detective
1. Eve Lipchik and Steve de Shazer, *"Purposeful Sequences for Beginning the Solution-Focused Interview."*

Chapter 8. Do Something Different for a Change
1. Steve de Shazer, *Keys to Solution in Brief Therapy*, pp. 122–23.

Notes

Chapter 10. Keeping It Up
1. Eve Lipchik and Steve de Shazer, *"Purposeful Sequences for Beginning the Solution-Focused Interview."*

Chapter 12. The Surprise Ending
1. Jack Canfield and Mark Hansen, *Chicken Soup for the Soul*, p. 72.

Bibliography

Akers, Paul. "Deadbeat Dads, Meet Your Counterpart: Walkaway Wives." Scripps Howard News Service, December 2, 1996.

Andrews and McMeel, *Disney's Magic Eye*. New York: Scholastic Inc., 1994.

Baer, Ted. *Communicating with Your Dog: A Humane Approach to Dog Training*. New York: Barron's, 1989.

Butler, Kay. "The Anatomy of Resilience." *Family Therapy Networker.* March/April 1997.

Canfield, Jack, and Mark Hansen. *Chicken Soup for the Soul*. Deerfield Beach, FL: Health Communications Inc., 1993.

Chopra, Deepak, M.D. *Ageless Body, Timeless Mind*. New York: Random House, 1993.

Crenshaw, Theresa L., M.D. *Alchemy of Love and Lust*. New York: Putnam, 1996.

de Shazer, Steve. *Keys to Solution in Brief Therapy*. New York: W. W. Norton, 1985.

Farrelly, Frank, and Jeffrey M. Brandsma. *Provocative Therapy*. Fort Collins, CO: Shields, 1974.

Gottman, John. *Why Marriages Succeed or Fail*. New York: Pocket Books, 1995.

Gray, John. *Men Are from Mars, Women Are from Venus*. New York: HarperCollins, 1992.

Kübler-Ross, Elisabeth. *On Death and Dying*. New York: Simon & Schuster, 1991.

Lipchik, Eve, and Steve de Shazer. "Purposeful Sequences for Beginning the Solution-Focused Interview." In E. Lipchik, *Interviewing*. Rockville, MD: Aspen, 1988.

Pittman, Frank III, M.D. *Man Enough*. New York: G. P. Putnam's Sons, 1993.

Prochaska, James O., Ph.D., John C. Norcross, Ph.D., and Carlo D. Diclemente, Ph.D. *Changing for Good: A Revolutionary Six-Stage Program for Overcoming Bad Habits and Moving Your Life Positively Forward*. New York: Avon, 1994.

Robbins, Anthony. *Unlimited Power*. New York: Simon & Schuster, 1991.

Spadafori, Gina. *Dogs for Dummies*. Foster City, CA: IDG Books Worldwide Inc., 1996.

Tanenbaum, Joe. *Male and Female Realities: Understanding the Opposite Sex*. Sugarland, Texas: Candle Publishing, 1989.

Thorton, Jim. *Chore Wars: How Households Can Share the Work and Keep the Peace*. Berkeley, CA: Conari Press, 1997.

Ullman, Leonard P., and Leonard Krasner. *A Psychological Approach to Abnormal Behavior*. Englewood Cliffs, NJ: Prentice-Hall, Inc., 1969.

Weiner-Davis, Michele. *Divorce Busting: A Step-by-Step Approach to Making Your Marriage Loving Again*. New York: Simon & Schuster, 1992.

———. *Change Your Life and Everyone in It*. New York: Fireside, 1996.

Wolin, Steven, and Sophie Wolin. *The Resilient Self: How Survivors in Troubled Families Rise Above Diversity*. New York: Villard Books, 1993.

About the Author

M ichele Weiner-Davis is an internationally renowned relationship expert, best-selling author, and psycho-therapist in private practice. She specializes in a revolutionary therapy approach—Solution-Oriented Brief Therapy—aimed at helping people change their lives quickly and painlessly. She is author of *Divorce Busting* and *Change Your Life and Everyone in It*, and is coauthor of *In Search of Solutions*. She is also the creator of the *Keeping Love Alive* program.

Weiner-Davis's work with couples has been featured in nearly every major newspaper and magazine. She offers clear, energetic, and entertaining seminars to professional and lay audiences nationally and internationally. Her book *In Search of Solutions* is often required reading in university courses. She has been instrumental in spearheading the popular movement urging couples to make their marriages work and keep their families together. She lives in Woodstock, Illinois, with her husband and their two children.